MENTAL HEALTH TREATMENT FOR CHILDREN AND ADOLESCENTS

EVIDENCE-BASED PRACTICES SERIES

SERIES EDITORS:

David E. Biegel, Ph.D.
Elizabeth M. Tracy, Ph.D.
Mandel School of Applied Social Sciences,
Case Western Reserve University

Family Psychoeducation for Serious Mental Illness
Harriet P. Lefley

School Social Work
An Evidence-Informed Framework for Practice
Michael S. Kelly, James C. Raines, Susan Stone, and Andy Frey

Mental Health Treatment for Children and Adolescents
Jacqueline Corcoran

The Evidence-Based Practices Series is published in collaboration with the Mandel School of Applied Social Sciences at Case Western Reserve University.

MENTAL HEALTH TREATMENT FOR CHILDREN AND ADOLESCENTS

Jacqueline Corcoran

OXFORD
UNIVERSITY PRESS

2011

OXFORD
UNIVERSITY PRESS

Oxford University Press, Inc., publishes works that further
Oxford University's objective of excellence
in research, scholarship, and education.

Oxford New York

Auckland   Cape Town   Dar es Salaam   Hong Kong   Karachi
Kuala Lumpur   Madrid   Melbourne   Mexico City   Nairobi
New Delhi   Shanghai   Taipei   Toronto

With offices in

Argentina   Austria   Brazil   Chile   Czech Republic   France   Greece
Guatemala   Hungary   Italy   Japan   Poland   Portugal   Singapore
South Korea   Switzerland   Thailand   Turkey   Ukraine   Vietnam

Copyright © 2011 by Oxford University Press, Inc.

Published by Oxford University Press, Inc.
198 Madison Avenue, New York, New York 10016
www.oup.com

Oxford is a registered trademark of Oxford University Press.

Library of Congress Cataloging-in-Publication Data

Corcoran, Jacqueline.
Mental health treatment for children and adolescents / Jacqueline Corcoran.
p. ; cm. — (Evidence-based practices series)
Includes bibliographical references and indexes.
ISBN 978-0-19-537571-8
1.   Child psychiatry. 2.   Adolescent psychiatry. 3.   Evidence-based psychiatry.
I.   Title. II.   Series: Evidence-based practices series.
[DNLM: 1.   Mental Disorders–therapy. 2.   Adolescent. 3.   Child.
4.   Evidence-Based Medicine.   WS 463 C793 2011]
RJ499.C647 2011
618.92'89–dc22
2010007427

1 3 5 7 9 8 6 4 2

Printed in the United States of America
on acid-free paper

To my children, Alexa Sian and Miles Rhys: that they grow up healthy and happy.

ACKNOWLEDGMENTS

I sincerely thank David Biegel and Elizabeth Tracy, the editors for the *Evidence-Based Practices Series*, for inviting me to be part of this important line of books for Oxford University Press. I also wanted to send my appreciation to Maura Roessner, Senior Editor at Oxford, who has always been supportive of my work and unfailingly professional. My appreciation further goes to the following MSW students who contributed vital case information that served to enliven this book: Treva Bower, Angela Corriveau, Gidget Fields, Michelle Mintling, Laura Savitsky, Amelia Schor, and LeAnn Smuthkochorn. Additional appreciation goes toward my co-authors on chapters, doctoral students at the Virginia Commonwealth University, Robert Broce and Jennifer Shadik, for their hard work and fine contributions.

I am grateful to my husband, Mark Rosman, for his support in the writing of this book, and my father, Patrick Corcoran, as always, deserves credit for painstaking proofreading and his attention to detail.

CONTENTS

Conclusion

MENTAL HEALTH TREATMENT FOR
CHILDREN AND ADOLESCENTS

1

INTRODUCTION AND OVERVIEW

The median estimate of the prevalence of child and adolescent mental health disorders is 12% of the U.S. population, which translates into a substantial proportion of youth who are afflicted by mental health disorders (Costello, Egger, & Angold, 2005). Children of vulnerable populations, such as those in the child welfare or juvenile justice systems, demonstrate even higher rates than those in the general population (Burns, Phillips, Wagner, et al., 2004; Fazell, Doll, & Langstrom, 2008; McMillen, Scott, Zima, et al., 2004). Most mental disorders have their onset in childhood (Costello et al., 2005). Furthermore, people with a disorder whose onset is in childhood or adolescence are more likely to have mental health problems in adulthood with the commensurate risks for impairment in educational, occupational, and relational domains (Grant, Hasin, Blanco, et al., 2005; Kessler, Adler, Barkley, et al., 2005; Lemery & Doelger, 2005) as well as increased rates for suicide (Pompili, Mancinelli, Girardi, et al., 2004). Because of their prevalence and potentially dire consequences, mental health disorders in childhood must be recognized and addressed effectively when they first occur to aid in recovery and improved adjustment.

Several reports have centered on the mental health needs of children in the United States and have suggested the use of "evidence-based practice" (Knitzer, 1982; Cooper, Aratani, Knitzer, et al., 2008; President's New Freedom Commission on Mental Health, 2003). Evidence-based practice (EBP) began in medicine in the early 1990s (Sackett et al., 1997) and was defined as the integration of the best available research knowledge with clinical expertise and consumer values. In other words, evidence-based treatment is a process of using research knowledge to make decisions about particular cases.

The process of gathering the available research knowledge involves formulating specific questions, locating the relevant studies, assessing their credibility, and integrating credible results with findings from previous studies (Sackett et al., 1997). In the current environment, however, the term "evidence-based" practice has come to mean that there is an empirical basis to treatments and services (Zlotnik, 2007). The process of clinical decision making according to evidence-based practice is therefore distinguished from the product, which involves compilations of the research evidence (Proctor, 2007). Furthermore, engaging in evidence-based practice, including finding studies, evaluating their worth, and synthesizing their findings, may be too complex and onerous a process for practitioners to undertake while maintaining responsibility for client caseloads. Additionally, this process has become increasingly difficult as results of research studies and other information have accumulated rapidly. Therefore, compilations of best available evidence are needed for graduate students and practitioners in the mental health and social service professions. *Mental Health Treatment for Children and Adolescents* has been written to address this need, with its main purpose to present and critically review the evidence for the treatment of youth with mental health disorders.

In addition to the controversies about how to define evidence-based practice is the debate about how much evidence is sufficient to recommend a certain treatment for a particular person and the standard that will be used to determine "evidence" (Norcross et al., 2005). In this volume, "evidence" will be appraised in terms of two different conceptualizations, the American Psychiatric Association Psychological Division 12 Task Force Criteria and systematic reviews/meta-analyses. Furthermore, treatments will be examined to the extent that they address the individual and environmental factors known to result in the development of mental health disorders and that also influence treatment and recovery.

DEFINITIONS

This book will be organized around certain concepts that are defined in more detail in this section: The *American Psychiatric Association Diagnostic and Statistical Manual of Mental Disorders* (DSM):

- empirically supported treatment
- systematic reviews and meta-analyses
- the risk and resilience framework

Case illustrations will show some of the complexity in weaving these elements together and the challenges of implementing evidence-based practice in real-life settings.

DSM

The various mental health disorders are catalogued and described in the *Diagnostic and Statistical Manual of Mental Disorders* (DSM) (APA, 2000). The DSM, published by the American Psychiatric Association, is the standard resource for clinical diagnosis in the United States. The definition of *mental disorder* in the DSM is a "significant behavioral or psychological syndrome or pattern that occurs in an individual and that is associated with present distress (e.g., a painful symptom) or disability (i.e., impairment in one or more important areas of functioning) or with significantly increased risk of suffering death, pain, disability, or an important loss of freedom" (p. xxxi). A disorder "must currently be considered a manifestation of behavioral, psychological, or biological dysfunction in the individual" (p. xxxi). The DSM represents a medical perspective, which is only one of many possible perspectives on human behavior. The medical definition focuses on underlying disturbances *within* the person and is sometimes referred to as the *disease model* of abnormality. This implies that the abnormal person must experience changes within the self (rather than create environmental change) to be considered "normal" again.

The DSM, originating from the field of medicine, approaches mental disorders in the same fashion as physical disorders, which takes an individualistic focus on problems (i.e., they develop from individual dysfunction). Disorders are diagnosed from their manifestation—their symptoms—as well as functional impairment (U.S. Department of Health and Human Services, 1999).

There are many criticisms of the DSM, which have been delineated elsewhere (Caplan & Cosgrove, 2004; Kutchins & Kirk, 1997). Germane for children, the DSM approach might pose other problems (DHHS, 1999). Children may not be able to convey their experiences verbally. As a result, practitioners rely on parents and teachers who may be unable to detect the internal experience of children. Additionally, DSM criteria for disorders were often developed with adults in mind, and, therefore, may not be relevant for children. Although the criticisms of the DSM have merit, this book will nonetheless be organized according to DSM-defined disorders, as the DSM is the standard reference point for diagnosis in the United States.

Because as many as 150 disorders in the *DSM-IV TR* apply to youth (Weisz, Jensen, & Mcleod, 2005), the following criteria were used to determine whether a disorder and its treatment would be included in this volume. First, disorders were chosen that are relatively common for children and adolescents seen in clinical settings rather than representing obscure and rare presentations. Furthermore, selected disorders were those typically treated in a psychosocial context. For example, elimination disorders are often treated medically and, therefore, were not part of this book. Another important criterion was that the treatment of the disorder had to possess sufficient study to warrant an in-depth discussion. For this reason, reactive attachment disorder, which has not been subject to controlled treatment outcome research, was not included in this volume.

Disorders not only had to have sufficient evidence for their treatment, they had to represent valid disorders in youth. For example, bipolar disorder is a controversial diagnosis for children. Although many researchers believe that bipolar disorder can occur in childhood and adolescence, it may manifest differently in those age groups (Birmaher, Axelson, Strober, Gill, Valeri, et al., 2006). Therefore, the DSM criteria for bipolar disorder lacks validity for youth and other symptom presentations are being used to diagnose children. Controversy has intensified recently with a congressional investigation into the failure of leading psychiatrists in the area of bipolar disorder to disclose pharmaceutical drug company connections, while widely endorsing the use of antipsychotic medications in children (Harris & Carey, 2008).

As a result of these criteria, the following disorders were selected for inclusion in the volume:

- Attention Deficit Hyperactivity Disorder
- Oppositional Defiant Disorder
- Conduct Disorder
- Substance Use Disorders
- Anorexia Nervosa and Bulimia Nervosa
- Anxiety Disorders
- Posttraumatic Stress Disorder
- Depressive Disorders

EVIDENCE

Each chapter in *Mental Health Treatment for Children and Adolescents* will present the state of the research knowledge in terms of two perspectives that define the constitution of an "evidence" basis. The American Psychological Association (APA) developed the APA Division 12 Task Force Criteria for *empirically supported treatment* (Chambless & Hollon, 1998). In this criteria, "well-established" and "probably efficacious," "possibly efficacious," and "experimental" treatments have been delineated. For "well-established treatments," at least two group-design experiments, conducted by independent investigatory teams, show statistically significant findings over medication, psychosocial placebo, or another treatment. Alternatively, the treatment may be equivalent to an already established treatment in experiments with statistical power being sufficient to detect moderate differences. Furthermore, treatment is manualized and targeted for a specified problem and outcome measures are reliable and valid. Appropriate data analysis is also used.

For treatments defined as "probably efficacious," at least two studies must show that the intervention is more effective than no-treatment control. For "possibly efficacious," at least one study must indicate that a treatment is superior in the absence of conflicting evidence. Generally, only well-established or probably efficacious treatments will be discussed in this volume, unless discussion centers around treatment for certain vulnerable subpopulations, such as youth from ethnic minority backgrounds, in which case "possibly efficacious" treatments for certain disorders might represent the current state of the knowledge.

The APA Division 12 Task Force Criteria is the organizing framework for the series of which this book is part. However, this categorical system has its limitations. First, empirically supported treatment has been defined only in terms of psychosocial, rather than pharmacological interventions, and this book will focus on both psychosocial and pharmacological treatment for child mental health disorders. Second, the inclusion and search process for studies is not typically made transparent, nor are authors required to demonstrate that their search has been comprehensive (Littell, 2005). As a result, one limitation of the APA Division 12 Task Force Criteria is that studies tend to be only those that are published and written in the English language. If only certain studies are located, results may be biased toward the findings of those studies, and the bias toward positive findings in published research is well-known (e.g., Dickersin, 2005).

A further limitation of the APA categorization system is that it relies on a vote counting method to tally the results of studies. Results are counted as "positive" if statistically significant results are found, and "null" if negative or null results are reported. A major limitation of vote counting is its reliance on tests of statistical significance, which are affected by sample size (Littell et al., 2008). In studies with very large samples, *clinically* insignificant differences will be *statistically* significant. Significance tests (p-values) do not reveal the strength or magnitude of the effect, so vote counting may tally positive scores that do not really matter. Conversely, studies based on small samples often lack the statistical power needed to detect meaningful effects. Thus, clinically significant effects can be missed when small studies are combined with vote counting (Littell et al., 2008).

Another limitation of vote counting statistically significant results involves the fact that many studies use multiple outcome measures. It is not clear what APA Division 12 Task Force Criteria reviewers do when confronted by multiple outcomes. One choice is to include only the significance testing relating to their variable of interest (i.e., conduct problems), ignoring outcomes that are not as directly related to the presenting problem (i.e., peer relations or depression). In this case, significant outcomes may be missed that may bear important information on the impact of an intervention. A final limitation of vote counting is that moderators—participant, treatment, or study design characteristics that influence the variables under study—cannot systematically be taken under account (Littell et al., 2008).

To address these limitations, the other way this volume appraises evidence is through systematic reviews and meta-analysis. A *systematic review* aims to comprehensively locate and synthesize the research that bears on a particular question, using organized, transparent, and replicable procedures at each step in the process (Littell et al., 2008). *Meta-analysis* is a set of statistical methods for combining quantitative results from multiple studies to produce an overall summary of empirical knowledge on a given topic. (See Box 1.1 for additional information.) Whenever possible, Cochrane Collaboration systematic reviews are presented. The Cochrane Collaboration is an international, nonprofit organization devoted to high caliber systematic reviews on health and mental health care (see www.cochrane.org). Other published systematic reviews and meta-analyses are discussed in this volume in the absence of Cochrane reviews, although criteria for their inclusion were that they used conventional and up-to-date meta-analytic techniques, such as the appropriate between-group effect size calculation and weighting pooled effect sizes by the inverse variance. Therefore, if systematic reviews/meta-analyses did not use this accepted methodology, they were not included for discussion in this volume. The purpose is to draw on the best available evidence possible.

It is also recognized that part of evidence-based treatment is the assessment of child and adolescent mental health disorders in an evidence-based way. However, several excellent resources already exist for this purpose (see Mash & Barkley, 2007), and these will not be replicated here. As an aside, an argument has been made that the assessment of youth disorders should replicate the process used in treatment outcome studies, which is to use standardized diagnostic interviews [e.g., the Diagnostic Interview Schedule for Children (Shaffer et al., 1993; Doss & Weisz, 2008)]. The purpose is to improve the accuracy of diagnosis so that the treatment that follows is appropriate.

RISK AND RESILIENCE FRAMEWORK

The risk and resilience framework was formulated from several longitudinal studies in which at-risk youth were followed over time (e.g., Rutter, Maugham, Mortimore, & Ouston, 1979; Rutter, 1987; Wallerstein & Lewis, 1998; Werner, 2000; Werner & Smith, 1982, 2001). Despite the adversity they faced, some participants were found to show evidence of adaptation, which led to an examination of factors that may lead to such outcomes. The risk and resilience framework was therefore developed to consider the balance of risk and protective factors that interacts to determine an individual's propensity toward *resilience*, or the ability to function adaptively despite stressful life events. *Risks* can be understood as "hazards in the individual or the environment that increase the likelihood of a problem occurring" (Bogenschneider, 1996). *Protective* factors exist in the presence of risk factors, and involve the "personal, social, and institutional resources that foster competence,

---

BOX 1.1 INFORMATION ABOUT META-ANALYSIS AND EFFECT SIZES

Meta-analysis is used to analyze central trends and variations in results across studies and to correct for error and bias in a body of research. Results of the original studies are converted to one or more common metrics, called effect sizes, which indicate the strength or magnitude of the relationships between variables. In meta-analysis, effect sizes are calculated for each study, weighted by sample size, and then averaged to produce an overall effect. The choice of effect size (ES) measures is influenced by the purpose and design of a study and the format of the data and Lipsey and Wilson (2001) describe several. Most commonly discussed in this book will be *standardized mean differences* (SMD), also known as *Cohen's d* (Cohen, 1969), which is the mean difference divided by the pooled standard deviation of the two groups. For the SMD, a negligible effect is considered to range from 0.0 to 0.2, a small effect is between 0.2 and 0.5, a medium effect ranges from 0.5 to 0.8, and a large effect is considered to be greater than 0.8 (Cohen, 1988).

In the United States, the most commonly used effect size measure for dichotomous data is the *odds ratio* (OR), but in other countries the *risk ratio* is usually presented. The *odds ratio* is a comparison of two odds, that is, it is the odds that something will happen in one group compared with the odds that it will happen in the other. A negligible result is considered to range from 0.0 to 1.5. A small effect size is between 1.5 and 2.5; a medium effect size ranges from 2.5 to 4.3; and a large effect size is greater than 4.3 (Cohen, 1988). Like the odds ratio, the risk ratio compares the chance of an event in one group with the chance of that event in another group. The risk is the number of people who experience the event divided by the total number in the group.

The correlation coefficient *r* (formally called the *Pearson product–moment correlation coefficient*) expresses the strength and direction of an association between two continuous variables. Under 0.1 is considered negligible, small ranges from 0.1 to 0.25, medium is between 0.25 and 0.4, and large is greater than 0.4 (Cohen, 1988).

Adapted from Littell et al. (2008).

---

promote successful development, and thus decrease the likelihood of engaging in problem behavior" (Dekovic, 1999). Protective factors may counterbalance risk or act as a buffer against risk (Hawkins, Pollard, Catalano, & Baglioni, 2002; Werner, 2000).

In this book, each chapter will include a section on what will be referred to as the biopsychosocial risk and resilience framework. The biopsychosocial emphasis expands the focus beyond the individual to a recognition of contextual factors that create and ameliorate problems. For each disorder, risk and protective influences will be discussed. Because this literature is difficult to identify—it is often not categorized as belonging to risk and resilience—and instead involves studies on the many factors that can potentially contribute to mental health disorders, efforts were made to include the relevant studies and, whenever possible, existing systematic reviews and meta-analyses of this literature were presented for each disorder. Evidence-based treatments are assessed in terms of their ability to address these influences. It is recognized that a focus on risk and protective factors naturally leads to a discussion of prevention of these risks and enhancement of protective factors. Although prevention is certainly an important thrust in children's mental health (President's New Freedom Commission on Mental Health, 2003), this volume will emphasize treatment *after* a mental health disorder is already present in a child or adolescent.

CASE ILLUSTRATIONS

Although most academics from the mental health-treating disciples, when surveyed, say they support evidence-based practice (Rubin & Parrish, 2007), the implementation of such treatments may be a more complex process. This complexity in *Mental Health Treatment for Children and Adolescents* will be demonstrated by case illustrations, which will be threaded throughout each chapter. The case studies will also highlight the myriad treatment settings through which children receive mental health services. Outpatient therapy is the most commonly used, with the treatment outcome research focusing on university-affiliated settings (DHHS, 1999). Traditionally, outpatient therapy has been delivered in a clinic or office, but other community-based interventions (e.g., case management, home-based therapy, school-based services) have not received as much attention. Outpatient therapy is followed in level of care by partial hospitalization or day treatment and then by residential treatment and inpatient hospitalization. The case studies will show the challenges of implementing evidence-based practices in these settings with youth from vulnerable populations, such as those living in poverty and from ethnic minority groups, and will indicate the adaptations that may be considered.

A concluding chapter will explore some of the cross-cutting themes that emerge from each chapter's presentation. The barriers and facilitators for the implementation of evidence-based practice will be discussed. Finally, recommendations for future research and for education and training of professionals, programming, and service system delivery will be advanced.

I

EXTERNALIZING DISORDERS

2

ATTENTION DEFICIT
HYPERACTIVITY DISORDER

Attention deficit hyperactivity disorder (ADHD), one of the disruptive behavior disorders, is characterized by a chronic pattern of *inattention* or *hyperactive/impulsive behavior* (or both) that is more severe than what is typically observed in peers (APA, 2000). Persons with the "inattention" subtype of the disorder manifest a failure to attend to details and make many careless mistakes, whereas those with the "hyperactive" subtype are characterized by restlessness and impulsivity. A recent study by the United States Centers for Disease Control (Centers for Disease Control and Prevention, 2005) reported a 7.8% prevalence of ADHD among children aged 4–17 years. The worldwide prevalence for ADHD is 5.29% (Polanczyk, de Lima, Horta, Biederman, & Rohde, 2007). European rates are similar to those of the United States whereas rates in Africa and the Middle East were lower.

In line with ADHD being posed as a heritable neurodevelopmental disorder, the treatment outcome research includes both psychopharmacological and psychological approaches and will be reviewed here, along with their application to a case study. Other influences on the disorder are discussed, as well as contextual factors that impact adjustment, treatment, and recovery. Based on these discussions, research recommendations for the treatment of ADHD are advanced.

STATE OF THE EVIDENCE

The evidence for treatment of ADHD mainly centers around medication and one type of psychosocial treatment, behavioral therapy. Within these somewhat limited options, there is some controversy among professional groups about which should be the first-line treatment (Pelham & Fabiano, 2008).

The empirical literature on family intervention for ADHD mainly involves parent training (Barkley & Murphy, 2006). This is a brief treatment model involving about 12 sessions in either individual or group formats in which parents receive information about ADHD, its medications, effective parenting behaviorally based parenting practices, how to reinforce children's coping strategies, and how to manage parental stress. Through positive reinforcement, children learn prosocial behavior such as following directions, completing homework, doing household chores, and getting along with siblings. Parents are taught to respond to children's negative behaviors by ignoring or punishing the child so that he or she will suffer negative consequences for engaging in the behavior. Parents are taught these principles through didactic instruction, behavioral rehearsal, modeling, and role-plays. Because children with ADHD have problems with schoolwork, other interventions for parents include structuring the home environment (so that the child has a place to work relatively free of distractions), regular teacher verification of satisfactory homework completion, and a home-based reinforcement system featuring regular school–home note exchanges (DuPaul & Power, 2000).

Systematic Reviews/Meta-Analyses

Systematic reviews and meta-analyses on the treatment outcome literature are accumulating (see Table 2.1). Bjornstad and Montgomery (2005) assessed the impact of family therapy with children with ADHD and their parents. Family therapy was defined as the therapist, at least for some of the work, having parents and child(ren) in the session at the same time. Family therapy was limited in this review to those that had a behavioral component (i.e., behavioral, cognitive–behavioral, or functional family therapy). However, many behaviorally oriented treatments were excluded because in them, parents were seen alone. Many behavioral parent training programs, however, involve parents only (see Chapter 3). Given Bjornstad and Montgomery's (2005) inclusion criteria that studies had to be randomized in nature, only two studies were located. Findings were therefore limited as the studies could not be quantitatively synthesized.

Another meta-analysis of relevance to this literature used broader criteria in that parents had to be involved in treatment for their child's ADHD (Corcoran & Dattalo, 2006). Studies could either be experimental or quasiexperimental in design. Sixteen studies were located with all being behavioral in nature. Compared to control and comparison conditions, parent-involved treatment (parent training) of ADHD had a low to moderate effect on ADHD and externalizing symptoms. It must be recognized that some of the control conditions involved viable treatments, such as medication and child treatment; therefore, the fact that parent-involved treatment produced overall gains above and beyond these control

TABLE 2.1 SUMMARIES OF SYSTEMATIC REVIEWS AND META-ANALYSES ON PSYCHOSOCIAL TREATMENT FOR ATTENTION DEFICIT HYPERACTIVITY DISORDER (ADHD)

Author and Purpose	*Inclusion Criteria*	*Main Findings*
Bjornstaad and Montgomery (2005)	**Participants** Children or adolescents with diagnoses of ADHD or a cut-off score on a well-validated assessment measure. Children must not be taking medication for their symptoms during the trials. **Intervention** Family therapy interventions that include functional family therapy, cognitive–behavioral family therapy, or behavioral family therapy, all of which must include components with at least one parent and the child participating in some therapy sessions with the therapist. Treatment methods that involved interventions with parents exclusively were excluded as were participants who received medication. **Studies** Randomized controlled trials investigating the efficacy of family therapy for children with ADHD. **Outcome** The incidence or severity of symptoms of inattention, impulsivity, and hyperactivity. Outcome measures considered for inclusion were ratings on standard, psychometrically sound and validated assessment questionnaires measuring changes in attentional, impulsive, and hyperactive symptoms over time.	*N* = 2 studies Only two studies were located, which limits the generalizability of the findings.

(continued)

Author and Purpose

Corcoran and Datallo (2006)

To determine the magnitude and direction of the overall effect size for parent-involved treatment of ADHD for a child internalizing, externalizing, ADHD, social competence, family functioning, self-control, and academic performance and to determine the moderators involved

Inclusion Criteria

Participants

Youth ages 18 years and under who have ADHD.

Intervention

Interventions had to have parental involvement.

Studies

Quasiexperimental or experimental designs in published English language journals.

Outcomes

Child internalizing, externalizing, ADHD, social competence, family functioning, self-control, and academic performance.

Main Findings

N = 16 studies met inclusion criteria

In order, parent-involved treatment affected the following: academic performance (8.20) based on three studies; family functioning (0.67); internalizing (0.63)

Teacher-reported outcomes had the largest effect size (0.75); child-reported outcomes had the smallest (0.11).

Two-parent families did better with parent-involved treatment and older age of children.

treatments is noteworthy. Parent-involved treatment had an even higher effect on child internalizing symptoms and family functioning. There were few studies assessing academic performance, but these showed that academic performance might be an outcome that family treatment positively benefits. Child social skills, on the other hand, were not affected by family treatment, despite the thrust of many programs, which was to improve such skills. Because children with ADHD struggle with deficits in attention and have high impulsivity, they have a hard time waiting, taking turns, and solving social interaction dilemmas. These core deficits seem difficult to alter, even when programs center on the development of social skills.

APA Psychological Task Force Criteria

A 10-year update was conducted on psychosocial treatments for ADHD. No treatment outcome studies were identified that supported the use of nonbehavioral therapies (i.e., individual therapy, play therapy, cognitive therapy) (Pelham & Fabiano, 2008). Three treatments met the criteria for well-established treatment: behavioral parent training, school-based behavioral reinforcement, and a summer day treatment program focusing on social skills.

The school-based behavioral reinforcement involved teachers implementing point systems and rewards, as well as time out (Pelham & Fabiano, 2008). While social skills training appears to be ineffectual in clinic-based weekly sessions (Pelham & Fabiano, 2008), confirming the results of Corcoran and Datallo (2006), a day treatment program focusing on social skills was categorized as "well-established." This is an intensive treatment, delivering 200 to 400 hours of treatment compared to only 10 to 20 hours in a weekly program. However, this day treatment program is also more expensive than other treatment options and is not available in most communities. Furthermore, this program is often offered as a part of another intervention [behavioral therapy for the MTA study (discussed below) or medication], and the reviewers are the leading researchers of the program. Therefore, an independent review of this treatment may be needed.

MEDICATION

Systematic Reviews/Meta-Analyses

The primary psychostimulant drugs for ADHD include methylphenidate (71% of cases), the amphetamines, and pemoline (Bentley & Walsh, 2006). King, Griffin, Hodges, et al. (2006) recently undertook a review of the stimulants for the National Institute of Clinical Excellence in the United Kingdom. Quantitative synthesis on efficacy was not able to be conducted due to their method of dividing dose levels (low, medium, and high) and separating immediate- from extended-release versions of medications. However, they concluded that overall, medication outperformed placebo. Few differences between the different stimulants emerged in terms of efficacy or side effects, but authors also noted that methodological rigor of some studies were weak, precluding analysis of differences. In addition to affecting ADHD symptoms, the stimulants also seem to help curb aggression in youth with ADHD (Connor, Glatt, Lopez, Jackson, & Melloni, 2002).

Schachter, Pham, King, Langford, and Moher (2001) conducted a meta-analysis of the randomized, controlled trials in the English-language published literature of short-acting methylphenidate with youth under age 18 years. Sixty-two trials were included involving 2897 participants. The impact of medication compared to placebo was 0.78 for teacher-report (a large effect size) and 0.54 for parent report (a moderate effect size).

Limitations were apparent in studies. Trials were short (on average 3 weeks); many studies had methodological problems, and there was an indication of publication bias, meaning that the focus on published studies may conceal the fact that unpublished studies may contradict these findings. Adverse side effects were also reported. For example, decreased appetite was common according to both parent and teacher reports and was statistically significant compared to placebo.

Although medication seems to benefit many children, concerns have also been raised about its use, which, in addition to adverse reactions, include (Brown et al., 2007) the following:

1. Stimulant treatment does not affect the long-term (adult) outcome of ADHD.
2. Many individuals will not respond to medications.
3. For nonstimulant medications, short-term safety data are lacking.
4. There is a negative effect of stimulant treatment on growth (see Faraone, Biederman, Morley, & Spencer, 2008, for a review).
5. There is a lack of long-term evidence that medication is safe when taken over a number of years.

Although the stimulants have traditionally been the drug of first choice in treating ADHD, alternatives are sometimes necessary due to side effects or lack of positive impact. Some typical alternatives are bupropion (Wellbutrin) and atomoxetine (Strattera), a selective norepinephrine reuptake inhibitor. Atomoxetine has been studied extensively since the last edition of this book. Cheng, Chen, Ko, and Ng (2007) performed a meta-analysis on nine randomized, controlled trials of atomoxetine and found a standardized mean difference of –0.699, favoring the medication over placebo. Therefore, it appears that atomoxetine may be helpful for youth who are prescribed it (Table 2.2).

COMBINED PSYCHOSOCIAL AND MEDICATION TREATMENT

To shed light on the differential efficacy of combined treatment over medication and behavioral treatment, the Multi-modal Treatment Study (MTA) of Children

TABLE 2.2 SUMMARIES OF SYSTEMATIC REVIEWS AND META-ANALYSES ON PHARMACOLOGICAL TREATMENT FOR ATTENTION DEFICIT HYPERACTIVITY DISORDER (ADHD)

Author and Purpose	Inclusion Criteria	Main Findings
Cheng, Chen, Ko, and Ng (2007) To evaluate the efficacy and safety of atomoxetine in youth with ADHD	**Participants** Children and adolescents **Intervention** Atomoxetine was used to treat ADHD **Studies** Randomized, controlled with a placebo as the control group **Outcome** Attention-Deficit/Hyperactivity Disorder Rating Scale IV and other standardized measures of ADHD (teacher, clinician, and parent report)	$N = 9$ Compared to placebo, the standardized mean difference for atomoxetine was −0.699 for ADHD-IV (with atomexetine faring better than placebo)
Schachter, Pham, King, Langford, and Moher (2001) To examine the efficacy of short-acting methylphenidate with youth under age 18 years	**Participants** Youth under age 18 years **Intervention** Short-acting methylphenidate **Studies** Randomized, controlled trials in the English-language published literature **Outcomes** ADHD	$N = 62$ involving 2897 participants The impact of medication compared to placebo was 0.78 for teacher-report (a large effect size) and 0.54 for parent report (a moderate effect size).

with Attention-deficit/Hyperactivity Disorder Cooperative Group Study, the largest study to date on the treatment of youth ADHD ($N = 579$), has been undertaken. In the MTA study, children were randomized to four groups:

- Medication, which was delivered in an intensive and carefully monitored fashion);
- Behavior therapy delivered in the following modalities: parent training (8 individual sessions and 27 group treatment sessions), teacher consultation on behavioral methods with the child, and child-focused therapy offered in a summer treatment program (8-week, 5 days a week, 9 hours a day);
- Combined medication and behavior therapy as described above;
- Community control (families were free to receive treatment from providers in the community).

Treatment was provided for a 14-month period. At this point time, the combined treatment (medication and behavior therapy) performed better than behavior therapy alone in terms of reduction in ADHD symptoms, but not in a statistically significant way from medication alone (Swanson, Arnold, Kraemer, et al., 2008). Children in the combination group were taking a 20% lower dose than those in the medication group. This suggests that the addition of behavior therapy allowed children to take a lower dose and still have the same benefits (Swanson et al., 2008). At 24 months, the medication groups still maintained an advantage over the behavior therapy and community control groups, though to a lesser extent. At 36-month follow-up, any advantages of medication had disappeared. There was a protective effect for behavior therapy against early substance use. Weight and height were diminished in children now ages 11–13 years who had taken medication. It is unknown whether they would catch up by early adulthood in terms of their growth.

The findings from the MTA study do not provide clear guidelines on treatment and do not resolve the controversies about appropriate treatment. The American Academy of Child and Adolescent Psychiatry (2007) recommends medication as a first-line treatment, whereas psychologists typically suggest behavioral interventions (Pelham & Fabiano, 2008). Indeed, authors of the MTA study disagree among themselves about appropriate treatment and whether behavioral treatment or medication should be offered (Vedantam, 2009).

BIOPSYCHOSOCIAL RISK AND PROTECTIVE INFLUENCES

ONSET OF ADHD

Biological Influences

The consensus seems to be that ADHD involves cognitive or neuropsychological impairment with problems in executive functioning related to response inhibition, vigilance, working memory, and planning for the future (AACAP, 2007). At the same time, not all those with ADHD show executive function deficits. Furthermore, researchers have not yet specified the mechanisms involved in neuropsychological theory.

Despite the limitations of this theory, broad support exists for the fact that child factors, rather than family, neighborhood, and other socioeconomic status (SES) influences, are responsible for ADHD (Ford, Goodman, & Meltzer, 2004). Specifically, ADHD represents an inherited genetic disorder. In a review of 20 twin studies, the heritability of ADHD was estimated at 76% (Faraone et al., 2005). Similarly, another review indicated heritability estimates to be between 70% and 90% (Polderman, Derks, Hudziak et al., 2007). The precise genetic mechanisms that contribute to the onset of ADHD are not known, but dopamine transmitter and receptor genes, as well as several serotonin transporter and receptor genes, have been linked (Faraone & Khan, 2006; Levy, Hay, & Bennett, 2006). Along with neurobiological risk for the development of the disorder, there may also be protective factors related to the development of the prefrontal cortex (certain gene systems and response inhibition or the capacity to inhibit impulsive behaviors) that may help children, in the face of environmental stressors, avoid ADHD (Nigg, Nikolass, Friderici, et al., 2007).

Aside from genetics, other biological influences may play a role in the development of ADHD. Children who are born preterm are at twice the risk for ADHD as full-term children (Bhutta, Cleves, Casey, Cradock, & Anand, 2002). Maternal smoking and drinking during pregnancy may independently act as predisposing influences (Biederman, 2005; Kahn, Khoury, Nichols, & Lanphear, 2003). Lead exposure is also thought to increase the number of ADHD cases by 290,000 in the United States alone (Braun, Kahm, Froehlich, et al., 2006).

Social Influences

Although many vigorously assert that ADHD is a neuropsychological disorder, others suggest that attachment patterns between parent and child and other family dynamics may contribute to the onset of ADHD. Severe early deprivation, as often occurs in institutional rearing, may be one way this occurs (Kreppner, O'Connor, & Rutter, 2001). In another study, hostile family interactions when the child was 2 years old and for boys, enmeshed family patterns, predicted child ADHD at age 7 years (Jacobvitz, Hazen, Curran, & Hichtens, 2004). One factor is whether symptoms of ADHD were already present in toddlers, contributing to family hostility and enmeshment.

Family adversity was related to ADHD symptoms independently of problems with conduct in a recent study, suggesting that family and social risk influences may be both a cause as well as a consequence of ADHD (Counts, Nigg, Stawicki, et al., 2005). It is also likely that certain risk factors, such as family adversity, affect children who have a genetic vulnerability to develop ADHD (Laucht, Skowronek, & Becker, et al., 2007).

TREATMENT AND RECOVERY

Biological Influences

DEVELOPMENTAL STAGE. Most studies on ADHD treatment outcome research have been conducted on children (Barkley et al., 2004). Adolescents are less likely than children to receive mental health services and are often noncompliant with services. Still, it is estimated that at least two-thirds of males in their early to mid-teens who have had ADHD as children continue to meet diagnostic criteria for ADHD, with academic, cognitive, or behavioral problems (Mannuzza & Klein, 1999;

Wolraich, Wibbelsman, Brown, et al., 2005). In late adolescence, 40% of youth may still display significant symptoms. Furthermore, personality disorders may emerge in adolescence (Miller, Flory, Miller, et al., 2008)

Some adaptations can be made for parent training in working with adolescents. First, consequences must be chosen that are meaningful and motivating for the individual at that particular stage of development. For example, time out may be a less appropriate punishment for adolescents, and loss of privileges or activities (e.g., talking on the telephone, going to the mall with friends, obtaining access to the car) may be substituted instead (Chronis et al., 2007). In contrast, tangible consequences should be offered on a frequent basis for young children. Reinforcement should also be presented immediately following the behavior so that children understand the connection between their behavior and the consequence.

GENDER. ADHD is more prominent among boys by approximately a 2.5:1 ratio (CDC, 2005), and more research has been done on boys (Rucklidge & Tannock, 2001). Boys may have a greater genetic liability for the disorder (Derks, Dolan, Hudziak, et al., 2007) and their disruptive behavior more often comes to the attention of professionals.

The validity of the DSM criteria for females has also been challenged. Fewer girls tend to be diagnosed with the disorder even controlling for referral bias. Females have a lower base level of inattentiveness and hyperactivity than their male counterparts, and thus they have to deviate much further from girls without symptoms to be diagnosed (Arnold, 1996). As a result, discussion has centered on appropriate diagnostic criteria for females, so that girls can be identified for services (Ohan & Johnston, 2005).

A recent study of females with ADHD compared them 5 years after they had been diagnosed to girls their ages without ADHD (Hinshaw, Owens, Sami, & Fargeon, 2006). Those with ADHD had significantly more impairment across all the symptom domains, including externalizing, internalizing, substance use disorders, eating problems, peer relations, and academic performance. Girls diagnosed with ADHD in childhood seem at particular risk for anxiety and depression by the time they reach adolescence (Biederman, Ball, Monuteaux, et al., 2008; Lahey, Hartung, & Loney, 2007). They are also more at risk for future diagnosis of conduct disorder in adolescence (Monteaux, Faraone, Gross, & Biederman, 2007). These researchers also found that girls with ADHD had more maltreatment (mostly sexual abuse and neglect) when they were younger than the comparison girls (Briscoe-Smith & Hinshaw, 2006). It is uncertain whether the abuse was a causal factor in the ADHD. These findings indicate the seriousness of ADHD symptoms in girls and the importance of proper diagnosis and treatment.

In the MTA study, girls did better than boys over the 36-month period in which they were followed after undergoing intervention for 14 months (Jensen et al., 2007). This is encouraging; girls may perform at least as well as boys when they receive treatment.

On the topic of gender, Fabiano (2007) reviewed the behavioral parent training literature and found that mothers were the participants and outcome raters only in a majority of the studies (87%). Clearly, fathers will need to play a greater role in parent training in future studies as coparticipants in treatment and for the provision of outcome information.

Psychological Influences

COMORBIDITY. ADHD commonly cooccurs with other childhood disorders, particularly oppositional defiant disorder (ODD), conduct disorder (CD), and learning disorders, and to a somewhat lesser extent with internalizing disorders, such as anxiety (Pliszka, 2000). In fact, in the MTA study, only 31.8% of the participants had a diagnosis of ADHD alone; 29.5% were diagnosed with ADHD and either ODD or CD, 14% were diagnosed with both ADHD and an anxiety disorder, and 24.7% were diagnosed with ADHD, ODD, or CD and an anxiety disorder (Jensen et al., 2007). Comorbid ODD puts a child at risk for continued ODD and depression in early adulthood (Biederman et al., 2008). Comorbid CD puts a child at risk for substance use disorders, bipolar disorder, and smoking in early adulthood.

Some evidence indicates that certain comorbid disorders could by targeted by particular treatment components. In the MTA study, children with ODD or CD continued to be impaired, but this group tended to improve when medication was one of the components (Jensen, Arnold, Swanson, et al., 2007). In contrast, children with comorbid ADHD and anxiety responded best to interventions including behavior therapy. In fact, for children with comorbid anxiety disorders, behavioral treatment alone yielded effects comparable to medication alone and to combined treatment on *both* ADHD and anxiety symptoms.

PATTERNS OF ADHD SYMPTOMS. More severe ADHD is more persistent (Kessler et al., 2005) and is associated with worse outcomes (Barkley et al., 2006). Types of ADHD include Inattentive Type, Hyperactive-Impulsive Type, and Combined Type. Most research has centered on the combined type with the inattentive type almost ignored (Pfiffner, Mikami, Huang-Pollock, et al., 2007). The little research that has been conducted on the inattentive type focuses on its treatment with stimulant medication, with initial positive results (Stein et al., 2003).

In the first randomized trial of the inattentive type, 69 school-aged children were randomized to either a home and school behavioral treatment or no treatment. Experimental participants showed reductions on symptoms and impairment both at posttest and at 5-month follow-up (Pfiffner et al., 2007). The authors suggest that the gains made were similar to those typically resulting from medication and were greater than generally observed for the combined type of ADHD.

Social Influences

FAMILY FACTORS.   Parental expressed emotion may moderate the genetic effect associated with ADHD (Sonuga-Burke, Lasky-Su, Neale, et al. (2008). Specifically, maternal warmth and criticism may protect against ADHD becoming severe or from the development of conduct disorder, respectively. Indeed, any parental or family difficulties that contribute to inconsistent, coercive, or decreased efforts at managing the child's behavior may increase problem behaviors in the child (Weiss & Trokenberg-Hechtman, 1993) and may eventually lead to ODD or CD, which presents further risk. At the same time, having a child with ADHD puts a strain on marriages. Wymbs, Pelham, Molina, et al. (2008) found that parents with a child with ADHD were more likely to divorce than parents without an ADHD child.

In the MTA study, good outcomes were mediated by parents' effective discipline (Hinshaw, 2007). On the other side, maternal depression predicts a worse improvement outcome (Owens et al., 2003). These findings are not surprising given that distressed individuals often lack the motivation or organization to complete effortful tasks that require ongoing work, such as the consistent implementation of behavioral management techniques.

Chronis, Gamble, Roberts, and Pelham (2006) conducted a randomized, controlled study of cognitive–behavioral treatment of mothers of children with ADHD to prevent depression. They found that compared to those on a wait-list mothers who received the intervention showed less depression, more self-esteem, improved cognitions related to their child, and less family impairment at posttest. These gains were also maintained at follow-up. This study suggests that depression in parents can be targeted for intervention.

Another factor identified in families involves household composition. A two-parent home may be a protective influence because two parents are more likely to successfully manage the stress related to having a child with ADHD (Cuffe et al., 2001). In the meta-analysis of family interventions for ADHD, a child's living in a single-parent home contributed to worse outcomes for family treatment (Corcoran & Datallo, 2006).

ETHNICITY.   Here ethnicity will be explored in terms of prevalence of ADHD in ethnic minority groups. Information on treatment as applied to these youth will also be discussed, when available.

Although African-American youth are rated by parents and teachers as having more ADHD symptoms than white youth, they are diagnosed with the disorder at two-thirds the rate of white youth (Miller, Nigg, & Miller, 2009). Although low SES itself did not explain the differences in symptom levels, Miller et al. (2009) recommend the need for exploring whether risk factors, such as low birth weight and lead exposure, might account for the variation. One reason offered by Miller et al. (2009) for the lower diagnosis rates is that symptoms may not be viewed as a serious problem among African-American parents and teachers. Additionally, parental factors could be operating, such as lack of education about symptoms, treatment, and the consequences of untreated ADHD. Other barriers relate to the healthcare system, involving the lack of culturally competent healthcare providers, racial stereotyping by professionals, and the failure of clinicians to evaluate the child in multiple settings before diagnosis. In the MTA study, African-Americans performed best when they were offered medication and behavioral treatment (Arnold et al., 2003).

Few population prevalence studies of ADHD have been done with the Latino population. One estimate by the National Center for Health Statistics reported a prevalence of is 3.3% in Latinos and 6.5% in whites (Bloom & Dey, 2006). The incidence of ADHD may truly be lower in Latino children, but underdiagnosis may also explain the differential rates (Rothe, 2005). Other explanations for differences in these rates include language barriers that interfere with the ability to report ADHD symptoms, the family's degree of acculturation (less acculturated mothers may not recognize symptoms of ADHD), different developmental expectations by Latina mothers, or physician bias that may cause dismissal of concerns regarding symptoms in the Latino population. Of the Latinos who are diagnosed, many are undertreated.

The research on outcome by ethnicity is limited. In the Corcoran and Dattalo (2006) meta-analysis, ethnicity did not emerge as a moderator variable. In the MTA study, combined treatment (behavioral treatment with medication) was more effective for African-American and Latino participants than either medication alone or community services. However, no other studies address the effectiveness of psychosocial treatment for youth of ethnic minorities who have been diagnosed with ADHD (Huey & Polo, 2008).

SES. People in poverty tend to do worse than their nonpoor counterparts in terms of improvement on ADHD (Jensen et al., 2007). It may be due to lack of access to health care. Alternatively, it could be that managing the stressors of poverty may be seen as the priority in comparison to a child's symptoms of ADHD.

TREATMENT SETTINGS. Some of the dissipation of the positive effects of medication is due to the fact that medication was being provided according to community standards; that is, it was no longer necessary to closely monitor and adjust dosages. Indeed, a study using a large claims database from U.S. managed healthcare organizations showed that the titration of dosage in usual practice is less than that at recommended levels, suggesting that children are not receiving optimal treatment (Olfson, Marcus, & Wan, 2009).

It must also be noted that the behavior treatment offered in the MTA study is much more intensive than is typically used in studies. For instance, parents received eight individual sessions and 27 group sessions, children were in a summer camp program for 8 weeks, and a consultant also worked with the child's teacher on behavioral management to coordinate efforts between the parents and the school.

RESEARCH RECOMMENDATIONS

Although it is widely believed that ADHD requires multimodal interventions, including parent training, medication, and school-based interventions (e.g., Conners, Epstein, March, et al., 2001; Multimodal Treatment Study of Children with Attention Deficit/Hyperactivity Disorder Cooperative Group, 1999), it is not known whether this is indeed the case. The Academy of Child and Adolescent Psychiatry (2007) consensus guidelines state that for some youth who do well on medication, no other treatment is required. However, researchers from the discipline of clinical psychology disagree and support behavioral treatment, either alone or in combination with medication (Pelham & Fabiano, 2008). A case, based on the available evidence, can be made for either position. Further testing needs to shed light on this issue with large-scale studies such as the MTA with long-term follow-up included. This is particularly important because the long-term safety of medication has not been established (Brown et al., 2007).

Future research also needs to determine the sequencing of treatment (Brown et al., 2007) and the aspects of intervention that are most critical for the types of problems and the characteristics children with ADHD and their families bring. One characteristic is gender. More exploration is needed to determine appropriate diagnostic criteria for girls, as well as how females do in treatment. The MTA study suggests they do just as well, but research could more routinely track girls in treatment and report their outcomes, particularly given how poor the adjustment is for girls with compared to girls without ADHD.

A similar need is represented for the treatment of clients that are from different ethnic groups. Do existing treatments developed and tested on white children perform as well for ethnic minority children? The initial research represented by the MTA study indicated that African-Americans did better with behavioral treatment combined with medication rather than medication alone, but further investigation is required.

Moreover, comorbidity is high among youth with ADHD, so an important area of future research involves the treatment approaches that are best suited for certain patterns of comorbidity. Additionally, further research on adolescents is required since a significant number of childhood cases persist into adolescence.

Treatment manuals also need to address how intervention should proceed when a parent has ADHD, when there is partner conflict, or when a parent is heading a single-parent home—all factors associated with poor outcome. Managing the stressors attendant to poverty are also not covered in existing treatment manuals. Although developing a manualized treatment encompassing these many potential factors would be a complex process, addressing these factors is crucial to ensure the success of the suggested evidence-based practice.

The previous section of this chapter detailed the different aspects of the client and the environment that may impact the course of treatment. To test interventions with people in these various circumstances, research needs to center on effectiveness research that is carried out in the community, rather than in university-based clinics. The latter types of settings tend to include intact, middle- to upper-middle-class samples. They also provide prompts and incentives so that participants continue in the research treatment. Often, these studies fail to include lower-SES families that may have problems with service attainment, compliance, and response (Weisz & Hawley, 1998). Importantly for medication outcomes, the type of treatment provided in the MTA study involved careful titration of doses and close monitoring, which is often not available for community doctors. Indeed, in the community control condition in the MTA study, participants and their families were free to seek medication (or other treatments), but this control condition did not stand up well to the experimental conditions that were part of the study.

Another recommendation for research is to improve the quality of systematic reviews and meta-analyses in the area of treatment for child ADHD. Recent meta-analyses have been published on psychosocial treatment and combined treatments, areas of study that urgently need answers. However, these were not discussed in this chapter because of outdated or unconventional meta-analytic techniques, which would compromise any results and conclusions made.

CONCLUSIONS

This chapter has surveyed the research evidence for the treatment of ADHD in youth. The controversy over whether psychostimulant medication should be a first-line intervention is ongoing. Among other recommendations posed in this chapter, further research needs to establish whether there are certain populations or subtypes that are associated with particular types of intervention. Another controversy centers on the role of psychosocial influences on the development of

ADHD, although certain contextual factors are associated with enhanced outcomes, which have been discussed in this chapter.

CASE STUDY

Trevor is an 11-year-old biracial male who was referred to the agency for home-based treatment. He lives with his intact biological family. His father, who is African-American, works as a delivery truck driver and his mother, who is white, is a secretary for a government agency, a job that she has held for nearly 20 years. Trevor has one brother who is 3 years old.

Trevor's family lives in a spacious apartment located in a safe neighborhood. The family income is adequate for the needs of the children and the family. The family has access to health care through Trevor's mother's job as a government employee. Trevor's parents and sibling are of average intelligence.

Trevor was referred by his school to this agency because of his inability to manage himself in a classroom setting, which has been a problem since the first grade. Although he is in a self-contained classroom in a specialized school for children with emotional and learning disabilities, Trevor was still acting out on a consistent basis. The school believed that Trevor would benefit from mentoring and more structure in the home environment. The family, who is frustrated by Trevor's acting out behaviors and excessive outbursts, were willing to try home-based counseling. Because both parents are employed full-time, Trevor and his younger brother spend a lot of time after school with their maternal grandparents, who are willing to participate in the home-based intervention.

At school, Trevor becomes frustrated easily when given new tasks. He is often distracted by activities of other children in the classroom. He has few friends but talks excessively to them during class. Trevor often interrupts the teacher during lessons and becomes angered when redirected from such behaviors. He also gets up in class, throws objects, taps his pencil, and engages in other behaviors that are distracting to the class. He curses and calls his classmates names, but fails to see the connection between his actions and his lack of friends.

Trevor has shown physical aggression towards staff and peers at school, such as pushing, hitting, and kicking when he is unable to get his way (with students) or when he is being removed from the classroom for behavioral issues (with staff). Trevor is behind grade level in several areas, especially written expression and reading comprehension.

At home Trevor is verbally abusive and physically aggressive toward his mother and his younger brother, pushing or hitting them when he is unable to get his way. He refuses to follow rules in the household and often does not complete his assigned chores or homework. Trevor is typically unable to sit through dinner or a TV show without getting up and usually returns with a toy or something to play.

Trevor's grandparents are particularly worried about his outbursts in their home. Because of their fears of being physically or verbally attacked by Trevor, they do not emphasize boundaries or limits with him. His parents are firmer with Trevor, but also give in to his demands when he is upset. For example, his mother will often tell Trevor that he has lost TV or game privileges for the day because of his behavior. She will later find him playing the game or watching TV and will confront him about it. If Trevor begins to throw a tantrum, she will let him continue to play the game or watch TV because it is easier than arguing with him. Normally the family uses a system of rewards (i.e., family outings, movies, games, and going out to eat) and punishments (i.e., losing privileges for TV and games) in relation to their "chore chart," but this is not always consistently enforced. The family indicates that they do not use physical punishment with the children.

Trevor's father has little involvement in the lives of the children, which he says is because of fatigue from his labor-intensive job and because of his "severe asthma." (Although otherwise healthy, Trevor also has asthma, which is controlled by the use of an inhaler.) Trevor's father rarely pays attention to his son and is sometimes verbally abusive to him, calling him curse words. Recently, Trevor's father dragged him by his feet across the floor, making a rug burn on the back of his neck. Trevor's father explained this incident as not being a punishment, but an attempt to keep the younger son safe because Trevor was threatening to physically harm him. A counselor reported the incident to Child Protective Services (CPS). An investigation took place and it was closed with no further involvement from CPS. After this incident the family decided to maintain a "hands-off" policy with Trevor in the future.

At home, Trevor is preoccupied with germs. He requests that the toilet seat be washed before he sits on it. When done toileting, he washes his hands excessively and uses a hand sanitizer. He carries hand sanitizers with him at all times and uses them when he feels that he has "gotten germs."

Trevor enjoys playing video games and quickly masters age-appropriate games. Other activities Trevor enjoys involve arts and crafts and music. He is easily able to learn song lyrics. In addition, he would like to be involved in playing sports in the future.

Trevor's behaviors were noted from a young age, as evidenced by his early placement in a special school program. His mother says that she is "tired" and "overwhelmed" and feels that her relationship with her extended family has suffered because of her son's behaviors at family functions. She also believes that her marriage has been strained because of Trevor's constant disruptions in the household. Trevor's mom hopes to be able to get her son's behaviors under control so their lives can go "back to normal." See Box 2.1 for the DSM diagnosis assigned in this case.

BOX 2.1 MULTIAXIAL DIAGNOSIS

Axis I: 314.01 Attention Deficit/Hyperactivity Disorder, Combined Type

A. 1. Trevor exhibits symptoms of inattention that have persisted for over 6 months to a degree that is maladaptive and inconsistent with his developmental level. Six or more symptoms must be present and he exhibits eight symptoms. Specifically, Trevor often:

(a) Fails to give close attention to details given by his teacher in school and often makes careless mistakes with chores and homework at home.

(b) Is unable to focus on school tasks. He often interrupts the teacher and other students when he loses focus on tasks.

(c) Fails to listen to his teacher when he is being spoken to and also fails to listen to his mother when she is giving him instructions.

(d) Fails to complete his homework and sometimes does not turn in completed work.

(e) Avoids schoolwork at school by talking to his peers and looking out the window. At home Trevor avoids homework by watching TV or playing with toys when not under direct supervision.

(f) Often loses his homework on the way to school or before going to class. He fails to turn in work that has been completed because it is "lost."

(g) Is easily distracted by stimuli in his environment. He is unable to focus if he feels others are doing something that he would rather be doing.

(h) Forgets to do chores given at home even though there is a consistent schedule.

Hyperactivity–Impulsivity

2. Trevor exhibits symptoms of hyperactivity–impulsivity that have persisted for over 6 months to a degree that is maladaptive and inconsistent with his developmental level. Six or more symptoms must be present and Trevor exhibits six symptoms. He:

(a) Fidgets in the classroom and at home. He is not content to sit through a television program or dinner without having something else to do.

(b) Is rambunctious in the household and in the classroom. He is often too rough with his brother when he is overstimulated and needs to be reminded to be gentle with others.

(c) Is loud and does not play quietly with his brother or cousins. He is often loud and needs to be reminded to use his "inside voice."

(d) Talks excessively at home and in the classroom. The teacher often has to remind Trevor of the classroom rules regarding talking out of turn.

(e) Often answers questions in class without raising his hand and gets frustrated with his teacher when he is redirected from this behavior.

(f) Has difficulty waiting his turn. Trevor has difficulties with interrupting conversations and does not like to take turns or share with his younger brother.

B. Trevor exhibited symptoms of hyperactivity/impulsivity before the age of 7 years. He has been in a special education setting since the age of 6 years.

C. Trevor exhibits symptoms of ADHD in both the home and school environment.

D. Trevor's impairment is moderate. He has few friends, does poorly in school, and often gets in trouble at home because of his inattention to details and his lack of compliance with family rules.

E. Trevor does not meet the criteria for Pervasive Development Disorder, Schizophrenia, or other Psychotic Disorders and his symptoms are not accounted for by another mental disorder.

(continued)

BOX 2.1 MULTIAXIAL DIAGNOSIS CONT'D

313.81 Oppositional Defiant Disorder

A. Trevor has a pattern of negative and defiant behaviors both at home and in the school environment that has lasted over 6 months. Four symptoms are needed to meet the criteria and he exhibits all of them. These behaviors occur more frequently and with more severity than with other children of his age and developmental level. Specifically, he:

(1) Loses his temper at home and at school. He is physically aggressive to teachers and parents when he is unable to get what he wants. He flies into a rage at times and is difficult to calm down.

(2) Argues with adults at home and in the school environment. He often argues with his mother and grandparents if he is unable to get his way. He also argues with his teacher and other authority figures at school.

(3) Defies class rules and refuses to listen to instruction from his caretakers. Although rules are clearly defined in these situations, Trevor still refuses to comply with classroom and house rules. He often ignores requests from his mother, grandparents, and teachers.

(4) Often deliberately annoys people around him. He constantly picks on his brother in hopes that he will be able to make him "cry." He deliberately engages in activities that he knows will receive a negative response from his mother.

(5) Is upset by the reactions of his peers at school to his behaviors. Although he does and says things to annoy his classmates (such as calling them names and using curse words), he is still upset when they do not want to associate with him. At times he is annoyed by their reactions and often starts arguments with his classmates.

(6) Is often angry with his situation and shuts down emotionally as a way to cope with his anger. Trevor picks physical fights or arguments with his peers and brother.

B. Trevor's behaviors severely limit his interactions with his peers. He is often left out of activities with children in his classroom and has few friends. His behaviors strain his relationships with his parents, brother, and grandparents.

C. Trevor does not meet the criteria for a Psychotic or Mood Disorder.

D. Trevor does not yet meet the criteria for a Conduct Disorder.

315.2 Disorder of Written Expression

A. Trevor was given diagnostic tests for learning disabilities as part of his Individualized Learning Plan (IEP) and scored in a range that indicates problems in written expression.

B. Trevor struggles with reading comprehension, which affects his schoolwork in all subjects. He is currently in a special needs classroom that helps with his needs.

C. Trevor does not have a sensory deficit issue.

Axis II: V71.09 No Diagnosis

Axis III: 493.90 Asthma (according to physician's report)

Axis IV: Problems with primary support group (inadequate and inconsistent discipline, father is uninvolved and emotionally unsupportive), problems with the social environment (lacks friendships), educational problems (academic difficulties)

Axis V: GAF: 63

Although Trevor has some moderate symptoms, such as few friends and conflicts with peers, he is able to attend school daily and interacts with his family. He also has meaningful relationships with others, such as his mother, brother, and his school mentor.

HOW RESEARCH EVIDENCE CAN INFORM THE CASE

Given his comorbid Oppositional Defiant Disorder and significant symptoms of Obsessive–Compulsive Disorder, a combined approach, involving both behavioral treatment and medication, may be indicated (Jensen et al., 2007). Parent training was developed in response to the types of antisocial behaviors Trevor evidences.

APPLICATION

Parent training for ADHD involves psychoeducation about the disorder as well as discipline strategies based on operant behavioral principles. The psychoeducation aspect involves providing Trevor's parents and grandparents with a description of ADHD, its symptoms, prevalence, and causes, as well as possible interventions. Normalization of some of Trevor's behaviors as symptoms of ADHD rather than as actions he takes to deliberately involve others can reduce some of the blame and ill-will that is held toward the child. Education about the disorder also helps family members revise their often too-high expectations for Trevor. For example, if Trevor needs to get up during dinner or when watching TV and get a toy that helps him to focus, this may be allowed.

Another important piece of psychoeducation involves assisting caregivers in reducing their stress as the diagnosis of ADHD in a child brings significant challenge to family functioning in terms of increased parenting stress, conflict with siblings, depression in mothers, marital conflict, and an increased likelihood toward separation and divorce of parents. For example, Trevor's mother talks about feeling "tired" and just wanting "peace and quiet," and speaks of marital strain that she attributes to Trevor's difficult behavior and its impact on the family. Trevor's father, in his frustration, has resorted to name-calling of his son, and at least one physical incident. Trevor's grandparents appear to fear him. As can be seen, Trevor's caregivers are experiencing a range of unpleasant reactions to Trevor's behaviors.

The treatment needs of children with ADHD and their families are often complex and intensive, requiring medication, psychosocial interventions for both child and parent, and school-based approaches; education helps caregivers understand this array of potential services.

Parent training involves principles of operant behavioral therapy, including positive reinforcement, rewards, ignoring, and punishment. Trevor's parents and grandparents would be taught the necessity of a system of positive reinforcement. When they talked about the discipline strategies they had in place, it appeared to feature punishment (taking away privileges). Although punishment has its place in parent training, it should play a less significant role than positive reinforcement. Punishment may be reserved for serious infractions, such as hitting his mother, verbally abusing her, and harming his younger brother. Trevor's parents and grandparents would be taught a program of reinforcement, including how to praise him, and to provide high-probability activities (such as TV shows and videogaming) for desirable behaviors, such as getting along with his brother, doing chores, and completing homework. A token economy for these behaviors could also be devised with rewards chosen by Trevor, such as spending time playing ball with his father.

Parents and grandparents would be taught how to make constructive use of commands, as opposed to his father's demeaning comments as a way to "get through" to him. Trevor's caregivers would also be educated on coercive cycles: when Trevor's father erupts angrily at his son, he is actually training Trevor to refrain from behaving until his father reacts violently; when his grandparents and mother give in to Trevor's demands, he learns that if he escalates his behavior, he can get what he wants.

Parent training relies on instruction, modeling by the therapist, and behavioral rehearsal by caregivers. Behavioral rehearsal will play a key role for this family; the parents seem to have some appropriate knowledge about discipline, but they need help on the actual implementation of these strategies.

HOW THE RESEARCH EVIDENCE DOES NOT FIT

Characteristics of Youth

Many studies of parent training are based on white youth; Trevor is of biracial status and therefore does not fit the "typical" participant in terms of his ethnic background. It is unknown if different cultural values operating between his mother and father are part of their contrasting parenting styles and whether racial identity issues play into Trevor's behavioral problems.

As mentioned, the concurrent oppositional defiant disorder will be addressed in the parent training package; however, Trevor also seems to suffer from significant obsessive–compulsive anxiety symptoms. Although parent training and the evidence-based treatment for anxiety share behavioral principles, the treatment for Trevor's anxiety focuses on exposure. He would be exposed to "germy places" and then not allowed to wash himself afterward. Exposure to "germs" and response prevention of cleaning behavior during sports may also help alleviate Trevor's symptoms of anxiety. Parents would have to be taught how to promote nonobsessional behaviors and compulsions in Trevor. For example, they would be taught not to enable him by refusing to clean the toilet seat and to encourage him not to give in to the compulsion to clean.

Characteristics of Context

Several aspects of this family's context may present challenges; these include the setting for treatment, the extent to which the family is voluntary, the targeted unit of change, and the level of anger that Trevor's father demonstrates toward him.

Most studies on parent training have been conducted in university and clinic-based settings rather than through home-based services. Although home-based services may offer several advantages (it may more directly promote the generalization of skills to the home environment, caregivers practice in the naturalistic environment, and alleviate time for transportation and therefore may be more convenient), it is unknown whether parent training provided in this way is as effective as parent training studied in university and clinic research settings.

Studies on parent training have also been based on families voluntarily seeking treatment for their children's behavior. Although the family, in this case, is amenable to treatment, they were referred by the school system. Reyno and McGrath (2006) in their meta-analysis indicated that when families are referred by the school, they tend to benefit less well from parent training.

Given Trevor's father's hostility toward him and the recent physical escalation of discipline, anger management techniques might be indicated for Trevor's father so that he is able to calmly enact recommended behavioral strategies. The relationship with Trevor and his father also needs more positive development. Only one parent training program, Parent–Child Interaction Therapy, focuses on the development of positive relationships between parent and child, and this program is indicated for young children only (between the ages of 2 and 7 years) and is implemented in a play therapy room, not the home.

Parent training is typically conducted with one parent, the mother, although involvement of the father has been urged (see Lundahl, Tollefson, Risser, & Lovejoy, 2008). In Trevor's case, his grandparents are also involved in taking care of him and are willing to be involved in his intervention. For this to act as a strength rather than a detriment (further inconsistency in the discipline), parent training needs to involve the parents and the grandparents, but manuals, although focused on behavioral principles, have not been tailored to this level of family involvement. Furthermore, parent training manuals do not emphasize how to help parents work together when their styles are at odds and when fathers are disengaged.

DOES THE EVIDENCE-BASED TREATMENT TAKE ADVANTAGE OF STRENGTHS?

This family purports to already use some of the techniques that will be part of any parent training program, such as positive reinforcement and punishment. Therefore, a basis of knowledge has already been established. Their main problem seems to be following through with the agreed-on discipline program and consistency among caregivers. Modeling and behavioral rehearsal of skills and involvement of all caregivers in the home-based services seem most salient in this regard. If all caregivers can be consistent with discipline, the burden of care can be shifted among several adults, meaning that no one person will be taxed with the demands of the discipline program.

Another way in which strengths may be utilized with parent training is to have it based on the behavioral principle of positive reinforcement. Trevor's prosocial and on-task behavior will be recognized through a system of positive reinforcement—praise, tokens, and privileges. The parent training program may take advantage of Trevor's interests. For example, he wants to spend more time with his father, so a reward may be to play sports with his father or watch sporting events together. Trevor enjoys videogaming, so he could earn such privileges by completing homework and chores.

CONCLUSIONS

The members of Trevor's family are good candidates for parent training because they are motivated to participate in treatment and they have much of the knowledge and many of the behavioral methods skills already in place. Trevor's father's level of disengagement and anger toward Trevor may not, however, be contained with a focus on appropriate methods of discipline. Also, the addition of grandparents involved in his after-school care may present challenges in the level of consistency they are able to provide. Finally, more research needs to be conducted on in-home delivery of parent training as home-based services have become increasingly popular as ways to serve families for more restrictive services.

3

OPPOSITIONAL DEFIANT DISORDER AND CONDUCT DISORDER IN CHILDREN

With Robert Broce and Jennifer Shadik

This chapter, as well as Chapter 4, will summarize and critically review the state of the knowledge of the treatment outcome research on oppositional defiant disorder (ODD) and conduct disorder (CD) in youth. ODD is characterized by a pattern of negativistic, hostile, and defiant behaviors toward authority figures such as parents and teachers. These behaviors persist for at least 6 months and occur more frequently than is typically observed in children of a comparable age and developmental level. ODD had a lifetime prevalence of 10.2% in the U.S. population when adults were surveyed retrospectively about their symptoms (Nock, Kazdin, Hiripi, & Kessler, 2007). For preschoolers, estimates for the rates of ODD range between 4% and 16.8% (Egger & Angold, 2006). Over 40% of those with ODD end up developing conduct disorder.

CD also involves an entrenched pattern of behavior, but in this diagnosis the basic rights of others or major age-appropriate societal norms or rules are violated (APA, 2000). The *DSM-IV* includes subtypes of conduct disorder based on age of onset and the number and intensity of symptoms. These include childhood onset conduct disorder, in which at least one criterion is present before age 10 years, and adolescent onset conduct disorder, in which no criterion emerges before the age of 10 years. The median age of onset of CD is 11.6 years.

The particular focus of this chapter is these disorders in children (up to age 12 years); Chapter 4 relates to treatment with adolescents. The original goal was to include a chapter on ODD and CD separately; however, previous reviews of the literature have noted that treatment outcome studies are rarely organized according to diagnosis (Weisz, Doss, & Hawley, 2005). Instead, ODD is often combined with CD in studies (Angold et al., 1999). Indeed, most of the systematic reviews, meta-analyses, and treatment outcome studies have aggression, antisocial behavior,

behavior problems, conduct problems, disruptive behaviors, externalizing symptoms, or delinquency rather than the diagnoses of ODD and CD as their targets.

This chapter reports on the treatment outcome literature for both psychosocial and pharmacological interventions for child antisocial behavior. The evidence will be evaluated in terms of the extent to which it addresses the biopsychosocial risk influences that lead to the development of ODD and CD, as well as the factors influencing treatment and recovery. The chapter concludes with research recommendations.

STATE OF THE EVIDENCE

This chapter will be organized according to psychosocial and psychopharmacological interventions. Within the psychosocial section, interventions will be categorized by whether they have an individual or family focus and whether the evidence stems from systematic reviews/meta-analyses or APA Psychological Task Force Criteria reviews.

PSYCHOSOCIAL INTERVENTIONS

Child-Focused Interventions

Cognitive–behavioral therapy has been the most researched child-focused intervention for youth disruptive behaviors. Cognitive–behavioral approaches derive philosophically, theoretically and empirically from four theories of learning: respondent conditioning (associative learning, e.g., of sexual arousal and trauma), operant conditioning (the effect of the environment on patterns of behavior, particularly reinforcement and punishment), observational learning (learning by imitation), and cognitive learning (the impact of thought patterns on feelings and behavior) (Macdonald et al., 2006). For conduct problems, cognitive–behavioral treatment involves training parents in the application of operant conditioning techniques with their children (parent training is discussed under family-focused treatment) and cognitive learning approaches with the child. All cognitive–behavioral therapy (CBT) approaches share the importance of practitioner modeling to introduce skills being learned and behavioral rehearsal so that youth can practice new skills.

One type of cognitive intervention, social information processing (Baker & Scarth, 2002), underlies many of the studies to be discussed. Social information processing involves training children in at least one of a number of thinking processes (Dodge, 1986). These steps include encoding and then interpreting situational and internal cues, setting goals, determining possible responses, and role-playing the behavioral responses. Anger Control Training (Lochman, Barry, & Pardini, 2003) is one program with social information processing as its basis for use with elementary school-aged children with disruptive behavior. In weekly group sessions, children discuss vignettes of social encounters with peers and the social cues and possible motives of individuals in the vignettes. Children learn to use problem solving for dealing with anger-provoking social situations, and they practice appropriate social responses and self-statements in response to different problem situations, first by behavioral rehearsal of the situations with feedback for correct responses. Later in treatment, in anger-provoking situations children practice their use of new anger control strategies.

SYSTEMATIC REVIEWS/META-ANALYSES. Bradley and Mandell (2005) performed a meta-analysis of the published treatment outcome studies (randomized, controlled trials) that involved children with ODD (see Table 3.1). Due to the inclusion criteria (published studies from 1990 to 2004), bias may have been introduced in the studies selected. The particular focus on ODD is unique, however; most studies, as noted, talk about antisocial problems in general rather than the specific diagnoses of ODD and CD and collapse the ODD and CD diagnoses together when the DSM system is used. The authors found that Webster-Stratton's child problem-solving training for preschoolers made up a majority (four) of the seven studies they found (e.g., Webster-Stratton, Reid, & Hammond, 2004). Like the Webster-Stratton parent training program described below, the child problem-solving training involves a videotape program. In over 100 vignettes, young children and fantasy characters (lifesize puppets) are posed in a variety of interpersonal situations that may challenge children with ODD. Modeled skills involve the use of social skills, conflict resolution, positive attributions, and perspective taking. Child-only interventions resulted in a large effect size [standardized mean difference (SMD = 0.93)] on child behaviors in the home and a medium effect on social functioning (SMD = 0.55); yet the effect size for academic performance and child behaviors in the school was not found to be statistically significant.

McCart et al. (2006) conducted a meta-analysis of 41 studies of both parent training and individually focused CBT to discover the differential effectiveness of each. Overall, child-focused CBT was helpful in reducing aggression in youth, but at a small effect at both posttest (0.35) and follow-up (0.31) (see Table 3.1). This effect size was smaller than for the parent training intervention (0.47) for the age range of children (6–12 years) for which both interventions were offered.

Wilson and Lipsey (2007) conducted a meta-analysis of CBT targeting youth anger in the school setting, including both published and nonpublished reports. They found that the effect of anger interventions varied according to the target population. In 249 school-based studies that used aggressive and disruptive behavior as an outcome, selected/indicated programs were the most effective, although the overall effect size was small (0.29). Selected/indicated interventions involved individual or group treatment outside of the classroom for students who had been

Author and Purpose	Inclusion Criteria	Main Findings

Bradley and Mandell (2005)
Conduct a meta-analysis of the effects of various treatment domains for oppositional defiant disorder (ODD)
	Participants
	Parents of, or school-aged children (preschool to 12th grade) previously diagnosed with ODD [but not conduct disorder (CD)] using either DSM criteria or a "t-score" of over 55 on the aggression subscale of the child behavior checklist (CBCL).
	
	Interventions
	ODD treatment that is nonresidential and nonpharamacological.
	
	Studies
	Randomized controlled trials published in English between 1990 and 2004 that use at least one nonobservational outcome measure and publish quantifiable results.
	
	Outcomes
	Symptoms at home, symptoms at school, academic functioning, social functioning, parent stress/strain, and environment across intervention targets.
		N = 7 studies
		Symptoms at home:
		  Parent, 1.06
		  Child, 0.93
		  Both, 0.25
		Symptoms at school:
		  Parent, 0.31
		  Child, 0.31
		  Both, 0.07
		Academic functioning:
		  Parent, 0.18
		  Child, 0.34
		  Both, 0.09
		Social functioning:
		  Parent, 0.14
		  Child, 0.55
		  Both, 0.20
		Parent strain/stress:
		  Parent, 0.88
		  Child, 0.50
		  Both, 0.25
		Environment:
		  Parent, 0.85
		  Child, 0.68
		  Both, 0.20
		Intervening with symptoms at home with either children or parents is most effective for ODD.

(continued)

Author and Purpose	Inclusion Criteria	Main Findings
Dretze et al. (2009) To examine the differential effectiveness of parenting training programs for children with conduct problems	**Participants** Parents of youth 18 years and younger in which at least 50% of the children had a conduct problem (either a diagnosis or a clinical cutoff on a standardized measure). **Intervention.** Manualized parenting program **Studies** Randomized, controlled trials **Outcome** Standardized measures of child behavior	$N = 24$ According to parent's report, a standardized mean effect of –0.67, favoring the parent training intervention; the differential effectiveness of programs could not be established.

Lundahl, Risser, and Lovejoy (2005)
Examination of behavioral and nonbehavioral parent training programs for the treatment of disruptive behavior problems in children
	Participants
	Parents of children with disruptive behavior problems (excluding children not developmentally or cognitively delayed).
	
	Interventions
	Parent training targeting disruptive child behaviors.
	
	Studies
	Peer reviewed studies conducted outside of a laboratory setting and published in English between 1974 and 2003. Treatment and control group of at least five participants in each.
	
	Outcomes
	Child behavior
	Parent behavior
	Parent perception of parenting
		$N = 63$
		Effect sizes (ESs) by outcome category and intervention type.
		Child behavior, 0.42
		  Behavioral, 0.42
		  Nonbehavioral, 0.44
		Parent behavior, 0.47
		  Behavioral, 0.45
		  Nonbehavioral, 0.66
		Parent perception, 0.53
		  Behavioral, 0.53
		  Nonbehavioral, 0.48
		ESs for up to 1 year follow-up for behavioral programs remained in the small to moderate range (0.21 for child behavior, 0.25 for parent behavior, and 0.45 for parental perceptions).

McCart et al. (2006)

To investigate the effectiveness of cognitive–behavioral therapy (CBT) and behavioral parent training (BPT) on antisocial behavior in children

To explore the moderating effect of demographic factors

Participants

Youth 18 years or younger with antisocial behavior

Interventions

BPT or CBT for antisocial behavior

Studies

Published studies

Compared treatment to a control group

Outcomes

Behavioral outcome measures of antisocial behavior

Significant moderating effects within categories

In the child behavior category higher socioeconomic status (SES), higher pretreatment levels of behavior problems, having two parents, and individual vs. group delivery significantly improved effect.

In the parent behavior category higher SES, lower family adversity, and parent-only intervention significantly improved effect.

In the parent perception category higher SES and parent-only intervention significantly improved effect.

Among economically disadvantaged families, individual training was significantly more effective than group training across all three categories.

N = 76

Overall ES for BPT and CBT, 0.40

Overall ES for BPT, 0.47

Overall ES for CBT, 0.35

For ages 6–12 years only:

ES for BPT, 0.45

ES for CBT, 0.23

(continued)

Author and Purpose	Inclusion Criteria	Main Findings
Mytton et al. (2006) To examine the effectiveness of school-based programs to prevent violence in children identified at risk	**Participants** Youth in grades K–12 or international equivalent **Intervention** A school-based intervention "designed to reduce aggression, violence, bullying, conflict or anger or focused on Conduct Disorder or Oppositional Defiant Disorder" (p. 4) **Studies** Randomized, controlled studies (excluded cluster randomized trials) **Outcomes** Aggressive or violent behaviors measured by standardized measures, counts of aggressive behavior through observation, school or agency responses to aggressive behavior, violent injuries.	$N = 34$ studies contributed to meta-analysis The intervention produced gains over the control groups on child aggression (SMD of −0.41) and was maintained in the seven studies reporting 12-month follow-up (SMD = −0.40). The intervention also reduced school or agency disciplinary actions (SMD = −0.48, $N = 9$) although it was not maintained. The most effective programs focused on relationship improvement or social skills. Mixed-gender groups were as effective as groups composed only of boys, as were those designed for elementary and secondary school students.
Weisz, Jensen-Doss, and Hawley (2006) Determine the overall effect size of evidence-based treatments (EBTs) when compared with usual services (UC) Explore the relationships between EBTs and UC	**Participants** Mean of children's ages between 3 and 18 years with psychological problems or maladaptive behavior. **Interventions** EBT; an intervention previously being listed as showing beneficial effects. UC; a control condition typically provided by the agency or organization. **Studies** Youth treatment outcome studies published in journals or dissertations later than 1960; treatment (EBT) and control (UC) groups were randomly assigned. **Outcomes** Youth treatment for psychological or behavioral problems.	$N = 32$ randomized trials Overall mean ES of 0.30 EBTs across categories of severity (inpatient and incarcerated vs. outpatient) were equally effective.

| Wilson and Lipsey (2006a) Examine studies of the effectiveness of programs aimed at improving social information processing for reducing aggressive behavior | **Participants** Specially selected school-aged children K to 12 at risk for antisocial behavior or evident behavior problems. **Interventions** Social information processing programs universally delivered in regular school settings during school hours. **Studies** Studies used a control group, and if not randomized had some method of matching. **Outcomes** Aggressive behavior | *N* = 73 studies Overall mean effect size, 0.21 Programs with more frequent weekly sessions were more effective than those with less frequency. |
| Wilson and Lipsey (2006b) Examine studies of the effectiveness of programs aimed at improving social information processing for reducing aggressive behavior | **Participants** Specially selected school-aged children K to 12 at risk for antisocial behavior or evident behavior problems. **Interventions** Social information processing programs delivered to identified or indicated students in regular school settings during school hours. **Studies** Published after 1970. Studies used a control group, and if not randomized had some method of matching. **Outcomes** Aggressive behavior | *N* = 47 studies Overall mean effect size, 0.26 Programs were less effective for special education students. There was a greater reduction in aggression in higher risk students. |

referred for help with anger or aggression. Universal, or general in class programs combining cognitive, behavioral, and social skills elements also showed a small effect (0.21). The investigators found that alternative high schools and special education classes for behavioral problems showed a negligible effect at 0.11. Comprehensive and multimodal interventions that combined special parent and teacher training with student interventions were not shown to be effective.

Wilson and Lipsey (2006) also examined the effectiveness of a specific type of CBT—social information processing programs—implemented in the school setting for youth identified as having anger and behavior problems. The youth in this study were between the ages of 9 and 11 years, and the interventions were typically conducted in groups. Social information processing involves training children in at least one of a number of thinking processes. The meta-analysis of 47 studies examined social information processing programs that were implemented with students who were selected, or indicated as already having behavioral problems. The overall effect for these interventions was 0.26.

Taking these systematic reviews together, it appears that cognitive–behavioral interventions have a minimal effect on child behaviors. Another systematic review concentrated on school-based secondary prevention of violence; that is, interventions targeted at children identified as aggressive or at risk of being aggressive, including those diagnosed with CD or ODD (Mytton, Diguiseppi, Gough, Taylor, Logan, et al., 2006). In all, 34 studies were meta-analyzed and the experimental interventions had a small to moderate effect size on child aggression over control conditions (SMD = –0.41). Even more importantly, effects found were maintained at 12-month follow-up. The most effective types of programs were those focusing on improving relationships with others and building social skills. This systematic review appears to justify the belief that research expand beyond CBT in its emphasis of study.

APA PSYCHOLOGICAL TASK FORCE CRITERIA. In a review of psychosocial treatments for conduct disorder in children and adolescents, Eyberg, Nelson, and Boggs (2008) conducted an update of the Brestan and Eyberg (1998) review, and identified 16 treatments, of which 15 met criteria for probably efficacious and only one met criteria for well-established (see family focused treatment). Listed here are all those that target preschool and elementary age children. The treatments focused on adolescents will be discussed in Chapter 4.

None of the child-focused treatments was well-established, and the ones that were rated "probably efficacious" were all cognitive–behavioral in nature. Problem-solving skills training (PSST) is designed for children ages 7–13 years with disruptive behavior and is based on the social information-processing model of anger control (Kazdin, 2003). Treatment usually consists of 20–25 sessions (40–50 minutes each) conducted with the child, with occasional parent contact.

In PSST, children are taught problem-solving strategies and encouraged to generalize these strategies to real-life problems. Skills include identifying the problem, generating solutions, weighing the pros and cons of each possible solution, making a decision, and evaluating the outcome. Therapists use in-session practice, modeling, role-playing, corrective feedback, social reinforcement, and token response cost to develop the problem-solving skills gradually, beginning with academic tasks and games and moving to more complex interpersonal situations through role-play. Two other versions of this treatment have added practice and parent management training. All three versions have been rated as "probably efficacious."

Eyberg, Nelson, and Boggs (2008) also reviewed the two well-conducted studies of Anger Control Training (Lochman, Barry, & Pardini, 2003) (described above). Treatment length varied between 15 sessions (Robinson, Smith, & Miller, 2002) and 30 sessions (Lochman, Coie, Underwood, & Terry, 1993). Both studies found the Anger Control Training superior to no-treatment control conditions in reducing disruptive behavior. Because these studies, by different research teams, were compared to no-treatment control conditions rather than alternative treatment or placebo control conditions, this evidence-based treatment meets criteria for a probably efficacious treatment

Family-Focused Interventions

Family-focused interventions for child antisocial behavior are dominated by parent training, in which the underlying theoretical framework is behavioral theory. It is postulated in this theory that the coercive cycles between parent and child are under the influence of behavioral principles. The cycle typically begins with the parent issuing a directive to the child. The child then responds in a coercive manner through noncompliance, whining, or yelling. At that point, the parent may withdraw the command, which acts to negatively reinforce a child's disobedient behavior. Negative reinforcement is defined as the termination of an aversive event; in this case, if a parental command is withdrawn, the child's noncompliance is increased. The parent may also be negatively reinforced for coercive behavior. If, following noncompliance, the parent escalates the command (raises the voice, uses physical aggression), the child may obey, which reinforces the parent's use of these aversive tactics. According to the principles of operant conditioning, positive reinforcement also plays a role in that parents attend to child deviant rather than prosocial behaviors, which increases the likelihood of future deviant behavior.

In parent training programs, behavioral principles are applied to increase child positive behaviors and decrease negative behaviors. Desirable and appropriate child behaviors are encouraged through the use of positive reinforcement techniques such as attention, praise, token economies, and privileges. Undesirable behaviors are decreased through ignoring and punishment, such as time-out from reinforcement. Parents are taught these tactics through the use of didactic presentations, modeling, role-plays, and homework assignments.

SYSTEMATIC REVIEWS/META-ANALYSES. Four recent meta-analyses have been conducted on parent interventions for child behavior problems. The first involved the aforementioned meta-analysis on treatment for ODD that resulted in a total of only seven randomized controlled trials (Bradley & Mandell, 2005). When parents were provided with an intervention, a strong effect was found for child behaviors in the home (SMD = 1.06) and for parenting stress, but no statistically significant effect was found for child academic performance, child school behavior, or child social functioning.

A second meta-analysis was performed on 63 studies of parent training programs. They included attention deficit hyperactivity disorder (ADHD) samples as long as externalizing outcomes were reported. They also included nonbehavioral programs, even though parent training is typically defined as having a basis in behavioral theory. Nonbehavioral programs involved those emphasizing healthy parent–child communications, democratic parenting, and problem-solving between the parent and child, and included Parent Effectiveness Training (Gordon, 1970) and Systematic Training for Effective Parenting (Dinkmeyer & McKay, 1976). Of note is that the Lundahl et al. (2006) meta-analysis violated the assumption of independence (citation) in that when more than one treatment group was included in a study, each of the treatment groups was compared with the control group. This violation means that results of the meta-analysis may be flawed and can be viewed as only tentative.

At posttest, effect size for child behaviors (e.g., compliance, problematic behaviors) was 0.42 and for parent behaviors (e.g., praise, spanking) was 0.47. Parental perceptions (e.g., parenting stress, parenting confidence) were 0.53. At follow-up, child behavior was 0.21 and parent behavior was 0.25, while parent perception was 0.45. "(T)he attenuation of effects over time . . . suggests that families with disruptive children may be best treated with continuing care models of service delivery, which may help parents better maintain their skills and modify them in response to developmental change" (Lundahl et al., 2006).

Although behavioral parent training programs and nonbehavioral programs showed similar success, because behavioral parent training programs comprised the majority of studies and had the strongest methodological rigor, Lundahl et al. (2006) suggest that these should be considered first-line treatments over nonbehavioral programs.

Another meta-analysis was conducted on behavioral parent training programs ($N = 30$ studies) with a focus on child aggression as the outcome (McCart, Priester,

Davies, & Azen, 2006). A small effect (0.47) for reducing child aggression and a small effect size for its impact on parental distress (0.33) were found. These effect sizes are comparable to the ones found by Lundahl et al. (2006), lending support to each other's results. Sufficient information was not available to conduct a follow-up effect size. It must be noted that parent training shows a small to moderate effect on outcomes, which is a higher effect size than found in other interventions for ODD and CD for youth.

Due to some of the limitations of these meta-analyses—including only the published literature, the time restriction of Bradley and Mandell (2005), the fact that McCart et al. (2006) targeted only aggression, that Lundahl et al. (2006) spanned more than the behavioral literature, and some of the problems with the statistical methods of these meta-analyses—Dretzke, Davenport, Frew, et al. (2009) conducted a systematic review of the parenting programs for children with conduct problems. When they pooled 24 randomized, controlled studies, they found that parents in these programs rated their children's behavior as improved compared to comparison groups with a medium effect size of −0.67. Taken together, the quantitative reviews of the parent training literature indicate that these programs are effective for positively influencing child behavior at a small to medium effect.

APA PSYCHOLOGICAL TASK FORCE CRITERIA. In the meta-analyses discussed above, parent training programs are aggregated together as they follow a similar theory and intervention base. However, in the review based on the APA Psychological Task Force Criteria, programs were considered separately. The purpose of the review was to determine the status of treatments for child and adolescent disruptive behaviors since the last update 10 years ago (Eyberg, Nelsen, & Boggs, 2008). Only one, the Parent Management Training Oregon Model (PMTO; Patterson, Reid, Jones, & Conger, 1975), was considered "well-established" because the research had been done by different investigative teams (Bernal, Klinnert, & Schultz, 1980; Patterson, Chamberlain, & Reid, 1982). In PMTO, therapists meet individually with the parents of children between ages 3 and 12 years in 10 (Bernal et al., 1980) to 17 hours of treatment (Patterson et al., 1982). Other parent training models were considered "probably efficacious." These include Helping the Noncompliant Child (Forehand & McMahon, 1981), which is a treatment for preschool and early school-aged children (ages 3–8 years) administered to parent–child dyads over 10 weekly session.

The Incredible Years (IY) (Webster-Stratton & Reid, 2003) is a series of videotaped treatment programs with modeling theory as its basis. There are three distinct treatment programs—one for parents, one for children, and one for teachers. Behavioral techniques for the parents of children ages 3–8 years are modeled through brief videotaped vignettes in the context of a discussion group. Discussion revolves around the correct implementation of techniques by involving parents in problem-solving, role-playing, and rehearsal. The programs for children focus on videotapes that provide training in social skills and problem-solving. Videotaped vignettes show young children and life-sized puppets in a variety of interpersonal situations that may challenge children with conduct problems. In a group setting, children view vignettes and discuss options for coping and the application of techniques learned to their own situations. The three programs have been tested for efficacy individually and in all possible combinations. Both the IY Parent Training Program and the IY Child Training Program are probably efficacious (Eyberg et al., 2008).

Parent–child interaction therapy (PCIT) (Zisser & Eyberg, 2010) is a parenting skills training program for young children (ages 2–7 years) with disruptive behavior disorders that targets change in parent–child interaction patterns. Families meet for weekly 1-hour sessions for an average of 12–16 sessions, during which parents learn two basic interaction patterns. In the child-directed interaction phase of treatment they learn specific positive attention skills (emphasizing behavioral descriptions, reflections, and labeled praises) and active ignoring skills, which they use in applying differential social attention to positive and negative child behaviors during a play situation. The emphasis in this phase of treatment is on increasing positive parenting and warmth in the parent–child interaction as the foundation for discipline skills that are introduced in the second phase, the parent-directed interaction phase of treatment. In this second phase, and within the child-directed context, parents learn and practice giving clear instructions to their child when needed and following through with praise or time-out during *in vivo* discipline situations. Therapists coach the parents as they interact with their child during the treatment sessions, teaching them to apply the skills calmly and consistently in the clinic until they achieve competency and are ready to use the procedures on their own. Parent-directed interaction homework assignments proceed gradually from brief practice sessions during play to application at just those times when it is necessary for the child to obey.

In two well-conducted studies, PCIT was found to be superior to waitlist control conditions in reducing disruptive behavior in young children. Although the studies were conducted by independent research teams, neither study compared the target treatment to an alternative treatment or placebo treatment condition. This evidence-based treatment therefore meets criteria as a probably efficacious treatment for 3- to 6-year-old children with disruptive behavior.

The Positive Parenting Program (called Triple P) (Sanders, 1999) has different versions (in content, number of sessions, type of provider, depending on the level of need (ranging from prevention to severe behavior problems), but all are based around parent training. Both the Standard Triple P (a maximum of 12 sessions in group, individual, and self-help formats delivered by mental health providers) and the Enhanced Triple P, as well as increasing parenting skills, also work to target family stressors such as parental depression or partner relational problems.

MEDICATION

Several classes of medication have been studied for their impact on children and adolescents with disruptive disorders and their cooccurring conditions, including the stimulants, selective norepinephrine reuptake inhibitors, antipsychotics, mood stabilizers, and α_2-agonists. Other classes of medication, such as antidepressants or β-blockers, have either not been studied sufficiently or show little evidence of effectiveness (Pappadopulos, Woolston, Chait, et al., 2006).

In one meta-analysis of 14 studies exploring the effectiveness of pharmacotherapy for disruptive behavioral disorders in general, Ipser and Stein (2007) found a strong overall treatment response compared to control (RR = 2.39). Aggression was reduced with medication (SMD = −1.93). However, the benefits of medication are accompanied by the possibility of side effects that may differ with each category of medication (Pappadopulos, Woolston, Chait, et al., 2006).

Stimulants

Stimulants are the most widely prescribed medication for youth (see Chapter 2). In a meta-analysis, Pappadopulos and her colleagues (2006) found that stimulants had a moderate to large effect on reducing aggression overall and that higher doses were related to greater effect (see Table 3.2). Ipser and Stein (2007) also found stimulants to be effective in reducing aggression in their meta-analysis with children's disruptive behavior disorders. Stimulants have been noted to be specifically effective in children with comorbid ADHD and aggression.

Selective Norepinephrine Reuptake Inhibitors (SNRIs)

Pappadopulos et al. (2006) explored the effectiveness of atomoxetine, a nonstimulant ADHD intervention categorized as an SNRI (Strattera). Only a small effect size (0.18) was shown for reducing maladaptive aggression. Patterns of prescription, however, as noted in a study of 905 juvenile patients, showed that atomoxetine is prescribed more commonly than stimulants when ADHD is comorbid with conduct disturbances and externalizing behavior. This may be due to the concern about substance abuse history or other unwanted effects from stimulants (Christman, Fermo, & Markowitz, 2004).

Antipsychotics

Both typical and atypical antipsychotic medications have been studied in relation to antisocial problems in youth. Of these, the atypical antipsychotic medications are increasingly prescribed for child and adolescent psychiatric problems

TABLE 3.2 SUMMARIES OF META-ANALYSES AND SYSTEMATIC REVIEWS – PHARMACOLOGICAL TREATMENTS

Author and Purpose	Inclusion Criteria	Main Findings

Ipser and Stein (2007)
 	
To test the treatment response, global symptom severity, reduction of aggression, and patient dropout across medication categories
	Participants
	Children 0–18 years old diagnosed with disruptive behavior disorders by ICD or DSM standards, with a majority IQ not ≤70.
	
	Interventions
	Medication trials on pediatric disruptive behavior disorders.
	
	Studies
	Randomized controlled trial (RCT) studies published after 1980 that were not medication-augmenting trials.
	
	Outcomes
	Treatment response, global symptom severity, reduction of aggression, patient dropout.
		$N = 14$ studies
		Overall treatment response to medication:
		Relative risk (RR) of difference = 2.39
		Response to lithium:
		   RR = 4.22
		Overall aggression reduction: standardized mean difference (SMD) = −1.93
		Methylphenidate (MPH) (stimulant) reduction of aggression:
		   SMD = −4.55
		Risperidone reduction of aggression:
		   SMD = −2.52

Pappadopulos et al. (2006)
To compare the effect sizes of categories of psychotropic medications for treating pediatric aggression

Participants
Children less than 19 years old with maladaptive aggression.

Interventions
Medication trials that specifically addressed overt aggression in children.

Studies
English published studies in peer-reviewed journals that used an RCT design with a drug-free washout period.

Outcomes
Measures of aggression, ODD, or CD

N = 45 studies
Stimulants:
  Overall stimulant effect size 0.78 for pediatric aggression.
  MPH was the most effective at ES = 0.9
Selective norepinephrine reuptake inhibitors (SNRIs):
  Mean effect size (ES) = 0.18
Atypical psychotics:
  Mean ES = 0.9, increasing with study durations.
Typical antipsychotics:
  Mean ES = 0.7
  Haloperidol ES = 0.8
  Thioridazine ES = 0.35
Mood stabilizers:
  Mean ES = 0.4
  Lithium ES = 0.0 at 2 weeks and 0.9 at 40 days
α_2-Agonists:
  Mean ES = 0.5
Antidepressants:
  Mean ES = 0.3
β-Blockers:
  No significant effect

(Pappadopulos et al., 2002). Risperidone (Risperdal) is the most thoroughly studied, and has been shown to substantially reduce aggression in youth with CD and subaverage IQ (Aman, Binder, & Turgay, 2004). In the meta-analysis of Pappadopulos et al. (2006), results showed that the overall effect size for atypicals was very high (0.9) and tended to increase over time. Ipser and Stein (2007) similarly found in their meta-analysis that risperidone effectively reduced aggression. Health risks, however, may include cardiac rhythm concerns, significant weight gain, and type II diabetes (Schur et al., 2003).

Typical antipsychotic agents have also produced large effect sizes (mean ES = 0.7) for the treatment of aggression (Pappadopulos et al., 2006). Haloperidol and thioridazine made the most significant contributions with effect sizes of 0.8 and 0.35, respectively. There is significant documentation, however, that these medications produce debilitating dyskinesia and extrapyramidal symptoms in children and adolescents and therefore are prescribed infrequently (Connor, Fletcher, & Wood, 2001).

Mood Stabilizers

Mood stabilizers are another category of psychotropic medication found to be effective by Pappadopulos and her colleagues (2006). Lithium was the most significant of these, having an overall effect size of 0.4 on aggression. However, lithium was not effective until a therapeutic dose was reached. Lithium also showed a high treatment response in young people with impulse control and disruptive behavioral disorders (RR = 4.22) (Ipser & Stein, 2007). Side effects, including nausea and vomiting, ataxia, fatigue, weight gain, and cognitive dulling, coupled with the requirement of frequent blood draws, hinder the use of this medication for young people (Bassarath, 2003).

α_2-Agonists

The final category of medication that may be effective for CD and aggression, α_2-agonists, is increasingly being used in combination with stimulants. Pappadopulos and her associates (2006) found a moderate mean effect size for aggression (0.5) across two studies, one with clonidine (Catapres) and the other with guanficine. Noted side effects for α_2-agonists include dizziness and drowsiness; however, these can balance out the effects of stimulant treatment.

Summary

Youth with ODD and CD are prescribed a variety of psychotropics for the treatment of their symptoms, but no one particular medication has been singled out for its effectiveness. Many classes of these medications have significant side effects that may outweigh any potential benefits. Additionally, psychiatrists in practice often prescribe more than one class of medicine simultaneously; such combinations have not been tested in randomized, controlled trials.

BIOPSYCHOSOCIAL RISK AND RESILIENCE INFLUENCES

ONSET

The development of oppositional defiant disorder and conduct disorder involves an interplay of factors. More research has been done on risk influences for CD than ODD, but the disorders share similar influences (Burke et al., 2002), so they will be discussed together.

Biological

Biological aspects influencing the development of antisocial behaviors include genetics, male gender, temperament, and intelligence quotient (IQ). Evidence indicates that genetics may account for at least 50% of the variance in conduct disorder (Gelhorn, Stallings, Young, et al., 2006). However, heritability is contextual in nature and sensitive to environmental circumstances (Legrand, Keyes, McGue, et al., 2008). Early difficult temperament (defined as negative emotionality, intense and reactive responding to stress and frustration, and inflexibility) predicts conduct problems (Nigg & Huang-Pollock, 2003), whereas an inhibited or approach-withdrawal temperament is protective against antisocial behaviors (Burke et al., 2002; Lahey & Waldman, 2003). Low IQ, especially verbal deficits, may give rise to the development of antisocial behaviors (Hill, 2002; Nigg & Huang-Pollack, 2003; Wachs, 2000). Children unable to identify emotions in themselves and others and who cannot reason well verbally may react aggressively rather than talking about their feelings, seeking comfort, or problem solving.

Psychological Influences

Personality traits marked by a lack of guilt, empathy, emotional expression, and exhibiting low harm avoidance and a preference for novel, exciting, and dangerous activities are associated with more severe and chronic conduct problems and poorer treatment outcome. These traits are found in about a third of treatment-referred children with early-onset conduct problems (Frick, 2006). However, the dominant personality profile for child-onset type features impulsivity, low verbal IQ, and a lack of emotional regulation, coupled with higher rates of family problems. Problems with emotional regulation result in impulsive and reactively aggressive behaviors. Other psychological factors conferring risk include hyper-activity (Frick, 2006), early aggression, and for girls, high stress and poor coping (Burke et al., 2002).

Furthermore, youth with conduct problems display several distortions in the way they perceive and code their social experiences (Dodge, 1986). These distortions include an inability to produce a variety of strategies to manage interpersonal problems, difficulty figuring out ways to achieve a particular desired outcome, difficulty identifying the consequences of a particular action and its effects on others, a tendency to attribute hostile motivations to the actions of others, and misunderstanding how others feel. The combination of perceived threat and lim-ited options for managing social situations makes antisocial youth more likely to respond with aggression rather than prosocial problem-solving strategies.

Social Influences

Social influences that may lead to a disruptive behavior disorder in children include family problems, deviant peers, low socioeconomic status (SES), and being African-American. These influences are explored further below.

FAMILY. Family characteristics and family functioning are strongly implicated in the development of conduct problems. Reviews of the literature indicate that children with a greater genetic predisposition to conduct problems are, unfortunately, more likely to encounter environments that foster antisocial behavior (Loeber et al., 2002). Children predisposed to CD are likely to be raised by ineffective (and sometimes abusive) parents with histories of antisocial behavior, substance abuse problems, and other psychopathology. With regard to mating, the likelihood of persons with particular characteristics selectively partnering and producing children is substantial for antisocial behavior (Ehrensaft, 2005).

Family functioning variables that are risk influences involve parental conflict, separation, violence, and high parental stress (Loeber, Farrington, Stouthamer-Loeber, Moffitt, & Caspi, 1998). Conversely, family stability, stable parental rela-tionships, and parental social support are protective. Any parental psychopathology (such as depression, substance use problems, antisocial personality disorder, and criminal offending) is also a risk influence (Steinberg, 2001). In addition, parental rejection of the child, lack of supervision, and lack of involvement in a child's activ-ities are risk influences for the disruptive disorders. Moreover, child physical abuse and sexual abuse, which often occur in the context of the family, are associated with conduct problems (McGee & Williams, 1999). A large-scale twin study recently established that maltreatment along with the presence of genetic risk increases the rate of conduct problems by 24%, whereas maltreatment without such risk increases the rate of conduct problems by only 2% (Jaffee, Caspi, Moffitt, et al., 2005).

Characteristics of family structure that may give rise to child conduct problems include single-parent families and inconsistent parent figures. Large family size (four or more children) is another risk (Werner, 2000), since financial and parenting resources are taxed considerably in large families.

PEERS. Peer relationships can act as either a risk or protective mechanism for the onset of (Hill, 2002) and recovery from conduct problems (Dekovic, 1999). Children diagnosed with conduct problems often experience rejection by peers for their aggression and lack of social skills. As a result, delinquent youth often consort together, also reinforcing their conduct problems.

Deviant peer relationships are a major pathway for adolescent-onset CD (Frick, 2006). In adolescence, the rate of ODD in females increases to that of boys, most likely because of girls' involvement with antisocial boyfriends (Burke et al., 2002; Moffitt, Caspi, Rutter, & Silva, 2001).

SES. Children who live in poor and disadvantaged communities experience substantial risks, including poverty, unemployment, community disorganization, availability of drugs, the presence of adults involved in crime, community violence, racial prejudice, overcrowding, poor and unresponsive schools, and lack of access to services, such as day care, after-school programs, and health and mental health services (Hankin, Abela, Auberbach, et al., 2005; Hill, 2002; Loeber et al., 2000). These stressors may overwhelm parenting abilities.

ETHNICITY. African-American children (after controlling for poverty) are more likely than white children to be diagnosed with disruptive and conduct-related problems (Nguyen, Huang, Arganza, & Lia, 2007). In the Nguyen study (*N* = 1200 youth), although disruptive behavioral diagnoses were more common among African-American youth, externalizing symptoms on the parent-rated Child Behavior Checklist (CBCL) were not elevated. This discrepancy could be due to the inconsistency between clinician-derived diagnosis and parents' report on the CBCL; parents might not view their children's behavior as disruptive, although clinicians might view this differently.

TREATMENT AND RECOVERY

Biological

Age and gender are classified here as influences at the biological level, although there are certainly psychosocial aspects to both of these.

AGE. The discussion of age as an influential factor has to do with both the age of onset of the disorder and age in terms of response to treatment. Early onset of antisocial problems tends to be related to the severity and the persistence of a disruptive behavioral disorder (Nock et al., 2007). The typical clinical presentation associated with an early-onset disorder includes impulsivity, low verbal IQ, and a lack of emotional regulation, coupled with higher rates of family problems. Problems with emotional regulation result in impulsive and reactively aggressive behaviors.

However, age does not seem be related to the ability of children to benefit from interventions, according to quantitative syntheses. Age of child was not a barrier in terms of dropout or outcome in the meta-analysis of predictors for parent training (Reyno & McGrath, 2006). In the Wilson and Lipsey (2007) meta-analysis on social processing interventions in the school system, adolescents (15–17 years) did better overall with an effect size of d = 0.74 compared to younger children (7–10 years), although this difference was not statistically significant. Similarly, Lundahl et al. (2006) did not find age-related findings in their meta-analysis of parent training programs.

However, in a direct comparison of parent training and cognitive–behavioral therapy, parent training was more effective for preschool and school-aged children, and cognitive–behavioral therapy was more effective for adolescents (McCart, Priester, Davies, & Azen, 2006). McCart and colleagues (2007) outlined some possible factors that may have influenced their age-related findings. Youth in the 6- to 12-year-old category may have had a greater response to behavioral parent training than older children because of their developmental level. First, they are younger and more dependent on their parents for direction and help than older youth. Second, they are also less developed cognitively, which interferes with their ability to engage in the self-reflection, consequential thinking, and consideration of future alternatives that are important to CBT.

GENDER. For ODD, the rate of diagnosis for males is 11.2% and for females is 9.2%. ODD is more prevalent for males than females at all ages, but the rate is not statistically significant (Nock et al., 2007). The persistence of ODD is related to being male. Males have a higher rate of CD than females (12% compared to 7.1%) (APA, 2000). The DSM criteria for CD include overt aggression, and, as a result of this focus, females may be underrecognized. The female presentation of CD tends to be less noticeable because indirect or relational aggressive behaviors are involved, such as the exclusion of others, threats of withdrawal from relationships, efforts to alienate, ostracize, or defame others, and rumor spreading (Ledingham, 1999; Loeber et al., 2000). Some have suggested that the diagnostic criteria for CD should be modified for females to include this presentation (Loeber et al., 2000; Ohan & Johnston, 2005), although others have argued that there are no gender differences in symptom patterns (Moffitt, Caspi, Rutter, & Silva, 2001).

Most studies of treatments for ODD and CD have focused on boys rather than girls, with males being represented at a 5:1 ratio (Brestan & Eyberg, 1998). None of the parent training or cognitive–behavioral studies included a predominantly female sample (McCart et al., 2006), and most studies in a review of school-based secondary violence prevention involved only boys (Mytton, Diguiseppi, Gough, Taylor, Logan, et al., 2006). Clearly there is a need for research into gender-specific treatment outcomes, particularly as the rates of ODD are equivalent in boys and girls.

Psychological

The severity of the disruptive behavior disorder plays a role in response to treatment. Although more severe child behaviors at baseline were associated with poor outcome for parent training (Reyno & McGrath, 2006), moderate behavior problems were associated with better outcomes in CBT interventions in the school setting than for those with mild behavior problems (Wilson & Lipsey, 2007). Similar to Wilson and Lipsey (2007), in the Lundahl et al. (2006) meta-analysis of parent training programs, those with clinically elevated symptoms did better than those without. When viewing this body of work together, it seems that interventions may perform better for those with clinical symptoms above mild. However, children with severe, as opposed to moderate, problems may not benefit as well.

Social

Social factors feature highly for treatment and recovery, as they do for the development of ODD and CD. Social influences include the family, SES, ethnicity, and treatment factors.

FAMILY. Many family factors, as discussed, play a role in the development of ODD and CD, and these may still exert an influence on the course of these disorders. A recent meta-analysis of the parent training research examined predictors associated with both outcome and dropout (Reyno & McGrath, 2006). Key family factors for outcome involved adverse parenting ($r = 0.22$), younger maternal age ($r = 0.21$), and maternal psychopathology ($r = 0.40$). Single-parent status was associated with poorer outcome in the Lundahl et al. (2006) meta-analysis of parent training programs.

SES. Low SES is associated with worse outcome for parent training. For dropout, the strongest predictors in the Reyno and McGrath (2006) meta-analysis involved small mean correlations with barriers to treatment ($r=0.29$), such as transportation problems, lack of child care, and so forth; low educational level ($r = 0.26$) and low income ($r = 0.21$); and minority race ($r = 0.20$). For predictors of outcome, low family income had a strong association with poor outcomes ($r = 0.52$). A related variable, barriers to treatment ($r = 0.33$), had a moderate association. Similarly, in the Lundahl et al. (2006) meta-analysis of parent training programs, low SES emerged as a moderator for worse outcome.

ETHNICITY. Several reviews have examined how ethnicity affects treatment outcome. Through meta-analysis, McCart and colleagues (2006) explored ethnicity as a moderating factor in the effectiveness of CBT and discovered a similar response between white and African-American youth. Weisz, Jensen-Doss, and Hawley (2006) examined the efficacy of evidence-based treatment in comparison to usual clinical services (see Table 3.1). Although their meta-analysis explored a range of youth problems, most of the studies involved youth antisocial behavior. When the percentage of minority youth in samples increased, effects sizes were not reduced at the level of statistical significance. Therefore, with minority samples, evidence-based treatment caused greater improvement over usual clinical services, albeit at a small effect.

Huey and Polo (2008) conducted a review according to APA Psychological Task Force Criteria of treatments for ethnic minority youth, reporting that four reached the status of probably efficacious, only needing replication by an independent investigative team. These are described in Table 3.3.

TREATMENT FACTORS. Several setting-related factors may influence outcome. Those who are mandated to treatment (referred by a school or social agency) seem to do worse with parent-training as compared to those who are self-referred (Reyno & McGrath, 2006). Lundahl et al. (2006) found that youth and parents did better when they were provided with individually-oriented parent training rather than group treatment. This effect was exacerbated for families with low SES backgrounds. Interestingly, self-directed parent training programs (using literature, audio/visual material, and/or computer-delivered material) performed as well as face-to-face treatments. The Lundahl et al. (2006) moderator analysis and the Bradley and Mandell (2005) examination of child and parent programs further showed that when parents or children were the sole recipients of treatment (as opposed to both children and parents being seen in treatment), outcomes were improved. A possible explanation for these findings is that when children are in concurrent treatment, parents may place the onus of responsibility for change on their children rather than viewing themselves as the primary agents of change (Lundahl et al., 2006).

RESEARCH RECOMMENDATIONS

From this review of the literature, certain recommendations can be advanced. First, studies could be strengthened methodologically. A typical inclusion criterion

Program	Target	Description	Cultural Responsivity
Lochman's coping power (Lochman, Curry, Dane, & Ellis, 2001; Lochman & Wells, 2003, 2004)	Aggressive problems in African-Americans	Group social skills in the school setting	African-American staff was involved in the development of the intervention
Brain Power: Attribution retraining (Hudley & Graham, 1993)	African-American elementary school children	Group attribution training held in the school system for 12 sessions	Implemented by African-American females
Brief strategic family therapy (BSFT) (Szapocznik, Hervis, & Schwartz, 2003)	Latino youth (primarily Cuban) with conduct problems	Based on the family systems work of Salvador Minuchin (Minuchin & Fishman, 1981), BSFT adopts strategies such as joining, reframing, and boundary shifting to restructure problematic family interactions	Informed by extensive background research on Cuban family values and conducted by Latino therapists (Miranda, et al., 2005)
Child-centered play therapy (Garza & Bratton, 2005)	Mexican-American youth	Child-centered play therapy offered on a short-term basis (15 sessions) and provided in the school system	Treatment was provided by bilingual counselors and toys were reflective of Latino culture
Anger management group training (Snyder, Kymissis, & Kessler, 1999).			

From Huey and Polo (2008).

for most systematic reviews, for instance, is that primary studies must be randomized controlled trials that report sufficient information to calculate an effect size.

This review has also indicated that interventions may need to be adjusted and adapted to increase their efficacy. The first involves the finding that intervention effects dissipate over time. Therefore, an important area of investigation is to enhance the durability of effects with extended treatment or booster session protocols. Because studies do not often collect follow-up data, a related recommendation is for future research to more routinely assess the impact of treatment over time.

Furthermore, the settings of intervention research are discrepant to where children with conduct-related problems are typically served. The majority of the research has been conducted in outpatient, office-based settings, although children are often served in the school or the child welfare system. The Mytton et al. (2006) systematic review provided encouraging results; school-based programs designed to reduce aggression in youth who showed antisocial problems were effective at a higher rate than control or comparison conditions. However, if youth are referred from the child welfare system, they may receive home-based services, which have not been tested with this population. Children with CD are also overrepresented in restrictive and expensive placements, such as residential treatment, which has not been the subject of research with this population.

Although the available research seems to indicate that interventions impact both males and females and children of ethnic minorities in similar ways, the lack of research involving these groups needs to be addressed. At the most basic level, studies should report the ethnic identity of their samples, and, if numbers allow, test the differential impact of interventions according to ethnicity. Culturally tailored interventions have not been well investigated and further work could be done in this area. The results of the Nguyen et al. (2007) study on the differing views of clinicians and ethnic minority parents toward child behavior imply certain research. "Because understanding impairment and arriving at diagnosis is integral to treatment planning and outcome, further study is needed to better understand the relationship of client and clinician culture to diagnosis" (Nguyen et al., 2007, p. 23).

Research also needs to expand to treatments that are used in clinical settings. Whereas parent training and CBT in individual and group interventions are often a focus of research, they are not so commonly used in clinical practice, where psychodynamic, family therapy, play therapy, and eclectic approaches may dominate. Furthermore, the results of individual and group CBT for behavior problems in children have fairly low effects according to the systematic reviews, which justifies the study of approaches more routinely implemented in practice. Indeed, the Mytton et al. (2007) review of school-based programs for child aggression was encouraging in this regard.

One interesting finding suggested by meta-analysis (Bradley & Mandell, 2005; Lundahl et al., 2006; Wilson & Lipsey, 2007) is that offering multimodal psychosocial treatment to both parents and children may not be more effective than targeting either parents or children. Such results need replication in systematic reviews that do not have publication bias.

Future research also needs to involve social factors as low SES has been associated with the development of ODD and CD and is correlated with worse outcomes. Some suggestions involve case management services, the provision of transportation and child care, or the use of home-based services. Any of these potential adaptations should be tested for their impact with low SES samples. Family risk influences, such as parental mental illness, also must be addressed in manualized treatment and then tested to meet the needs of such families. Other social barriers, such as living in a rural area or other places in which providers are not trained to provide parent training, may be targeted through self-directed programs (Lundahl et al., 2006). Preschoolers, in particular, may be more readily identified in primary care settings, which are generally ill-equipped to handle such problems in terms of both treatment and referral. Self-directed programs may offer a first line of intervention that could be tested for their effectiveness.

CONCLUSIONS

This chapter has focused on intervention with child ODD and CD. Treating preschoolers and children who meet criteria for these problems is necessary so that antisocial problems do not continue into adolescence and adulthood. Although evidence is limited at this time, it seems that social problem-solving programs in preschoolers may have more of an effect than when these children are in elementary school. Parent training has received more support than other interventions, and older children, as well as younger children may benefit. Other individual and contextual influences for the development of antisocial problems and their recovery were discussed, along with corresponding research implications. Chapter 4 will continue with ODD and CD in youth, addressing the presentation of these problems in adolescence.

CASE STUDY

George is a 10-year-old African-American child who was removed from his biological parents at the age of 4½ years due to a founded complaint of physical abuse by his father. George is part of a sibling group of seven and all of his siblings were taken into foster care. At present, George's siblings have been adopted, some of them with relatives. George has no contact with either parent, any of his siblings, or any relatives. He was especially close to his older brother William and misses him greatly. Because he lived in a non-open adoption state, no information could be obtained as to the whereabouts of George's siblings.

Soon after George was placed in foster care, he revealed that he had witnessed numerous incidents of domestic violence between his parents. Both parents also used drugs and alcohol and had trouble maintaining employment and stable housing. George's parents frequently left him and his siblings alone for long periods of time while they went out to use, sell, and buy drugs. The family did not always have enough to eat and the children sometimes shoplifted food to survive. It is suspected that George was exposed to alcohol prenatally.

During the incident that precipitated the removal, George's father slapped him across the face several times, leaving bruising, red marks, and swelling. George reports being hit, punched, and slapped on numerous occasions by his father in the past, as well. George also reports waking up in the night and seeing his mother having sex with various boyfriends.

Efforts were made to reunify George with his parents, but they did not follow through with recommended substance abuse treatment and mental health evaluations. They were also unable to obtain housing or keep employment. The domestic violence continued, and George's father was eventually arrested on drug charges and remained in prison for several years. George and his siblings were allowed to visit with their parents at Social Services, but the parents often failed to show, causing a great deal of distress and feelings of abandonment for the children.

Parental rights were terminated 3 years before. Since that time George has been free for adoption, and DSS has made extensive efforts to find a permanent home for him. Unfortunately, George has experienced severe behavior problems and has had six different placements since being in foster care. All of the foster parents eventually reached a stage at which they could no longer handle George's extreme behavior and requested that he be moved.

George was placed with Mrs. Jones and her 15-year-old son 8 months ago for the purposes of adoption. Mrs. Jones has gone through special training to become a therapeutic foster parent, which means that she has taken classes to learn how to manage the possible behaviors of traumatized and abused children. Intensive home-based therapy is being provided three times per week. George also sees a psychiatrist for medication management and sees an outpatient therapist every other week.

George is in a special education class at the public elementary school under the classification of emotional disturbance. He is in the fifth grade and his grades currently consist of Ds and Fs. George often refuses to do his work in class, refuses to do homework, or simply tears up his papers and/or books, then stomps on them. During the first month at his new school George's behavior was fine and he showed the ability to work on grade level, but now he spends so much time acting out that it consumes his day, and he no longer completes assignments. The possibility of placing George in an alternative school is currently under consideration. George's full scale IQ is 93, which is in the average range.

About 3 months after moving in with Mrs. Jones and her son, Andre, George again began having difficulties. He has been kicked off the school bus for threatening other students, hitting them, using racial slurs, spitting, running up and down the aisles, and cursing at the driver. Last week at school George became defiant when asked about his homework and began running through the halls screaming. He threatened to jump off of the balcony in the atrium of the school, then barricaded himself inside a classroom after turning over some desks and throwing books and backpacks. The police were called, Mrs. Jones came to the school, and together they were able to calm George down and take him home.

At home George has also been oppositional. He curses at his foster mother, refuses to follow her directives, calls her names, has pulled up all the flowers in her bed, threatened to hurt her new puppy (he did not follow through on the threat), and demands that she do things for him. On two occasions George has intentionally urinated on the floor of the bathroom instead of in the toilet. Two weeks ago he punched a hole in the living room wall when Mrs. Jones took away his TV privileges. When George gets angry he sometimes runs out of the house and sits in a tree in the back yard until he calms down. When confronted about his behavior he refuses to take responsibility for it, laughs it off, and blames others. For George's DSM multiaxial, see Box 3.1.

HOW THE EVIDENCE FITS

For school-aged children, such as George, parent training has been indicated as an evidence-based treatment for CD. Although there are various parent training programs available, the one to address George's particular needs—both the attachment and the conduct problems—might be PCIT (Brinkmeyer & Eyberg, 2003). The emphasis of PCIT, in contrast to some of the other parent training programs, is to initially build a positive relationship between parent and child, so that the parent can be more effective as a reinforcer for the child.

APPLICATION

PCIT is a parenting skills training program for young children (ages 2–7 years) with disruptive behavior disorders that targets change in parent–child interaction patterns. The foster parent would be heavily involved in this treatment. In the child-directed interaction phase of treatment, Ms. Jones would learn specific positive attention skills (emphasizing behavioral descriptions, reflections, and labeled praises) and active ignoring skills, which she would apply while allowing George to play in the therapy room. The emphasis in this phase of treatment is on increasing

BOX 3.1 MULTIAXIAL DIAGNOSIS

312.81, Conduct Disorder (CD), Mild

[A repetitive and persistent pattern of behavior that violates the basic rights of others or major age-appropriate social norms or rules (three or more criteria are required)]:

A. Aggression to people and animals

- George threatens and intimidates peers and adults, including his foster mother, and threatened to hurt her puppy.
- George has spit at and hit other children.

B. Destruction of property

- George has destroyed his foster mother's flower beds and school property (desks, books, backpacks).

C. Deceitfulness or theft

- George has lied and stolen.

Axis I: 313.89, Reactive Attachment Disorder (RAD) of Early Childhood, Inhibited Type

[Although George is not developmentally delayed (a screen-out criterion), he shows a persistent failure to initiate or respond in a developmentally appropriate fashion to most social interactions. He has experienced seven different placements due to his rejection, oppositionality, and aggression since being removed from his biological family at the age of 4 years (therefore, the behavior shows a pattern before the age of 5 years, as part of the criterion). He also is unable to make or retain same-age friendships.]

Axis II: V71.09

Axis III: None

Axis IV: Problems with primary support (removal from biological family, multiple placements, strained relationship with foster mother), social environment (does not have any friends), educational problems (inability to function appropriately in school or engage in academic pursuits)

Axis V: GAF = 40

[Major impairment in school (he has no friends, he is too aggressive to stay in the classroom, and he has had seven placements in 6 years.]

positive parenting and developing warmth in the parent–child interaction. This relationship-building stage is seen as the foundation for discipline skills that are introduced in the second phase of treatment. Here, Ms. Jones would learn and practice giving clear instructions to George and following through with praise or time-out during *in vivo* discipline situations. A therapist would coach Ms. Jones as she interacts with George, teaching her to apply the skills calmly and consistently in the clinic until she achieves competency and is prepared to use the procedures on her own.

A third characteristic is George's pattern of comorbidity. His diagnosis of Reactive Attachment Disorder means that it will be challenging for Ms. Jones to build a relationship with him before she becomes too overwhelmed or frustrated with his behavior. Part of his incurring the diagnosis of Reactive Attachment Disorder is due to the abuse and neglect he suffered in his early childhood. One question is whether the behavioral treatment would address the abuse and trauma issues or whether they would have to be dealt with more directly, as the treatment outcome research on sexual abuse has shown (Macdonald, Higgins, & Ramchandani, 2006). However, there have been some recent studies on PCIT with child welfare and community samples with high rates of abuse and neglect, and these showed positive outcomes for child behavior (Porter, Timmer, Klisanac, et al., 2009; Porter, Timmer, Urquiza, et al., 2009). Whether other child outcomes, such as attachment, depression, and anxiety, are affected is unknown, however.

CHARACTERISTICS OF THE CONTEXT

George is in foster care with Ms. Jones; therefore, they are not biological mother and son. The treatment outcome studies with PCIT have been performed with biological mothers and their children and have not been researched with foster parent–child units. On the PCIT website, however, it mentions that the treatment has been used with foster parents.

Another characteristic of the context is that George is being seen in a child welfare setting, where knowledge of evidence-based treatments (EBTs) for mental health problems might be minimal. Therefore, it is unknown if treatment service providers to foster care youth would have the necessary knowledge of EBTs and the training and supervision to competently administer them.

DOES THE EVIDENCE-BASED TREATMENT TAKE ADVANTAGE OF STRENGTHS?

PCIT takes advantage of strengths by enhancing the parent–child relationship so that parents become better reinforcers for their children's desirable behavior. The foundation of PCIT is the critical role that positive reinforcement plays in child behavior. George's prosocial and on-task behavior will be recognized through a system of positive reinforcement—praise, tokens, and privileges. In this way, he will learn that positive behaviors will earn him reinforcement and rewards. The foster parent's involvement is another strength in this case that can be enhanced through PCIT. George has a foster parent who is willing to care for him. Ms. Jones wants to improve their relationship and make the placement work. The PCIT model helps her learn and practice how to be a potentially effective agent of change with George.

4

ADOLESCENT DISRUPTIVE BEHAVIOR DISORDERS AND SUBSTANCE USE DISORDERS

This chapter continues the discussion of oppositional defiant disorder (ODD) and conduct disorder (CD), now focusing on their presentation in adolescence. Because there is significant comorbidity between antisocial behaviors and substance use problems in adolescence and because treatments for these disorders sometimes overlap, both adolescent conduct problems and substance use disorders will be considered in this chapter. Some have argued, in fact, that problematic substance use patterns should be incorporated into the diagnostic criteria for CD (Bukstein & Kaminer, 1994).

In the *Diagnostic and Statistical Manual* (DSM), *substance abuse* and *substance dependence*, fall under *substance-related disorders* and 11 classes of substances are named: alcohol, amphetamines, caffeine, cannabis, cocaine, hallucinogens, inhalants, nicotine, opioids, phencyclidine, and sedatives/hypnotics/anxiolytics (APA, 2000). The defining characteristic of *abuse* involves negative consequences of use; *dependence* involves compulsive use, despite serious consequences, and is often accompanied by tolerance and withdrawal.

The substance use disorders usually begin in late adolescence or early adulthood, with a median age of 20 years (Kessler, Berglund, Demler, et al., 2005). Many adolescents engage in problematic drinking, but only a subset fulfills the criteria for abuse or dependence. In 2004, the rate of substance dependence or abuse was 8.8% for youths aged 12–17 years (SAMHSA, 2006).

STATE OF THE EVIDENCE

The discussion on the state of the treatment outcome literature will focus on psychosocial interventions as treatment outcome studies of psychotropic medication with adolescents with antisocial problems or substance use disorders have not been conducted. Psychosocial interventions will be discussed based on whether they focus on the individual or the family.

INDIVIDUALLY ORIENTED TREATMENT

The only individually oriented treatment tested for adolescent antisocial behavior and substance use problems is cognitive–behavioral therapy (CBT). There are three ways in which substance use is conceptualized from a cognitive–behavioral theoretical approach with corresponding techniques, which are often used together in a package (Kaminer & Waldron, 2006). The first is classical conditioning, which involves the conditioning of certain cues that trigger substance use. Treatment involves identifying the cues and learning strategies for avoiding or managing these cues. A second is operant theory, which views alcohol and drug use as due primarily to the consequences that follow it (positive feelings, fun with others, ease with socializing). Techniques involve identifying and implementing alternative reinforcers, such as vouchers for drug-free urine tests that can be exchanged for rewards such as movie tickets (Higgins & Silverman, 2008). A third is social learning in which substances are used due to modeling from others (peers, adults) in combination with an individual's cognitive processes. Techniques involve modeling alternative behaviors by service providers and coping skills training (Kaminer & Waldron, 2006).

Cognitive–behavioral interventions for antisocial behavior have been described in Chapter 3, but particular programs for adolescents will be explored in more detail as they are discussed. Some overall outcomes will first be discussed from the results of meta-analyses and systematic reviews and then results of the APA Psychological Task Force 12 will be provided.

Systematic Reviews/Meta-Analyses

There have been no systematic reviews conducted on individually focused treatments for adolescent substance abuse. For antisocial adolescent behaviors, reviews have focused on CBT implemented in specific systems of care (Table 4.1). Armelius and Andreassen (2007) reviewed 12 studies on CBT with antisocial behavior in adolescents residing in residential treatment settings. When compared to standard treatment, CBT showed small positive gains (SMD = 0.25) for the reduction of recidivism.

Lipsey, Landenberger, and Wilson (2007) conducted a review of 58 studies of adolescent and adult offenders who received treatment while they were on probation. They found that the overall odds ratio for recidivism was 1.53 when comparing CBT and the control group, which was associated with a 25% reduction

TABLE 4.1 SUMMARIES OF SYSTEMATIC REVIEWS/META-ANALYSES FOR ADOLESCENT ANTISOCIAL BEHAVIOR

Author and Purpose	Inclusion Criteria	Main Findings
Armelius and Andreassen (2007) To explore the effectiveness of cognitive–behavioral therapy (CBT) with adolescents who are placed in residential treatment settings To investigate whether a focus on criminogenic needs is more effective than focusing just on cognition and behavior	**Participants** 12–22 years Antisocial behavior **Interventions** Residential treatment **Studies** Randomized controlled trials, or studies with nonrandom comparison groups Reported follow-up outcomes at least 6 months after treatment **Outcomes** Recidivism measured by: Police and court records Other reports of offenses Self-report of criminal behavior Offenses causing entry into a residential facility	N = 12 studies Effect size (ES) 0.25 (for CBT vs. standard treatment at 12-month follow-up)
Macdonald and Turner (2006) Cochrane review Describe the effectiveness of Treatment Foster Care (TFC) on psychosocial and behavioral outcomes, delinquency, placement stability, and discharge status for children and adolescents who require out-of-home placement	**Participants** Children and adolescents up to the age of 18 years who for reasons of severe medical, social, psychological, and behavioral problems are placed out of home. **Interventions** TFC programs providing individualized, therapeutic, community-based and foster family-based intensive services to children and adolescents.	N = 5 studies Child outcomes: TFC, compared to control, showed lower index offense scores, and felony assaults: Standardized mean difference (SMD), −0.54, −0.45 Caregivers' perceptions of girls engaging in delinquent acts or behaviors 1 year after treatment entry: SMD, −0.51 Days in a locked setting significantly less for TFC than for group care:

Designed to prevent multiple placements, and/or as an alternative to restrictive institutional placement options.

Studies

Included a random allocation or quasirandom allocation to a TFC intervention and control. The control group could be a no-treatment, wait-list control, or regular foster care. There were no language restrictions.

Outcomes

Looked-after child outcomes; behavioral, psychological functioning, educational, interpersonal functioning, mental health status, physical health status

Treatment foster care/family outcomes; measures of skills, interpersonal functioning

TFC agency outcomes; placement stability

1 year:
SMD, −0.62
2-year follow-up:
SMD, −0.92
Criminal referral rates significantly less for TFC than group care:
1-year follow-up:
SMD, −0.53
2-year follow-up:
SMD, −0.56
Girl's school attendance and homework scores significantly increased at 12 months postbaseline:
SMD, 0.54, 0.63
TFC agency outcomes
Time between referral to the study and placement outside the hospital was lower than a control:
SMD, −0.96
Number of children in permanent placements in the experimental group is higher compared to control:
SMD, 0.49
Number of days on the run compared to group care:
SMD, −0.52
Days in treatment favored multidimensional treatment foster care (MTFC) over group care:
1-year follow up:
SMD, 0.57
2-year follow up:
SMD 0.61
Living at home after MTFC compared to group care:
1-year follow-up:
SMD, 0.45

(continued)

TABLE 4.1 SUMMARIES OF SYSTEMATIC REVIEWS/META-ANALYSES FOR ADOLESCENT ANTISOCIAL BEHAVIOR (CONT'D)

Author and Purpose	Inclusion Criteria	Main Findings
Wilson, Lipsey, and Soyden (2003) To determine the overall effectiveness of mainstream delinquency interventions for minority youth To compare the overall effectiveness of delinquency interventions for majority and minority youth	**Participants** Delinquent or antisocial youth from age 12 to 21 years. **Interventions** Treatment for delinquency or antisocial behavior. **Studies** Published and unpublished studies between 1950 and 1996 that included at least one treatment group. Studies tailored to a specific cultural or ethnic group were excluded. Sample of 305 from 500 in data base; 141 with at least 60% minority, 164 with at least 60% white. **Outcomes** Academic achievement Attitude change Behavioral problems Employment status Family functioning Internalizing problems Peer relations Psychological adjustment School participation Self-esteem	N = 305 studies Mean ES for minority youth across outcomes, 0.11 (significant) The difference between the mean ESs of all outcomes for minority youth (0.11) and majority youth (0.17) was not statistically significant. No significant differences were found on any outcome between minority and majority youth. N = 6 studies Multisystemic therapy (MST), family behavior therapy (FBT), individual cognitive problem-solving therapy (ICPS) all effective with externalizing behavior; >0.80

McCart et al. (2006) To investigate the effectiveness of CBT and behavioral parent training (BPT) on antisocial behavior in children To explore the moderating effect of demographic factors	**Participants** 18 years or younger Antisocial behavior **Interventions** BPT or CBT for antisocial behavior **Studies** Published studies Compared treatment to a control group Provided enough data to calculate effect size **Outcomes** Behavioral outcome measures of antisocial behavior	IT, CBT, FBT, ICPS all effective with internalizing behavior; >0.80 FBT, ICPS, CBT, PET all effective with substance abuse; >0.80. FBT and ICPS had large effect sizes in all three domains of "dual-diagnosis" and maintained their effects at a 9-month follow-up. $N = 76$ studies Overall ES for BPT and CBT, 0.40 Overall ES for BPT, 0.47 Overall ES for CBT, 0.35 For ages 6–12 only: ES for BPT, 0.45 ES for CBT, 0.23
Woolfenden, Williams, and Peat (2001) Cochrane Review To determine the benefit of parent and family interventions for children with conduct disorder and delinquency	**Participants** 10–17 years Conduct disorder and delinquency **Interventions** Family and parenting interventions **Studies** Published or unpublished randomized controlled trials with comparison groups. **Outcomes** Objective outcome measures or validated measures.	$N = 8$ Parent and family interventions decreased amount of time spent in institutions (51.34 days)

in reoffending. Participants categorized as high risk for reoffending had a better response to treatment than those with lower risk, and adolescents performed as well as adults from undergoing CBT. Lipsey et al. (2007) also looked at commercial packages of CBT, such as Aggression Replacement Training (Goldstein, Glick, & Gibbs, 1998), which involves social skills training, feeling management, stress management, learning alternatives to aggressions and how to plan ahead, anger control, and moral education. There were no statistically significant benefits in using these types of commercial packages, however. Instead, implementation of the program was a key moderator. When programs were implemented as they had been designed, better outcomes were produced. Crucial elements of CBT were also identified. Anger control and interpersonal problem solving were important elements, whereas victim impact and behavior modification were not.

APA Psychological 12 Criteria

Waldron and Turner (2008) conducted a review of treatment outcome studies for adolescent substance use disorders using the APA Division 12 Task Force Criteria. They ranked CBT, both in individual and group formats, as "well-established." The seven studies that evaluated individual CBT models included three with a component of motivation enhancement therapy, and one with an adolescent community reinforcement approach (Azrin et al., 2001; Dennis et al., 2004; Hops et al., 2007; Liddle et al., 2003; Waldron et al., 2005, 2007; Waldron, Slesnick, et al., 2001; Waldron & Turner, 2008). However, four of the studies are not readily available (unpublished manuscripts, paper presentations), when generally APA Division 12 Task Force Reviews rely on the published literature. CBT has also applied in group modality, and these studies (Battjes et al., 2004; Dennis et al., 2004; Hops et al., 2007; Kaminer et al., 1998; Liddle et al., 2001, 2004; Smith et al., 2006; Stanton et al., 2007; Waldron et al., 2005) were also reviewed by Waldron and Turner (2008). Again, not all studies were published.

Eyberg, Nelson, and Boggs (2008) reviewed the psychosocial treatments for child and adolescent disruptive behavior according to the APA Division 12 Task Force criteria and found none that was "well-established." Two individually-oriented (CBT) treatments were identified as "probably efficacious" for adolescents with disruptive behavior disorders; both of these treatments were delivered in a group modality in the school setting.

The first probably efficacious treatment is the Rational-Emotive Mental Health (REMH) Program (Block, 1978), which was implemented in daily 45-minute small-group sessions for 12 consecutive weeks with eleventh and twelfth graders with disruptive school behavior. The primary focus was on cognitive restructuring through rational-emotive methods. In the one study in which it was tested,

REMH produced greater reductions in disruptive behavior and skipping classes than the control condition.

The other is Group Assertive Training (Huey & Rank, 1984), which involved 8 hours of training for eighth and ninth grade African-Americans who had shown aggression in the classroom. Two different versions (counselor-led and peer-led) produced superior effects on aggression over counselor-led discussion groups and no-treatment controls in the one well-conducted study (Huey & Rank, 1984). Both versions of Group Assertiveness Training therefore meet criteria as "probably efficacious" (Eyberg et al., 2008).

FAMILY AND PARENT INTERVENTIONS

Because many risk factors for antisocial behavior and substance use disorders involve family factors (see the discussion of risk and protective factors below), much of the treatment outcome research in this area focuses on parent and family-centered treatment. In an overall examination of these treatments for adolescents (ages 10–17 years) with conduct problems, Woolfenden, Williams, and Peat (2001) found eight trials. Most of the samples comprised youth involved with the juvenile justice system. Although parent- and family-focused treatment for youth reduced time spent in residential treatment and other institutional settings, incarceration and arrest rates were not reduced. Furthermore, no significant differences between parent/family interventions and other types of treatment emerged on psychosocial outcomes, such as family functioning and youth behavior. Substance abuse was not one of the outcomes studied.

Different types of family interventions have been the focus of other reviews, and these will be explored below.

Multisystemic Treatment (MST)

THEORETICAL APPROACH. Henggeler and colleagues (e.g., Henggeler & Lee, 2003) have created a model emphasizing the multiple systems that impact the development of delinquency. The Bronfenbrenner's (1979) theory of the social-ecological model of development postulates that the systems surrounding individuals influence their behavior in both direct and indirect ways. The microsystems (the most direct systems that impact the child, such as immediate and extended family) and mesosystems (more distal influences that the child and his or her microsystems are embedded within, such as the school or neighborhood) impact the child and are impacted by the child in a systemic fashion. Systems that affect and are affected by delinquent behavior include the child's own intrapersonal system (i.e., cognitive ability, social skills), the parent–child system, the family system, the school system (interactions with teachers), and the child–peer system (e.g., Henggeler, 1991).

SYSTEMATIC REVIEWS/META-ANALYSIS. Although MST has been touted as an evidence-based model by many sources, including federal entities, such as the National Institute on Drug Abuse, National Institute on Mental Health, Surgeon General's office, Center for Substance Abuse Prevention, the Office of Juvenile Justice and Delinquency Prevention, and the Substance Abuse and Mental Health Services Administration (see Littell, 2005), the systematic review of eight studies indicated that of several outcomes measures—arrests and time incarcerated, teen adjustment, parent adjustment, and prosocial involvement—none was significantly improved with MST compared to control (Littell, Popa, & Forsythe, 2005). Furthermore, treatment and control conditions (usual services or individual therapy) were not always comparable, despite claims of randomization to conditions in studies. This might have biased the findings toward the treatment group.

APA DIVISION 12 TASK FORCE REVIEWS. In the Eyberg et al. (2008) review of disruptive behavior disorders, MST earned the criteria for a "probably efficacious" treatment. Two well-conducted studies with adolescents who committed criminal offenses found MST superior to control conditions (Borduin et al., 1995; Henggeler et al., 1992), one showing superiority to usual community services and one showing superiority to alternative community treatments.

Additionally, Waldron and Turner (2008) examined MST as an intervention for adolescent substance abuse and claim that a number of studies have been conducted by the creators of the program. However, careful examination of Waldon and Turner's cited studies indicates that the two outcome studies reported in Henggeler et al. (1991) did not publish outcome data that allowed one to evaluate the results of the intervention. Furthermore, Henggeler, Clingempeel, Brondino, and Pickrel (2002) present 4-year follow-up data of Henggeler, Pickrel, and Brondino (1999) rather than standing as a study on its own. Note that Waldron and Turner (2008) had eliminated Henggeler, Halliday-Boykins, Cunningham, et al. (2006) from their review because of its focus on family drug court rather than MST per se. This means that there is only one study on which to evaluate the effect of MST on substance use outcomes.

Moreover, outcomes were not reported consistently across the follow-up periods in Henggeler et al. (1999) and Henggeler et al. (2002). Self-report for alcohol, marijuana, and other drugs was assessed in Henggeler et al. (1999), but in the 4-year follow-up study, Henggeler et al. (2002) presented self-report outcomes for marijuana and cocaine only. Drug screen outcomes were presented for cocaine and marijuana (these were not reported in the previous study).

Waldron and Turner (2008), in examining only Henggeler et al. (1991) and Henggeler et al. (2002), concluded that they met standards for a "probably efficacious" treatment and lacked only independent replication to become a "well-established" treatment. "Probably efficacious" treatment requires that there be at least two studies that show the intervention to be more effective than no-treatment control. Therefore, this requirement appears to be lacking for MST in terms of substance use disorders.

Treatment Foster Care

THEORETICAL APPROACH. Treatment foster care programs serve children and youth who are at risk for being placed in institutional or other restrictive, non-home settings due to their emotional, behavioral, medical, or developmental problems. Often these children face a series of progressively more restrictive placements. One type of treatment foster care, Multidimensional Treatment Foster Care (MTFC; Chamberlain & Smith, 2003), is targeted specifically for youth with severe and chronic delinquent behavior. MTFC is a community-based program originally developed as an alternative to institutional-, residential-, and group-care placements Youth are placed one per foster home for 6–9 months and given intensive support and treatment in the foster home setting. The foster parents receive a 20-hour preservice training conducted by experienced foster parents and learn to implement a daily token reinforcement system that involves frequent positive reinforcement and clear and consistent limits. During treatment, the foster parents report point levels on the token reinforcement system by daily telephone calls to program supervisors and meet weekly with supervisors for support and supervision (Eyberg et al., 2008).

Youth in MTFC meet at least weekly with individual therapists who provide support and advocacy and work with the youth on problem-solving skills, anger expression, social skills development, and educational or vocational planning. They also meet once or twice a week (2–6 hours per week) with behavioral support specialists trained in applied behavior analysis who focus on teaching and reinforcing prosocial behaviors during intensive one-on-one interactions in the community (e.g., restaurants, sports teams). Finally, youth have regular appointments with a consulting psychiatrist for medication management.

At the same time youth are in MTFC treatment, the biological parents (or other after-care resource) receive intensive parent management training designed to assist in the reintegration of youth back into their homes and communities after treatment.

SYSTEMATIC REVIEWS/META-ANALYSES. A recent Cochrane Collaboration review on treatment foster care located only five studies that met inclusion criteria

(Macdonald & Turner, 2008). Although results favored treatment foster care, studies typically did not assess similar outcome measures; quantitative synthesis, therefore, was difficult. The authors concluded that treatment foster care may be a successful alternative to more costly higher levels of care, such as residential treatment, and may help young people avoid some of the deleterious outcomes for children with CD (Macdonald & Turner, 2008). However, the authors also warn that the evidence is not as robust as the claims that have been made as there have been many published articles touting its effectiveness.

APA DIVISION 12 TASK FORCE CRITERIA. Honing in on MTFC has more relevance for this chapter because of its focus on delinquent youth. In the Eyberg et al. (2008) review, two well-conducted experiments, using treatment manuals and clearly defined sample criteria (Chamberlain & Reid,1998; Leve, Chamberlain, & Reid, 2005) contributed to MTFC being ranked as "probably efficacious." Both studies, using data from treatment records, criminal referral data, and youth self-report measures, found that with chronically delinquent adolescents, MFTC was significantly more effective that usual group home care. Of note is that there is some inconsistency in the documentation of delinquency outcomes in the follow-up of the original studies (Chamberlain, Leve, & DeGarmo, 2007; Eddy, Whaley, & Chamberlain, 2004). Although reports at follow-up were positive for MFTC, it raises the question of whether only positive results were being supplied.

Family Behavioral Treatment

THEORETICAL APPROACH. Family Behavioral Treatment (FBT) is an intervention for adolescents designed to reduce conduct problems and drug use (Donohue & Azrin, 2001; Donohue, Azrin, Allen, Romero, Hill, et al., 2009). Following a behavioral theoretical model, the initial process involves an assessment to identify the factors that contribute to the reinforcement of substance use, such as cognitive, verbal, social, and family concerns. These targets are analyzed and processed with the family, which may include siblings and peers, and a set of strategies is chosen to meet the individual needs of the client. Youth are taught strategies to avoid and manage triggers. Behavioral interventions with the parents include contracting to supervise the child's therapeutic homework tasks and providing rewards for child activities incompatible with drug use, including cooperation with monitoring. Treatment usually involves 16–20 sessions that may range in time from 1–2 hours and are spread out over as long as a 1-year period.

APA DIVISION 12 TASK FORCE CRITERIA. Because behavioral family therapy has not been subject to a systematic review or meta-analysis, only the results of the APA Division 12 Task Force Criteria according to Waldron and Turner (2008) will be reported here. Behavioral family therapy was categorized as a "probably efficacious" approach for adolescent substance abuse based on two randomized trials in terms of reduction in substance use and improvements in psychological adjustment and academic performance (Azrin et al., 2001; Azrin, Donohue, et al., 1994; Azrin, McMahon, & Donohue, 1994).

Functional Family Therapy

THEORETICAL APPROACH. Alexander and Parsons (1982) developed functional family therapy in which systems, cognitive, and behavioral theories are integrated. Juvenile offending and other clinical problems are conceptualized from the standpoint of the functions they serve for the family system as well as for individual family members (Alexander & Parsons, 1982). Behavior is viewed in the context of family relationships in which the individual may be attempting to achieve greater closeness, greater separation, or some balance between the two in the relationship. For example, behavior problems may unite parents around their child's difficult behavior; alternatively, conduct problems may be the child's attempt to signal that the family is too restrictive. Because maladaptive processes within the family develop in lieu of more direct means of fulfilling these functions, the goal of functional family therapy is to alter interaction and communication patterns so that more adaptive functioning is experienced. As well as communication patterns of the family, coercive interactions between parent and child are also targets for functional family intervention (Alexander & Parsons, 1982). With the combination of theoretical concepts, the model has also been referred to as behavioral-systems family therapy (Gordon, Arbuthnot, Gustafson, & McGreen, 1988).

Treatment is divided into three phases: assessment, therapy, and education (Alexander & Parsons, 1982). In the assessment phase, behavior patterns and the contingencies that reinforce behaviors are examined. Information is also obtained from collateral agencies, such as the school and the justice system. In the therapy phase, practitioners use many techniques to change the relationships between family members as well as the meaning the problem holds for the family (Alexander & Parsons, 1982). Techniques include changing beliefs, cognitions, expectations, and reactions between family members. Interactions between family members rather than the behavior of the adolescent are the focus of intervention, . The education phase involves the family members learning new skills, including parenting, communication, and problem-solving skills.

SYSTEMATIC REVIEWS/META-ANALYSES. Currently, a systematic review is being conducted on Functional Family Therapy (FFT) (see Littell, Bjørndal, Winsvold, & Hammerstrøm, 2008), but results are not yet available.

APA DIVISION 12 TASK FORCE CRITERIA. According to the review conducted by Waldron and Turner (2008), FFT has emerged as a "well-established" treatment. "Findings for FFT have been replicated by independent investigators and at multiple sites (Friedman, 1989; Hops et al., 2007; Waldron et al., 2001; Waldron, Ozechowski, Turner, & Brody, 2005; Waldron et al., 2007; see also Waldron & Kaminer, 2004)" (Waldron & Turner, 2008). However, only two of these studies are included in Waldron and Turner's (2008) list of outcome findings (Waldron et al., 2001, 2005). In the methodologically weaker Friedman study (Friedman, 1989), no differences emerged on outcome between the functional family therapy condition and the parent group condition. Therefore, according to the Chambless and Hollon (1998) criteria for empirically supported treatment, functional family therapy would meet criteria for "probably efficacious" because no independent investigation has replicated the positive results found in the two studies conducted by Waldron and colleagues.

Multidimensional Family Therapy

THEORETICAL APPROACH. As the name belies, Multidimensional Family Therapy (MDFT), like Family Behavioral Treatment, Functional Family Therapy, and MST, is a multicomponent intervention targeting individual, peer, school, and family risk factors associated with adolescent substance abuse (Liddle et al., 2001). The individual adolescent domain involves engaging teens in treatment and building communication skills, social competence, and alternatives to substance use. The *parent domain* engages parents in therapy, increases their behavioral and emotional involvement with the adolescents, and improves parental monitoring and limit setting. The *family interactional domain* focuses on decreasing conflict and improving emotional attachments, patterns of communication, and problem-solving techniques using multiparticipant family sessions. The *extrafamilial domain* fosters family competency and collaborative involvement within all social systems in which the teen participates (e.g., school, juvenile justice, recreational) (Liddle et al., 2009). The therapist meets with the adolescent, parents, or in cojoint sessions as needed. MDFT can be delivered from one to three times per week over the course of 3–6 months depending on the treatment setting—office-based, in-home, outpatient, day treatment, residential treatment—and the severity of adolescent problems and family functioning. Regardless of the version, therapists work simultaneously in four interdependent treatment domains according to the particular risk and protection profile of the adolescent and family.

APA DIVISION 12 TASK FORCE CRITERIA. Based on Waldron and Turner's review (2008), MDFT has been classified as a "well established" treatment for adolescent substance abuse mainly because it has involved more than one research team (Dennis et al., 2004; Liddle et al., 2001; Liddle, Dakof, Turner, & Tejeda, 2003; Liddle, Rowe, Dakof, Ungaro, & Henderson, 2004), with comparisons to one or more active treatment conditions, and has emerged as superior on reductions in substance use. No systematic review has been conducted on MDFT.

SUMMARY

In sum, no well-established treatment has emerged for antisocial adolescent behavior, although one family treatment (MST) and group CBT are categorized as "probably efficacious." CBT for adolescent substance abuse seems to have been subject to more research and has earned the categorization of "well-established." The Waldron and Turner (2008) APA Division 12 Task Force review of treatment outcome studies for adolescent substance abuse stated that MDFT, MST, and FFT "have emerged as well-established treatments." However, closer analysis determined that only MDFT may be classified as such.

BIOPSYCHOSOCIAL RISK AND RESILIENCE

ONSET

Risk and protective factors for the onset of adolescent substance *use* (not necessarily abuse or dependence, the focus of this chapter) are described in Table 4.2. Note that the majority of these factors overlap those that have been outlined for the development of childhood oppositional defiant and conduct disorder (see Chapter 3). In addition to the factors named in Table 4.2, early onset of drinking (before age 14 years) is associated with having a problem with substances (Hingson, Hereen, & Winter, 2006).

Most studies on risk and protective factors for adolescents have focused on the onset of ODD or CD in childhood, but a recent longitudinal study of risk and protective factors conducted primarily in African-American teens found that child factors of verbal IQ, verbal memory, and attention span, as well as social factors—good housing and low crime in the community, were protective for delinquency (Loeber et al., 2007). A recent study also demonstrates how environmental context may shape genetic factors. For males residing in urban areas, heritable factors explained a majority of the variance, but for males in rural areas, environmental effects played a larger role in the development of conduct disorder (Legrand, Keyes, McGue, et al., 2008). To explain these findings, it could be that stronger community norms operate in smaller towns or that parents might be able to more easily monitor their adolescents' behaviors in rural areas.

TABLE 4.2 RISK AND PROTECTIVE FACTORS FOR ADOLESCENT SUBSTANCE USE

System Level	Risk	Protective
Biological	Male	
	Genetics (moderately heritable)	
	Lesbian, gay, or bisexual sexual orientation	
Psychological	Impulsivity and attention deficit hyperactivity disorder (ADHD) symptoms	Goal direction
	Aggression and undercontrolled behavior in childhood	
	Sensation-seeking behavior	
	Low feelings of guilt	
	Conduct problems and delinquency	
Peers	Social impairment	Having abstinent friends
	Affiliation with deviant peers	
	Peer substance abuse	
School	Low achievement and academic failure	Positive connection to school
	Truancy	
	Suspension	
	Low motivation, negative attitude toward school	
Family	Parental substance abuse	Parental warnings about alcohol use and being close to parents
	Permissive parental values about teen alcohol and drug use	
	Sibling substance abuse	A warm and supportive family environment
	Harsh, inconsistent, and ineffective discipline strategies	Low level of family conflict
	Lack of monitoring and supervision	Parental control and supervision
	Child abuse and other trauma	
	Poor relationships with parents and siblings, low bonding	
	Unemployment, poor education of mother	
	Teens running away from home	
Community	Availability	Clear community prohibitions
Race	White (alcohol)	
	Hispanic (drug use)	

References for this table were drawn from the following sources: Farrell and White (1998); French, Finkbiner, and Duhamel (2002); Hawkins et al. (1992); Hingson, Hereen, and Winter (2006); Hopfer, Stallings, Hewitt, and Crowley (2003); Jessor et al. (1995); Kaplow et al. (2002); Kilpatrick et al. (2000); Latimer et al. (2000); Loeber et al. (1998); Marshal, Friedman, Stall, et al. (2008); Martin et al. (2002); National Institute on Drug Abuse (1997); Siebenbruner, Englund, Egeland, and Hudson (2006); Young, Rhee, Stallings, et al. (2006).

TREATMENT AND RECOVERY

The number of risk influences appears to affect how an adolescent may fare over time. In one study 2% of youth who had no childhood risk influences showed persistent delinquency in adolescence, compared with 71% of youth who had risk influences in five different areas of life (Frick, 2006). These findings imply that prevention of risk factors in childhood may have effects that continue into adolescence.

For substance use disorders, whereas psychosocial risk appears to be a more powerful predictor of onset for adolescent use, the relative importance of protective factors is greater for recovery (Latimer et al., 2000). Additionally, it appears that factors in play at the end of treatment, including participation in aftercare and AA meetings, a lack of substance-using peers, involvement in a variety of non-substance-related activities, use of coping strategies learned in treatment, and motivation to continue sobriety, positively influence recovery (Chung & Maisto, 2006). These findings are encouraging as they suggest that certain factors are malleable and can inform treatment efforts.

Both child and peer factors were identified as risk factors in a longitudinal study of males (over half of whom were African-American) followed from 7– 20 years of age. Ongoing delinquency involved tobacco use, high interpersonal callousness, and peer delinquency (Loeber, Pardini, Stouthamer-Loeber, & Raine, 2007). Interestingly, none of the cognitive, family, and neighborhood factors predicted desistance, although, as discussed, individual and social factors were implicated in the onset of delinquency.

Ethnicity

Research has indicated the ethnic disparities that exist in the juvenile justice system with ethnic minorities overrepresented (citation). Recent attention has been given to how well tested interventions apply to ethnic minority youth in both systematic reviews/meta-analyses and APA Psychological 12 Task Force criteria reviews. The role of ethnicity in treatment outcomes has been explored inconsistently across studies, leading to a lack of evidence (Eyberg, Nelson, & Boggs, 2008). Debate surrounds several questions relating to the effectiveness of mainstream services for minority clients, the possible need for culturally specific interventions, and the role of the helping professional's ethnicity (Wilson, Lipsey, & Soydan, 2003).

SYSTEMATIC REVIEWS/META-ANALYSES. One main question about intervening with people from ethnic minority groups involves whether interventions tested on the majority still retain their effectiveness. One meta-analysis focused on whether "mainstream" interventions for youth with juvenile justice system involvement were as effective for ethnic minority adolescents (Wilson et al., 2003).

Altogether 305 studies met the inclusion criteria, and the main finding was that no statistically significant difference emerged between outcomes for white youth and what ended up being primarily African-American samples when they were treated with mainstream delinquency interventions that had not been culturally tailored. However, the overall effect size for outcomes was negligible according to Cohen's standards (1988).

Ethnicity was studied in another meta-analysis, this one having to do with CBT. McCart and his colleagues (2006) explored ethnicity as a moderating factor in the effectiveness of CBT. The strength of their conclusion was limited because of the low criterion used in coding the studies (66%); however, they did find similar treatment responses among white and African-American youth.

APA PSYCHOLOGICAL 12 TASK FORCE CRITERIA. Huey and Polo (2008) examined the applicability of tested interventions for minority ethnic youth for both adolescent antisocial and substance use disorders. For behavioral problems, treatments considered to be probably efficacious for ethnic minority teens include two family-based treatments—MST (for conduct disorder) and MDFT (for substance abuse; Liddle, Rowe, Dakof, Ungaro, and Henderson, 2004)—and two cognitive–behavioral group treatments—Coping Power with parent training and Anger Management Group Training (Huey & Polo, 2008). The Coping Power program used a combination of training in social problem solving, coping with negative emotions, positive play, and group-entry skills. The program's efficacy with aggressive ethnic minority youth was tested in three studies with African-American youth. In the first, an earlier version of Coping Power showed more effectiveness than a no-treatment control group (Lochman, Coie, Underwood, & Terry, 1993). In subsequent studies (Lochman & Wells, 2003, 2004), a behavioral parent training component was included, and youth demonstrated more improvement than no treatment or usual treatment (Huey & Polo, 2008).

Anger Management group training was developed as a condensed four-session group delivered in 2 weeks. Participants were predominantly African-American males and females in a psychiatric hospital. Decreases in standardized anger management scores were significantly better than the control group.

In sum, although ethnic minority youth are still underrepresented in research, particularly for certain ethnic groups, the findings so far are encouraging that both interventions used for mainstream youth, as well as culturally adapted treatments, are helpful in improving teen behavior problems and reducing substance use.

Gender

It is important for females' conduct problems to be addressed as continued involvement with deviant partners might lead to a high risk of experiencing intimate partner violence (Maughan & Rutter, 2001). Although conduct problems predict earlier sexual involvement for both boys and girls, the consequences of sexual behavior are more serious for girls because they may become pregnant and drop out of school (Ledingham, 1999). Having children, however, is protective for females with CD in terms of the persistence of the disorder. The transition to motherhood may result in decreased opportunities for the adolescent's deviant behavior and a strengthening of social bonds through the child. These developments inhibit girls' willingness to engage in antisocial behavior (Ehrensaft, 2005). At the same time, mothers with CD often are harsh disciplinarians (Capaldi & Patterson, 1994; McMahon, 1994). This tendency, along with the effect of assertive mating and consequently increased genetic risk, puts their children at particular risk for the development of antisocial behavior (Ehrensaft, 2005).

As detailed in Chapter 3, the treatment outcome research for girls with ODD and CD lags behind that of males. Additionally, although rates of substance use disorders are comparable for teens of both genders (Reddy, Resnicow, Omardien, & Kambaran, 2007), there is little research evidence to guide the treatment of girls with substance use disorders. One treatment implication from a review of conduct problems in females is that priority should be given to stabilizing and structuring the home environment and building trust between clients and their caregivers (Ehrensaft, 2005). Girls with conduct problems are more likely to come from homes characterized by intense emotional conflict and unstable interpersonal relationships and are more likely to develop borderline personality disorder.

MTFC (as described above) is the only study conducted with an all-female (mostly white) delinquency sample. The researchers claim that reductions in delinquency for the MTFC group were maintained at 2-year follow-up when compared to the "group care" condition (Chamberlain, Leve, & DeGarmo, 2007).

Comorbidity

Adolescents have a 60% likelihood of being diagnosed with a psychiatric disorder, along with a substance use disorder. The disruptive disorders—conduct disorder, oppositional defiant disorder, and ADHD—are most common, followed by depression (Armstrong & Costello, 2002).

In a review of six studies of adolescents who were dually diagnosed with a substance use disorder and a mental health disorder such as CD, ODD, or posttraumatic stress disorder (PTSD), Bender, Springer, and Kim (2006) examined the effect of seven different interventions. In these studies, many of the interventions showed an effect of over 0.80 for an individual outcome, internalizing, externalizing, or substance abuse. Only individual cognitive problem solving (ICPS) and family behavioral treatment (FBT) were highly effective in all three areas that represent dual diagnosis. Improvement from both ICPS and FBT was also maintained over time as evidenced by a sustained effect size at 9-month follow-up.

RESEARCH RECOMMENDATIONS

Many of the research recommendations of relevance here have already been discussed in Chapter 3 on childhood ODD and CD, so only particular points deserve emphasis. One is the critical issue of addressing comorbidity in treatment when both a substance use disorder and ODD or CD are present. The current existence of two separate treatment systems (substance use and mental health) contributes to the fragmentation of service delivery and may leave salient issues unaddressed (American Psychological Association Task Force on Evidence-Based Practice for Children and Adolescents, 2008). As noted in the above review, Bender, Springer, and Kim (2006) located only six studies that targeted both substance use problems and another disorder. Therefore, future research suggestions for this area include the following:

1. more purposive targeting of comorbid disorders;
2. youth with substance use disorders could be allowed to enter into treatment outcome studies for other mental health disorders, such as eating disorders, depression, anxiety, as well as ODD and CD;
3. when examining adolescent substance use or antisocial behavior, both outcomes should be routinely included in studies, even when the focus is only on a particular population or problem.

Another recommendation particular to this literature relates to the fact that a confluence of risk factors interacts to give rise to adolescent antisocial and substance use. As a result, complex, multicomponent packages have been developed to treat these disorders. However, when faced with such a package, it is not clear what the critical components of the intervention are and whether one or two components might work as well as more expensive and complicated arrangements. Therefore, dismantling studies could pinpoint the components that are necessary to impact problematic behaviors.

A third recommendation for this literature is to subject more treatments to the Cochrane Collaboration systematic review process. As noted in the discussion above, although MST has been touted heavily as an "evidence-based treatment" for juvenile delinquency, there were no statistically significant differences when it came to effect sizes comparing MST to treatment as usual on any of the many outcomes that were studied. Although FFT is currently undergoing the same review process, other treatments, such as MDFT and CBT, could also undergo a similar process.

CONCLUSIONS

Adult antisocial behavior and diminished outcome for youth as they enter into adulthood can result from adolescent ODD and CD (Moffitt, Caspi, Harrington, & Milne, 2002). Similarly, substance use disorders can often be traced to adolescent onset (Rohde, Lewinsohn, Kahler, et al., 2001). The necessity, therefore, is to identify and disseminate those treatments that demonstrate effectiveness for adolescents with these problems. The disruptive behavior and substance use disorders have been considered together given their common risk factors and similar treatments—CBT and integrated family systems/behavioral models. More empirical studies and reviews should be undertaken of these treatments, particularly of those for substance abuse.

CASE STUDY

Kay is a 17-year-old Puerto Rican female who is currently in the 11th grade. She was born in Puerto Rico; however, 3 weeks following her birth she moved to the United States with her mother after her parents' relationship collapsed. Kay has not had contact with her biological father since that time, although she has heard that he sold drugs and was incarcerated on a few occasions (see Box 4.1).

When Kay was 6 months old her mother married a man named "Jose." At the age of 3 years, she was sent to live with her aunt and uncle in another state because her mother and Jose were unable to financially provide for her. At the age of 5 years, Kay was returned to her mother, who had since moved to another state with Jose and their two boys, who were 4 and 2 years old. Both Kay's mother and Jose frequently abused drugs and alcohol. Soon after Kay's arrival, Jose began to physically abuse Kay. Kay also witnessed him emotionally and physically abusing her mother and brothers. Kay said she survived by praying and by bonding with her brothers. When Kay was 9 years old, Jose sexually abused her. Kay reported the abuse to school personnel, but she was not believed until 2 years later.

After Child Protective Services became involved, Jose was prosecuted and sentenced to jail. Kay was once again sent to live with her aunt and uncle, who were much stricter than her mother and stepfather. While living there, Kay began running away, engaging in sexual activity, and drinking to the point of "blacking out." When Kay's uncle discovered she was sexually active, he became enraged, pushed Kay down the stairs, and administered blows with a belt while her aunt held her down and covered her mouth. Kay reported this incident to school personnel, and CPS investigated, but did not become further involved.

Six months later at the age of 14 years, Kay moved back to live with her mother. Kay's mother had divorced Jose, remarried, and given birth to another son who was an infant at the time. Kay's mother had continued to abuse drugs. While living with

---

BOX 4.1 *DSM-IV* DIAGNOSIS

Axis I: 312.82—Conduct Disorder, Unspecified Onset, Mild
V61.21, 995.54—Physical Abuse of Child (Victim)
V61.21, 995.53—Sexual Abuse of Child (Victim)
305.00 Alcohol Abuse

The diagnosis of Conduct Disorder was given because in the past 12 months Kay stole her stepfather's car, ran away from home, and cut a legal monitoring bracelet off her leg to escape the confines of her sentence. Furthermore, at least one of these behaviors occurred in the past 6 months.

There was no report of childhood history, so either the specifier Adolescent Onset or Unspecified Onset could be given. The severity of the disorder was mild because Kay met only minimal criteria. Conduct Disorder was listed first because this disorder is causing her the most impairment (recent multiple placements, poor school performance).

When looking at PTSD, Kay met some of the criteria. She experienced physical and sexual abuse by her stepfather and sexual assault by gang members. Kay also scored relatively high (total score of 35) on the Impact of Event Scale–Revised. Despite this, Kay did not meet the three or more required avoidance symptoms that are listed in the *DSM-IV*. She does avoid thoughts and feelings associated with the trauma, but has no other avoidance symptoms. Therefore, Kay was given the secondary diagnoses of Physical Abuse of a Child and Sexual Abuse of a Child, which are both V codes.

Alcohol Abuse was given as a diagnosis even though Kay denied it was a current issue. She said that it had been a problem when she was 14 through 16 years old and admitted it may have played a role in her running away, stealing cars, and sexual risk-taking in the past, but she denied current use. At the same time, she had been drinking when she ran away from her previous foster home to attend a party; therefore, it remains a current diagnosis rather than being indicated as "history."

Axis II: V71.09—No diagnosis

Axis III: Human papillomavirus (HPV)
Genital herpes

A medical doctor diagnosed Kay with HPV and genital herpes. Other than these diseases, Kay was found to be in overall good health at a recent physical.

Axis IV: Problems with primary support group (disruption of family by separation;removal from the home; estrangement from biological father; multiple placements)
Problems with the social environment (inadequate social support; discord with her foster sister)
Problem related to interaction with the legal system (the court is her legal guardian)

Axis V: GAF—65

---

her mother, Kay began hanging out with gang members and stopped attending school. She would steal her mother's car to attend parties, and ran away on several occasions. On one occasion, Kay was raped by two gang members and photographed in the nude. She did not report this incident to authorities because she was afraid that the rapists or other gang members would retaliate by harming her or her family.

As a result of stealing her mother's car, running away, and truancy, Kay became involved with the legal system. On three occasions the court ordered Kay to wear a monitoring ankle bracelet and each of these times Kay cut the ankle bracelet off to run away. Eventually, Kay was sentenced to a Juvenile Detention Center (JDC) for her illegal behaviors. Kay recalls getting into multiple physical altercations with the staff and other girls at JDC.

Kay was released from JDC after 6 months and was placed in a group home because of her out-of-control behavior and her mother's inability to provide a safe and stable home. She started "cutting" at this placement, and this behavior persisted for 1 year. After 2 months the group home shut down and she moved to another group home; there Kay reported that at times she felt suicidal. Many services were provided to Kay while living at this placement, including individual therapy, family therapy with her mother, and alcohol/drug counseling. The staff noted that Kay was "bright" and "insightful"; however, she could also be "manipulative," "impulsive," "disrespectful," and "moody." Kay was prescribed Zoloft but disliked taking it and did not feel that the medication benefited her.

After spending 15 months in the group home Kay, at the age of 17 years, successfully graduated from the program and went to live with her mother (now sober) and her new stepfather. At that time her two older brothers were living with their father, Jose, and her youngest brother was living with his grandmother in another state. Three weeks after arriving home, Kay ran away, taking her stepfather's car and driving it without having a license. Concurrently, Kay's mother made the decision to leave Kay's stepfather and move in with her Narcotics Anonymous sponsor. Kay's social worker decided that it was necessary to take Kay into custody, and she was admitted to a therapeutic foster care agency.

Kay was initially placed in a two-parent therapeutic foster home. The foster parents ran a strict household, and the foster father was especially demanding. Kay and her foster father had difficulty developing a positive relationship with one another. Three weeks after Kay moved into this foster home, she ran away to attend a party and admitted to drinking but claimed that she did not "get drunk." As a result of this incident, the foster parents decided to disrupt the placement.

Kay was subsequently placed in a single-parent therapeutic foster home. This household consists of a foster mother, a foster sister, and another female therapeutic foster care adolescent. Kay seemed to be adjusting well to the foster home. Although she did not get along well with the other foster adolescent in the home, Kay began to develop a close, trusting relationship with her current foster parent.

Recently, Kay had a physical examination and was found to be in good overall health, although she was diagnosed with human papilloma virus (HPV) and genital herpes.

Kay's history of truancy resulted in her failing ninth grade. She currently attends eleventh grade, where she is doing well in her classes. Her goal is to graduate from high school and attend college or a vocational school. She is particularly interested in studying cosmetology. Kay identifies herself as Christian, but reports that religion does not play a large part in her life. She has and continues to use prayer as an instrument to sustain herself during difficult times.

Kay reports that she consumed alcohol frequently between the ages of 14 and 16 years. She describes this as a "phase" and explained that she mainly consumed alcohol when she ran away. Kay insists she has never done drugs, including marijuana, because she has seen what drugs did to her mother.

Currently, visitations between Kay and her mother occur biweekly at her mother's request. Kay's mother explained that she could visit with Kay only every other week because she needs time for herself in order to maintain her sobriety. Kay describes her relationship with her mother as being loving but distant, due to their separation and communication problems. She had expressed a desire to develop better communication and a closer relationship with her mother.

Kay's two older brothers live with their father in one state and her younger brother lives in another state with his paternal grandmother. She often spends time with her older two brothers during visitations with her mother; however, she does not see her younger brother often because he lives far away. Kay states that she loves her brothers and misses them very much. She explained that she wants to help her mother maintain her sobriety. When Kay's mother spent Thanksgiving with her younger brother Kay never expressed her sadness and instead stated that her younger brother needed her mother more than she did. Additionally, when Kay's mother said that she only had $100 to spend on Christmas gifts, Kay requested that she spend the money on her brothers and not on her.

HOW THE EVIDENCE FITS

According to the accumulated evidence basis, Kay could receive treatment in foster care, which would involve intense foster home-based support and treatment for 6–9 months. Family interventions other than treatment foster care are not feasible because Kay's mother is not actively engaged in her treatment. Specifically, MTFC, as noted, has been found to be more effective for girls than boys, and is targeted toward delinquent youth.

APPLICATION

The implementation of MYFC would require Kay to transition over to another foster parent, since only one youth is allowed per foster home and her current placement involves two other foster children. Kay's foster parent(s) would be required to attend a 20-hour training program prior to Kay's participation. This training is critical because it teaches the parent(s) how to effectively implement a system of daily token reinforcements consisting of clear, consistent limits as well as rewards. As an example, Kay might find supervised driving privileges in preparation for a driver's license particularly rewarding. MTFC further involves the parent(s) reporting point levels to program staff on a daily basis over the phone, as well as meetings with staff intended to support and supervise the foster parent(s).

Kay, meanwhile, would receive treatment in weekly settings to develop her problem-solving skills, anger management, social skills, and planning for educational or vocational goals. In addition, she would receive support from a certified behavioral specialist experienced with Applied Behavior Analysis who would work with her outside in the community (shopping centers, restaurants) to reinforce prosocial behaviors. Even though Kay does not currently take medications, she would have the support of a psychiatrist to discuss the potential benefits, if she were interested.

Finally, Kay's mother would also receive parent training, as a way to prepare for the transition for when Kay is ready to return home. This would be helpful for Kay's mother because she could use support managing Kay's difficult behaviors and she could help reinforce the new behaviors Kay is learning. It would also be valuable if Kay's mother could be in communication with Kay's foster parent(s) on a regular basis in order to facilitate the transition. If these mandates seemed to be too intensive for Kay's mother to attend along with her sobriety requirements, perhaps another family member such as her grandparents could tackle the training.

HOW THE EVIDENCE DOES NOT FIT

Characteristics of Youth

Kay is part Puerto-Rican, although it is unknown from the case information with which ethnic group she identifies. The studies on MTFC have primarily been conducted with white youth. Therefore, it is not clear how well the treatment may apply to a person of her ethnicity.

As well as the externalizing and substance use behaviors that are common to juvenile offenders, the target population of MTFC, Kay shows elevated scores on a standardized measure of PTSD. Although she does not meet full-blown criteria for PTSD, the argument was made in Chapter 3 that subclinical PTSD must be treated. In addition to PTSD symptoms, sexual abuse might also lead to problematic sexual behaviors, depression, other anxiety symptoms, and the externalizing behaviors that Kay currently shows. Therefore, treatment of the sexual abuse appears critical. Because a part of MTFC is regular therapy sessions, it is hoped that the externalizing symptoms would not be the only focus of treatment, and that the trauma would be addressed as well. This is not explicitly stated in the description of MTFC, however.

Characteristics of Context

Although part of the treatment model involves training biological parents in the techniques as well, so that the teen can eventually transition back into the home, Kay's mother may be unable to meet these requirements. Currently, she does not participate in Kay's treatment because of her stated needs to concentrate on her sobriety. Because many of the risks to Kay occurred as a result of lack of stability of her mother's care, this may be an ongoing risk after the completion of MTFC.

HOW IT ADDRESSES STRENGTHS

The MTFC model is inclusive of strengths through its positive reinforcement system; as Kay displays desired behaviors, whether they are newly acquired or part of her current repertoire, these will be reinforced through positive feedback and rewards. For example, Kay is described as having positive social skills; when she shows such skills in public settings, they will be reinforced by the behavioral specialist.

II

INTERNALIZING DISORDERS

5

ANXIETY DISORDERS

Anxiety *disorders* are characterized by extreme, intense, almost unbearable fear that disrupts social or occupational functioning. The DSM describes 11 different anxiety disorders, as well as separation anxiety disorder, which is listed under disorders of infancy and childhood. See Table 5.1 for the different anxiety disorders and their prevalence. Although posttraumatic stress disorder (PTSD) and oppositional obsessive compulsive disorder (OCD) are often considered separately from the other anxiety disorders in children—Generalized Anxiety Disorder, Separation Anxiety Disorder, and Social Anxiety (e.g., Brown et al., 2007; James et al., 2005)—a lack of treatment outcome research for OCD means that it will be included here rather than in its own chapter. PTSD will be covered in Chapter 6.

After discussing the state of the research on the treatment of anxiety disorders, the individual and environmental influences on the development of the disorder, and factors leading to enhanced recovery and treatment will be explored with a case study illustrating their importance. From these discussions, research recommendations will be advanced.

STATE OF THE EVIDENCE

PSYCHOSOCIAL TREATMENT

The most widely studied intervention for child and adolescent anxiety disorders is cognitive–behavioral therapy (CBT) featuring exposure (James et al., 2005). *Exposure* is a process in which the client learns to face the feared object until the anxiety dissipates. Typically conducted in a graduated fashion, the practitioner helps the client construct a hierarchy of situations from least to most feared

TABLE 5.1 ANXIETY DISORDERS IN CHILDREN: DESCRIPTION AND PREVALENCE

Anxiety Disorder	Description	Prevalence (%)	
Separation anxiety disorder	Excessive anxiety about separation from a major attachment figure, often involving school refusal	0.2–3.6	3 month
		1.8–3.2	6 month
		3.1	12 month
		4.6	Lifetime
Panic disorders	Unpredictable anxiety attacks	0.1–1.8	3 month
		0.4–1.1	6 month
		0.6–3.0	12 month
		0.5–3.1	Lifetime
Agoraphobia with or without panic	The panic attacks arise from anxiety about being in places or circumstances from which escape might be difficult or embarrassing or attacks are not associated with particular situations but are characterized by fears of losing self-control or panic-like symptoms occur in places or situations from which escape might be difficult.	0.1–1.1	3 month
		2.2–3.3	6 month
		1.6–4.0	12 month
		2.6–9.1	Lifetime
Social phobia	Anxiety related to social situations; fear of negative evaluation from others is the overwhelming worry.	0.3–2.5	3 month
		2.0–9.2	6 month
		2.6–12.4	12 month
		1.6–13.1	Lifetime
Generalized anxiety disorder	Persistent, excessive worry that lasts for at least 6 months, occurring more days than not	1.4–3.9	3 month
		1.3–4.6	6 month
		0.3–2.4	12 month
		0.6–0.8	Lifetime
Obsessive–compulsive disorder	Recurring thoughts that cause marked anxiety and compulsive behaviors that temporarily serve to neutralize anxiety. The obsessions and compulsions are severe enough to be time consuming (greater than 1 hour per day) or cause marked distress or significant impairment.	0.1–0.3	3 month
		1.0	6 month (only one study reported)
		0.6–7.1	12 month
		0.7–1.7	Lifetime
Posttraumatic stress disorder (PTSD)	PTSD is characterized by symptoms of anxiety that follow exposure to a traumatic stressor. Three major symptom categories include reexperiencing of the trauma, avoidance and numbing, and increased arousal.	0.5–4.0	3 month (no studies reporting 6 month)
		0.7–0.8	12 month
		1.3–6.0	Lifetime

From Costello et al. (2005).

and then work through these in order, conquering smaller fears before going on to larger ones. Other components of CBT packages include the following (Gorman et al., 2002; Velting et al., 2004):

Psychoeducation: providing information about the nature of anxiety and how it can be controlled)

Monitoring anxiety symptoms for their frequency, duration, and triggers

Cognitive restructuring: identifying, challenging, and replacing maladaptive belief systems that contribute to anxiety

Breathing retraining: to distract clients from anxiety symptoms and provide a sense of control over them

Progressive muscle relaxation: to reduce tension in anxiety-provoking situations by alternately tightening and relaxing certain muscle groups

Problem solving: for generating a variety of practical solutions to life challenges.

Systematic Reviews

Three systematic reviews have been conducted on the treatment of youth anxiety disorders with CBT. James et al. (2005) conducted a Cochrane systematic review on social phobia, separation anxiety, panic disorder, and generalized anxiety disorder (excluding PTSD and OCD) (see Table 5.2). The intention to treat analysis comprised 475 treatment subjects and 290 controls in 13 studies. Results of meta-analysis indicated that for CBT, remission of the anxiety disorder occurred in 56% of cases versus 28.2% for controls. Similarly, in a meta-analysis of 24 published studies (German and English), 68.9% of children had remitted from their anxiety disorder compared to only 12.9% of children who were assigned to a waiting list (In-Albon & Schneider, 2007). Both meta-analyses showed that improvement increased at follow-up—a remission rate of 69% (James et al., 2005) and 72% (In-Albon & Schneider, 2007). When looking at reduction in anxiety symptom scores, effect sizes were in the moderate range (at 0.58 for James et al., 2005).

Because the treatment of anxiety involves exposure to the feared object, there is a concern with exposure-based CBT that people might be unwilling to undergo the intervention. However, James et al. (2005) found no differences in follow-up rates between treatment and control groups. They took this as evidence that both conditions were similarly acceptable.

The purpose of a third meta-analysis departed in that it focused on examining the theory basis of CBT by analyzing its effect on different theoretical outcomes (Chu & Harrison, 2007) (see Table 5.2). These researchers found a moderate effect similar to that of James at al. (2005) on anxiety symptom scores (0.64). CBT was especially effective in targeting behavioral outcomes for anxiety, but did not affect cognitive outcomes more than alternative conditions. This latter finding was surprising given the cognitive thrust of CBT programs.

TABLE 5.2 SUMMARIES OF SYSTEMATIC REVIEWS AND META-ANALYSES FOR PSYCHOSOCIAL TREATMENT OUTCOME STUDIES FOR NON-OBSESSIVE COMPULSIVE DISORDER (OCD) AND NON-POSTTRAUMATIC STRESS DISORDER (PTSD) ANXIETY DISORDERS

Author and Purpose	Inclusion Criteria	Main Findings
James et al. (2005) (Cochrane Review)	**Participants** Youth 6–18 years old with a diagnosis of anxiety, excluding PTSD, simple phobias, elective mutism, and OCD disorder. **Intervention** Manualized cognitive–behavioral therapy (CBT) of at least eight sessions **Studies** Randomized controlled trials **Outcome** A diagnosis of anxiety disorder; reduction in anxiety symptoms	N = 13 studies involved 519 subjects Remission of anxiety disorders occurred in 56% of cases versus 28.2% for controls at posttest and remission improved to 69% at follow-up. The effect size for the reduction of anxiety symptom scores was 0.58.
In-Albon and Schneider (2006) To examine the efficacy of psychotherapy for anxiety disorders in children	**Participants** Children had to have a diagnosed anxiety disorder. **Intervention** Treatment for anxiety with a written protocol **Studies** Peer-reviewed published studies written in English and German examining the efficacy of treatment for anxiety (excluding OCD and PTSD) against a control condition or a viable treatment, using randomized controlled trials **Outcome** Diagnosis of anxiety disorder, anxiety symptoms	N = 24 studies Across all active treatments, 68.9% of children who completed therapy no longer met the diagnostic criteria for their principal pretreatment anxiety disorder compared to only 12.9% of children who were assigned to a waiting list. At the follow-up assessment, the recovery rate of children who completed treatment increased slightly to 72%.
O'Kearney, Anstey, and von Sanden (2006) To examine the efficacy of behavioral therapy (BT)/	**Participants** 18 years of age or under with a diagnosis of OCD **Intervention** Behavioral or cognitive–behavioral techniques	N = 4 studies involving 222 participants Researchers call it a "promising" treatment although they could quantitatively combine very few studies.

CBT for child and adolescent OCD overall, and its differential efficacy over medication and whether benefits accrue from combining BT/CBT with medication

Studies

Randomized or quasirandomized published and nonpublished studies; the comparison conditions used appeared to be wait-list, pill placebo, other interventions, and medication.

Outcome

"Frequency, duration, and degree of distress of obsessions and compulsions are measured by clinician rated or self-monitored standard measures."

"Dichotomized primary outcomes included responders/nonresponders and diagnosis remitted/nonremitted."

Self-report measures of distress and disruption

"Adverse effects, drop-out from studies, and acceptability of treatment"

Chu and Harrison (2007)
To determine the effect that CBT has on cognitive and behavioral change, including behavioral, physiological and coping outcomes

Participants

6–18 year olds who had a clinical diagnosis of depression or anxiety or clinically significant symptoms

Intervention

CBT

Studies

Randomized, controlled trials published in English-language peer-reviewed journals

Outcome

Assessed anxiety or depression and at least one cognitive, coping, behavioral, or physiological target

$N = 14$ studies on anxiety

The effect size for anxiety was 0.64.

CBT was especially effective in targeting behavioral outcomes for anxiety but did not affect cognitive outcomes more than other conditions.

In a systematic review of CBT outcome research for OCD, O'Kearney, Anstey, and von Sanden (2007) found only four studies, which involved a total of 222 participants. They were unable to compute effect sizes for most outcomes because of the few number of studies that shared outcomes and the statistical heterogeneity in studies that precluded quantitative summary. The study with the highest quality on which to base findings was the Pediatric OCD Treatment Study (POTS, 2004). In this multisite, large-scale study, youth with OCD were randomized to either of four different conditions for 12 weeks: CBT alone, sertraline alone, combined CBT and sertraline, or pill placebo. They found that CBT was superior to pill placebo for the reduction of OCD symptoms and for remission of OCD. Although only two studies (including POTS) compared CBT with medication, CBT was equally as effective in these cases.

APA Task Force 12 Criteria

Two different reviews have been conducted according to APA Task Force 12 Criteria (Silverman et al., 2008; Verdeli et al., 2006). Although neither review found that any treatment was "well-established," different conclusions were reached on what was categorized as "probably efficacious." Verdeli et al. (2006) considered particular manualized treatments separately, even though they were all CBT programs, whereas Silverman et al. categorized treatments by modality. Verdeli et al. (2006) further divided studies on whether they targeted children or adolescents. Using these criteria, Verdeli et al. (2006) categorized Kendall's (1990) Coping Cat program, designed for youth ages 7 to 14 years with separation anxiety disorder, generalized anxiety disorder, and social phobia, as "probably efficacious." Adaptations of this program have emerged in Australia with Coping Koala and in Canada with Coping Bear. Additionally, Spence et al.'s (2006) children's CBT group for social phobia was categorized as "possibly efficacious." Verdeli et al. (2006) addressed simple phobia whereas the Silverman et al. (2008) did not, yet no treatment for simple phobia met criteria for well-established or probably efficacious. For adolescents, no treatment met the criteria for "probably efficacious" (Verdeli et al., 2006).

According to the Silverman et al. (2008) APA Psychological Task Force Criteria review, probably efficacious treatments for mixed anxiety disorders included the following: individual CBT (Barrett et al., 1996; Flannery-Schroeder & Kendall, 2000; Kendall, 1994; Kendall et al. 1997), group CBT (Barrett, 1998; Flannery-Schroeder & Kendall, 2000; Mendlowitz et al., 1999; Rapee et al. 2006), and group CBT with parents (Barrett, 1998; Mendlowitz et al., 1999; Silverman, Kurtines, Ginsburg, Weems, Lumpkin, et al., 1999; Spence et al., 2006).

The only specific anxiety disorder with empirically supported treatment was social anxiety, and these treatments were rated as probably efficacious: group

CBT for social anxiety (Gallagher et al., 2003; Hayward et al., 2000; Spence et al., 2000) and social effectiveness training for children with social anxiety disorder (Beidel & Turner 2000).

Some of the APA Psychological Task Force criteria reviews have also been conducted on OCD (Barrett et al., 2008; Verdeli et al., 2006). Barrett et al. (2008) found that only four studies were well designed methodologically. This review (as the O'Kearney, 2007, systematic review above) primarily based its findings on the POTS Team study (POTS, 2004) and concluded that individually administered CBT (March & Mulle, 1998) was "probably efficacious." Reviewing two randomized controlled trials, Verdeli et al. (2006) reached the same conclusion and categorized March's OCD CBT curriculum as "probably efficacious."

Summary of Psychosocial Evidence

The different results of the Silverman et al. (2008) and the Verdeli et al. (2006) APA Task Force 12 Criteria show how different ways of categorizing studies can lead to different conclusions about the state of the evidence. The Cochrane Collaboration systematic review process as followed by James et al. (2005) appears to be a more transparent and standardized process, and was able to synthesize the entire CBT literature for anxiety disorders. However, practitioners may find it more helpful to be told that a particular curriculum can be used for a certain anxiety disorder as in the APA Task Force 12 Categorization reviews. In either case, CBT has been the research focus and has been met with modest success.

MEDICATION

Several medications have evolved for the treatment of anxiety. The first of these is the benzodiazepines, which are believed to achieve their therapeutic effect by causing the γ-aminobutyric acid (GABA) neurotransmitter to bind more completely with its receptor site, possibly inciting the release of the body's natural benzodiazepines. Antidepressant medications are also used for anxiety. The tricyclic antidepressants (TCAs) are believed to work by blocking the reuptake of norepinephrine and serotonin and, to a lesser extent, dopamine. Reviews of the evidence of these medications have concluded that "[T]he relative lack of efficacy and adverse safety profiles of benzodiazapines and tricyclic antidepressants do not support their use in the treatment of children and adolescents with an anxiety disorder" (Brown et al., 2007). As a result, the focus here will be on the selective serotonin reuptake inhibitors (SSRIs), which have emerged as the medication of choice in practice. Research has accumulated on its effects and will be reported here.

TABLE 5.3 SUMMARIES OF SYSTEMATIC REVIEWS AND META-ANALYSES FOR PSYCHOPHARMACOLOGICAL TREATMENT OUTCOME STUDIES FOR NON-OBSESSIVE COMPULSIVE DISORDER (OCD) AND NON-POSTTRAUMATIC STRESS DISORDER (PTSD) ANXIETY DISORDERS

Author and Purpose	Inclusion Criteria	Main Findings
Bridge et al. (2007) To assess the efficacy and risk of reported suicidal ideation/suicide attempt of antidepressants for treatment of pediatric non-OCD anxiety disorders and for OCD.	**Studies**: randomized, placebo-controlled trials **Intervention**: selective serotonin reuptake inhibitors (SSRIs) and other second-generation agents **Participants**: children and adolescents (<19 years old) with major depressive disorder, OCD, or non-OCD anxiety disorders **Primary outcome**: suicidal ideation/suicide attempt	In six non-OCD anxiety disorders trials of 1136 participants, pooled rates of response were 69% in antidepressant-treated participants and 39% in those receiving placebo, and the pooled risk difference was 37%. In six OCD trials of 705 participants, pooled rates of response were 52% in SSRI-treated participants and 32% in those receiving placebo, and the pooled risk difference was 20%.

From AACAP (2007), Barrett et al. (2008), James et al. (2005), and Silverman et al. (2008).

In the Bridge, Iyengar, Salary, et al. (2007) meta-analysis of all available randomized clinical trials of antidepressant treatment of pediatric major depressive disorder (MDD), OCD, and non-OCD anxiety disorders, six studies were found for non-OCD anxiety disorders, which represented 1136 participants (see Table 5.3). In the antidepressant group, there was a 69% response rate compared to a 39% rate in those receiving placebo with a pooled risk difference of 37%. As with youth depression, there is an increased risk of suicidality with the treatment of antidepressants. Suicide ideations/attempts were higher in the antidepressant (1%) versus placebo groups (0.2%), with a pooled risk difference of 0.7%.

For OCD, two meta-analyses have been conducted for the use of SSRI medication in youth. In Geller et al. (2003), 12 published randomized controlled studies were found, comprising 1044 participants. A small to moderate effect size was determined (0.46). More recently, Bridge et al. (2007) conducted another meta-analysis. They included six randomized controlled studies involving 705 individuals. Rates of response in the SSRI-treated participants were 52%, and were 32% in those receiving placebo with a pooled risk difference of 20%. In general, Bridge et al. (2007) determined that the SSRIs were less effective for OCD than for other anxiety disorders, but were more effective than they were for depression.

COMBINED TREATMENT

Two multimodal studies examining the differential effectiveness of medication, cognitive–behavioral therapy (CBT), and their combination have been conducted. In the Child–Adolescent Anxiety Multimodal Study, 488 children between the ages of 7 and 17 years who had a primary diagnosis of separation anxiety disorder, generalized anxiety disorder, or social phobia were randomized to the following: CBT (14 sessions), sertraline, a combination of sertraline and CBT, or a placebo drug for 12 weeks (Walkup et al., 2008). The percentage of children rated as very much or much improved on a clinician-report scale was 80.7% for combination therapy, 59.7% for CBT, and 54.9% for sertraline; all therapies were superior to placebo (23.7%). Combination therapy was superior to both monotherapies, but the researchers concluded that parents and providers could choose from any one of the three treatments, depending on preferences and available resources.

For OCD specifically, the Pediatric Obsessive-Compulsive Disorder Treatment Study (POTS, 2004) randomly assigned participants (N = 112) at three academic sites to receive CBT alone, sertraline alone, combined CBT and sertraline, or pill placebo for 12 weeks. A statistically significant advantage was posed for CBT alone, sertraline alone, and combined treatment compared with placebo. Combined treatment also proved superior to CBT alone and to sertraline alone, which did not differ from each other. In examining this study, the APA Psychological 12 criteria review assigned combination treatment to "probably efficacious" status based on its greater effectiveness compared to sertraline (Barrett et al., 2008). However, the O'Kearney (2007) meta-analysis, in synthesizing the results of two studies for OCD (including POTS), found that combining CBT and medication did not appear to help beyond medication alone.

BIOPSYCHOSOCIAL RISK AND PROTECTIVE INFLUENCES

Looking at the context of the child with an anxiety disorder, there are factors intrinsic to the individual—biological and psychological influences—as well as the social environment that lead to the development of an anxiety disorder and that affect the outcome of the anxiety disorder. Although biological factors explain about 40% of the variation in the development of anxiety, this means that other factors, including social influences, account for the majority of the variation.

ONSET

Biological

Although genetic influences may account for the majority of variation in anxiety in young children, as they grow older, environmental influences assume a greater role

(Boomsma, van Beijsterveldt, & Hudziak, 2005). Temperamental factors identified with anxiety involve *anxiety sensitivity*, *temperamental sensitivity*, and *behavioral inhibition* (Donovan & Spence, 2000). Anxiety sensitivity is the tendency to respond fearfully to anxiety symptoms. Temperamental sensitivity is characterized by a range of emotional reactions toward negativity, including fear, sadness, self-dissatisfaction, hostility, and worry. This tendency predisposes people to both anxiety and depression, which often occur together. Behavioral inhibition involves timidity, shyness, emotional restraint, and withdrawal when introduced to unfamiliar situations (Kagan et al., 1988 as cited in Donovan & Spence, 2000). Behavioral inhibition has been associated with elevated physiological indices of arousal and has been shown to have a strong genetic component.

Another risk influence involves gender. Girls report more fears than boys, and generally have higher rates of anxiety disorders starting in adolescence and continuing through the lifespan. Whether the gender difference is due to biological factors, social factors (such as increased rates of sexual abuse), or a combination of the two is unknown (Hagopian & Ollendick, 1997; Ozer et al., 2003).

Psychological

A major psychological theory of anxiety involves *conditioning*, which is the process of developing patterns of behavior through responses to certain environmental stimuli or behavioral consequences (Kazdin, 2000). An initially neutral stimulus comes to produce a conditioned response after being paired repeatedly with a conditioned stimulus. For example, having a humiliating experience during a social event may make a person feel anxious in subsequent social situations. Although a client's initial symptoms may be incited by the original experience, ongoing symptoms may result from avoiding contact with a feared situation (in this example, avoiding social situations), which reinforces the maintenance of the anxiety through negative reinforcement.

Social

Social factors associated with the onset of child anxiety include the family, stressful life events, and societal conditions that have changed over time

The following family factors may play a role:

- Genetically based influences
- anxious attachment (Warren, Huston, Egeland, & Sroufe, 1997)
- parental overcontrol, overprotection, and criticism (Donovan & Spence, 2000)
- children of anxious parents may be more likely to observe anxious behavior in their parents and to have fearful behavior reinforced by their parents (Hagopian & Ollendick, 1997).

Despite the number of possible family factors involved, family factors explain only a modest percent (4%) of the variance in anxiety (McLeod, Weisz, & Wood, 2007). Parental overcontrol played a larger role than did parental rejection of the child.

Parental involvement may be indicated in the following circumstances (Velting et al., 2004), although there has been no research to determine whether these guidelines are appropriate:

- The youth's functioning is seriously compromised by anxiety or comorbidity.
- The child is young in age or developmental level.
- The parents or other family members engage in behavior that accommodates the anxiety.
- A parent has an anxiety disorder or another psychiatric disorder (if so, concurrent individual therapy for the parent is recommended).

Parent–child interventions may include improving the parent-child relationship, strengthening family problem solving, reducing parental anxiety, and helping parents to encourage the child to face new situations rather than withdraw, to refrain from excessive criticism and intrusiveness, to respond more directly to the child's needs, and to encourage the child to engage in activities despite anxiety. On the other hand, if a teenager presents for treatment but has generally good functioning and no comorbid disorder, less parental involvement is indicated. This helps the teen to address the developmental task of assuming self-responsibility.

Stressful life events also play a role in the development of anxiety (Bandelow et al., 2002). These often arise in the context of the family, such as frequent moves and changes of school, divorce and custody battles, and abuse.

Socioeconomic status (SES) and its link to anxiety, as well as depression, for youth aged 10–15 years, was studied in a systematic review (Lemstra, Neudof, D'Arcy, et al., 2008). Findings established a negative association; that is, the lower the SES the higher the rates of depression and anxiety.

Social influences were examined by Twenge (2000). She found that child anxiety had significantly increased between the early 1950s and the early 1990s, explaining about 20% of the variance. "The birth cohort change in anxiety is so large that by the 1980s normal child samples were scoring higher than child psychiatric patients from the 1950s" (p. 1017). When looking at the specific social influences that seemed to have contributed to the rise, Twenge (2000) found that it was not economic conditions, but low social connectedness and high environmental threat, such as from crime and the threat of terrorism or war.

TREATMENT AND RECOVERY

Biological

Developmental stage of the youth will be categorized here, although it may not be influenced only by biological factors (cognitive and hormonal). Social influences and expectations, such as about dating and the importance of having friends in adolescence, may also play a role in how anxiety is experienced at various stages. In general, fewer treatment outcome studies have been conducted on adolescents with anxiety disorders than with children (see Verdeli et al., 2006). In a review of studies, the American Academy of Child and Adolescent Psychiatry concluded that older youth have worse outcomes when they are treated with either CBT or SSRIs than do children (Connolly & Bernstein, 2007). These findings are not well understood and deserve further study.

Psychological

Certain presentations of the anxiety disorder may influence outcome. First, the particular type of anxiety disorder may need particular adaptations (see Table 5.4). Severity is another aspect, with the more severe the anxiety disorder, the worse the outcome (Connolly & Bernstein, 2007; Brown et al., 2007). Medication has been suggested for severe anxiety disorders, although this has not been researched.

Another aspect of the anxiety disorder itself pertinent to outcome is that complete remission of symptoms should be the goal of treatment. Any residual symptoms may present risk for relapse or the development of another anxiety disorder (Connolly & Bernstein, 2007). This information should be shared with clients to motivate them to continue treatment until no symptoms remain.

A final aspect of the anxiety disorder is the pattern of comorbidity. Comorbid disorders are common with childhood anxiety and are often associated with worse

TABLE 5.4 ADAPTATIONS OF COGNITIVE-BEHAVIORAL THERAPY FOR DIFFERENT ANXIETY DISORDERS

Disorder	Adaptation
Specific phobia	Focus on graded exposure and likely to include cognitive modification of unrealistic fears and participant modeling (demonstrations by therapist and parent of approaching feared objects or situations)
Social phobia	Inclusion of social skills training and increased social opportunities
Panic disorder	Interoceptive exposure (exposure to physical sensations associated with panic such as dizziness, shortness of breath, and sweating by using exercises that induce these sensations) and education about the physiological processes that lead to these physical sensations
Obsessive compulsive disorder	Features exposure to feared object and response prevention (the person is prevented from doing the compulsion)

outcome (Storch et al., 2008). There is no information from the available psycho-social evidence on how to handle particular comorbid disorders, such as depression or one of the disruptive behavior disorders, which may be particularly deleterious for outcome. According to a consensus statement by the American Academy of Child and Adolescent Psychiatry (2007), antidepressant medication can address both the anxiety and the depression, and atomoxetine (Strattera) may address both ADHD and anxiety.

Another factor categorized under psychological influences on recovery is the youth's motivation for treatment or the ability to engage in treatment. Exposure requires a certain amount of motivation to tolerate the discomfort that arises when faced with traumatic material. In cases in which there is low motivation, medication rather than CBT might be preferable (Connolly & Bernstein, 2007; Brown et al., 2007).

Social

At the environmental level, family factors, ethnicity, and certain aspects of treatment delivery may affect recovery. Parental anxiety is a risk factor for the child's outcome from an anxiety disorder. However, if a parent is anxiety free, the child may have more positive outcomes from treatment (Kendall, Hudson, Gosch, Flannery-Schroeder, & Suveg, 2008).

Family members are often involved in CBT treatment to varying degrees, depending on the developmental stage of the child and other clinical issues, as discussed above. The quantitative syntheses of the child anxiety treatment outcome literature found that family interventions showed the highest effects, although statistically significant differences did not show up between different modalities (In-Alban & Schneider, 2007; James et al., 2005).

Few treatment outcome studies have been conducted with ethnic minorities. Huey and Polo (2008) used the APA Task Force Criteria to evaluate the efficacy of treatments for children from ethnic minorities. Two studies indicate that group CBT is possibly efficacious for Latino and African-American youth with anxiety disorders (Ginsburg & Drake, 2002; Silverman et al., 1999). To address the needs of African-American youth in school settings, Ginsburg and Drake (2002) adapted group CBT by reducing the length of treatment, including only children in treatment, and altering examples to include experiences this population was likely to encounter, including neighborhood crime and violence, issues related to stepparents, and financial hardship. Compared to those assigned to an attention-support condition, African-American youth receiving CBT had lower levels of anxiety symptoms. However, the sample size was small ($n = 12$). Silverman et al. (1999) also found significant treatment effects for group CBT compared to waitlist control, and outcomes did not differ by ethnicity (white vs. Latino).

Another treatment was implemented with African-American youth with test anxiety (Wilson & Rotter, 1986). Participants were randomized to anxiety management training, study skills training, the combination of both, attention placebo, or no treatment. The three experimental conditions led to greater reductions in test anxiety than attention placebo or no treatment, with no differences between them, leading to the conclusion that this treatment is "possibly efficacious."

For OCD in particular, most studies have primarily included white participants; therefore, it is unclear whether available treatments would be effective for ethnic minority youth. One exception is Asbahr et al. (2005), which was conducted in Brazil. Participants in both the group CBT and the SSRI condition had significant improvement after 12 weeks of treatment. After the 9-month follow-up period, participants in the cognitive–behavioral condition had a significantly lower rate of symptom relapse than those in the SSRI group.

For the anxiety disorders in general and for OCD in particular, the only psychosocial treatment to receive adequate research support (CBT) does not have an adequately trained workforce to deliver treatment (Connolly & Bernstein, 2007; O'Kearney et al., 2006). Although treatment manuals are available, training and supervision are not.

RESEARCH RECOMMENDATIONS

Several limitations have emerged from this review, with corresponding recommendations. First, most CBT trials used wait-list (i.e., no treatment) control conditions, which provide no protection against the confound of therapist attention and positive expectations about treatment. Psychoeducation or bibliotherapy may provide plausible active controls in future studies, which would also not delay intervention for those in need (Brown et al., 2007). A related recommendation is to test other types of treatments, such as psychodynamic psychotherapy and the non-CBT family therapies that are often used in clinical practice, and discover whether CBT is superior to alternative psychosocial interventions.

The theory basis of CBT could also be improved. Chu and Harrison (2007) found that CBT was especially effective in targeting behavioral outcomes for anxiety but did not affect cognitive outcomes compared to other conditions. This finding was surprising in light of the cognitive emphasis of CBT, and calls into question its theory basis.

A continuing question involves the extent to which a particular modality of CBT is suited to certain characteristics of the child, as well as family and symptom presentations. Although the majority of the youth treatment protocols involve some degree of family participation, on the whole, the open-ended and flexible nature of this involvement has prevented rigorous examination of how this component contributes to outcome and in what child and family circumstances it should be used (Barrett et al., 2008).

Another recommendation is for research to determine the beneficial treatments for the different anxiety disorders and to test whether certain adaptations are necessary for a positive outcome. Separation anxiety disorder, in particular, warrants separate attention (which it has not received) because it often persists and is a risk for other disorders into adulthood.

A social justice concern is that rates of anxiety are higher in children living in low socioeconomic strata. Ameliorating these stressors is an important aspect, therefore, of intervention, and such work must be addressed in treatments that are developed for child anxiety disorders. Research could assess the differential impact of case management services for these youth compared to psychotherapy and their combination.

Relatedly, existing treatment outcome studies may not capture the response of clinic populations to treatment. Effectiveness research involving socially diverse clients, adolescents, and those with more severe disorders is needed to ensure that treatments designed for research conditions show the same level of impact and acceptability to clients in real-world settings.

CONCLUSIONS

The general consensus is that psychosocial treatment should be offered as a first-line treatment. Even the medically oriented American Academy of Child and Adolescent Psychiatry has argued this position, given the safety concerns about medication for youth (i.e., suicidality) and since the effects of medication do not persist beyond its administration (Connolly & Bernstein, 2007; Brown et al., 2007).

The psychosocial treatment that has been researched is CBT, which shows an impact on at least half of the children and adolescents with an anxiety disorder. In comparison, only one-third of youth in control groups will no longer meet the DSM diagnosis (James et al., 2005). There are also several "probably efficacious" treatments. Therefore, the results of CBT appear substantial, yet not overwhelming. A critical issue is whether CBT outperforms other treatments that are commonly applied in typical practice settings. Additionally, a major question is whether CBT will perform as well in real-life clinic settings where comorbidity, stressful life events, and suicidality may complicate the picture.

CASE STUDY

Brandon, an 8-year-old, white male, came into foster care 18 months ago. His older brother, who is now 10 years old, disclosed at the time that he had been sexually victimized by his and Brandon's father. Brandon and his two other siblings denied experiencing or witnessing sexual or physical abuse.

At the time of the disclosure, his mother did not believe the abuse had occurred and refused to have her husband leave the home. As a result, Brandon and his siblings were removed from the home and placed in separate foster care homes about 25 miles apart. Brandon quickly grew attached to his foster mother, a single woman who had no other children in the home. He began weekly individual therapy (nondirective play therapy), had mentoring services, and started having weekly supervised visits with his biological family. During the visits, Brandon hid underneath the table and often became oppositional with his mother. When she asked him to do something, he would respond "no" or simply dismiss what she said; at times, he wouldn't talk at all.. After visits with his family, his foster mother reported "tearful" episodes. Other times, Brandon would act angrily—pinching the family dog and breaking his toys. However, he would recover within a couple of hours after being with his foster mother again.

After Brandon's father was incarcerated for the sexual abuse, Brandon's mother moved into a one-bedroom apartment and started working 50 hours a week at a local restaurant. When asked why she wasn't following through on the Child Protective Services treatment plan to gain back custody of her children, which entailed individual therapy for herself, then family therapy with the children, she said, "I have to work if I'm going to support my kids. I can't get a bigger place that'll fit all of us without making some money first."

About 6 months into the placement, Brandon became clingy with his foster mother. He constantly asked where she was going and what time she would return. He started having unrealistic fears. He was terrified of thunder and lightening and was also scared of the dark; he often hid under his covers or bed at night. Although his appetite was normal, he complained of stomachaches before bedtime and had difficulty concentrating on school assignments or chores at home. The foster mother reported that she was concerned about his excessive worrying and fears. At this time, she began relaxation techniques with him at bedtime.

After 1 year, Brandon's biological mother had made little progress with her goals (having a less demanding job, living in a larger apartment, and obtaining therapy). In court, she was granted a 6-month extension to achieve these goals. At the 6-month point, however, she voluntarily gave up her parental rights.

At this time, which was a year after the onset of his symptoms, Brandon still experienced fears and worries, especially those revolving around his foster mother. He told his daycare staff, his case manager, and his teacher that he is "scared she will be in a car wreck or something will happen to her" when he went to school. Brandon still had visits with his biological mother; however, they were less frequent due to her lack of consistency and the negative reactions he has afterward. During visits, she would tell him she wants him back and that she will fight for him.

Brandon talks little about his family to his foster mother, caseworker, or therapist. He reports being "happy in his foster home" and wants to know why it is taking so long for his adoption to occur. Despite his lack of focus at times due to his worry, he is still able to maintain a B average. He has some friends with whom he plays at

BOX 5.1 MULTIAXIAL DIAGNOSIS FOR BRANDON

Axis I 309.21 Separation Anxiety Disorder

[Rationale: A. Developmentally inappropriate and excessive anxiety concerning separation from his foster mother, as evidenced by the following (three symptoms are required):
(1) Brandon experiences recurrent excessive distress when separation from his foster mother occurs or is anticipated.
(2) Brandon worries about losing, or about possible harm befalling, his foster mother.
(3) Brandon complains of stomachaches before bedtime when he will be sleeping in his own bed and separated from his foster mother.
B. The duration of the disturbance is a year, clearly in excess of the 4-week minimum requirement.
C. The onset is before age 18 years. Brandon was 7 years old when the symptoms began.
D. The disturbance causes clinically significant distress.]

V61.20 Parent–Child Relational Problem

[Rationale: Brandon's father has been incarcerated for sexually abusing Brandon's brother and Brandon avoids talking about him. He has difficulty seeing his mother since he entered foster care, becoming uncooperative during visits and tearful and angry. His mother gives him mixed messages: she voluntarily gave up her parental rights yet she says she will "fight for him."]

Axis II V71.09 No Diagnosis

Axis III None

Axis IV Problems with primary support (Brandon has been removed from his biological family and placed in foster care. His mother's parental rights have been terminated, and he is pending adoption).

[Rationale: He seems to experience a great deal of distress from his anxiety. However, he performs well in school and is able to relate to same-age peers.]

school and at daycare; however, he does not refer to them when he is not with them. Brandon recently underwent a physical examination and was found to be a healthy 8-year-old boy.

A multiaxial diagnosis for "Brandon" is provided in Box 5.1.

When examining the risk and protective factors operating in Brandon's case, the negative and stressful life events he has suffered, which include his brother's disclosure of sexual abuse by Brandon's father, his father's incarceration, and Brandon's being removed from his home and into foster care, seem the most salient. Little information is provided in general about his genetic history, his temperament, or other psychological variables that were in place before the onset of the anxiety disorder.

The risk and protective factors that might contribute to recovery from his anxiety disorder include the fact that Brandon has been placed with an apparently caring and supportive foster mother to whom he seems to feel attachment. At the same time, she is a single parent and has to work full-time, which limits the amount of time she can spend with him. In addition, the fact that he is not in a permanent home is a great source of anxiety for him.

Brandon maintains involvement with his biological family, a potential protective influence, although the nature of this involvement may be questionable. For instance, Brandon's mother still talks about him returning to live with her, even though her parental rights have been terminated.

On the protective side, Brandon receives services through his Child Protective Services case manager, including therapy and mentoring. He is an intelligent child who receives good grades in school. He also has playmates in the school and day-care setting.

Taking into account the risk and protective influences in his life, Brandon's case illustrates the environmental influence on problems, which is at odds with the medical model and its notion of internal dysfunction as the cause of a disorder. Therefore, the first necessary step involves an environmental intervention rather than a psychologically focused one, and that is to make a permanency plan for Brandon. The fact that he is in foster care rather than having been adopted into the home is obviously a great source of (realistic) distress for him.

Separation anxiety disorder has a potentially long-term course, so effective intervention is of the essence. A more psychologically focused goal is to treat the separation disorder through an empirically supported cognitive–behavioral protocol, such as the Coping Cat program (Kendall et al., 1990), which has been categorized as "probably efficacious." This program focuses on monitoring anxiety symptoms, identifying feelings, and developing coping skills (self-talk, problem solving, relaxation), which could help Brandon manage the difficult situation he faces. The program has adaptations for family members, and the foster mother should be included given Brandon's young age so she can help him practice the new skills at home. This suggests that, like Brandon, these children are plagued by more chronic environmental stressors

HOW THE EVIDENCE FITS?

For separation disorder, an evidence-based treatment involves a cognitive-behavioral package, such as the Coping Cat program (Kendall et al., 1990), which has been categorized as "probably efficacious." This program focuses on monitoring anxiety symptoms, identifying feelings, and developing coping skills (self-talk, problem solving, relaxation), which could help Brandon manage the difficult situation he faces.

APPLICATION

The Coping Cat program is designed not only for separation anxiety disorder, which Brandon demonstrates, but also generalized anxiety disorder and social phobia. Although Coping Cat can be implemented as an individual program, it also has adaptations for family members. Because of Brandon's young age and the fact that his fears mainly revolve around his foster mother, she can be part of treatment to help him practice new skills in the home.

A first step in the Coping Cat program is to help youth learn about anxiety and notice the way they experience it. In this way, they will know when their anxiety is triggered and use it a signal to enact strategies they learn in the program. The therapist will assist Brandon in discovering the following aspects to his anxiety: cognitive (his beliefs about what will happen to his foster mother when he is apart from her), somatic (stomach aches), emotional (fear, dread), and behaviors (sitting in foster mother's lap, asking for repeated reassurance).

The second phase of treatment is to design an individualized plan with the acronym FEAR, which stands for:

1. Feeling frightened—the recognition of his anxiety
2. Expecting bad things to happen—his beliefs about dire consequences
3. Attitudes and actions that help—having adaptable beliefs (e.g., my foster mom is okay, she's here to take care of me) and problem solving
4. Results and rewards—"I am doing a good job practicing what I have learned." "She will take me to McDonald's this weekend for my reward."

The next major part of treatment involves practicing the individualized FEAR program through in-session modeling by the therapist, behavioral rehearsal by Brandon, and homework assignments. Stickers are given as rewards for completing the exercises in the Coping Cat workbook. In session, Brandon will practice being exposed to various anxiety-provoking situations, such as imagining his foster mother being at work and absent from him and then working up to sessions in which she is actually at work. During these exposure incidents, he will rehearse the techniques he has acquired and his foster mother can help Brandon use his FEAR plan when he encounters anxiety.

HOW THE EVIDENCE DOES NOT FIT

There does not seem to be anything about Brandon's individual characteristics that preclude the use of the Coping Cat program. He is white, male, and does not present with comorbid disorders. However, there are many characteristics of his context that do not seem to be tailored for a psychologically focused program, such as Coping Cat. The fact that Brandon is not in a permanent home is a large source of realistic distress for him. Brandon maintains involvement with his biological family, a potential protective influence, although the nature of this involvement may be questionable. For instance, Brandon's mother still talks about him returning to live with her, even though her parental rights have been terminated.

Therefore, an individually focused anxiety disorder treatment program may not be as relevant as an environmental intervention—namely developing a permanency plan for Brandon.

HOW DOES THE EBT TAKE INTO ACCOUNT STRENGTHS?

Anxiety-focused treatment, such as Coping Cat, assumes that there are deficits in thinking patterns (distorted thinking) and behaviors (lack of problem solving, lack of social skills) that contribute to anxiety disorders. These factors emphasize people's deficits rather than their strengths. However, the underlying assumption is that once we learn about anxiety and certain techniques for managing it, anxiety can be remedied. The educational aspect to it non pathologizes the youth, and the instructional material is presented through child-friendly cartoons and simple explanations.

Although the Coping Cat program can be implemented on an individual basis with the child, it also allows for parental involvement as necessary. In this case, the availability of a seemingly supportive foster parent would be an asset to the treatment. Furthermore, the extension of the treatment to Brandon's foster mother will involve the environmental conditions that give rise to his anxiety.

6

POSTTRAUMATIC STRESS
DISORDER

This chapter discusses the evidence basis for treatment of posttraumatic stress disorder (PTSD), which is a type of anxiety disorder that follows exposure to an extreme traumatic stressor (APA, 2000). PTSD has been separated from the other anxiety disorders in this volume as it has been in other systematic reviews and meta-analyses (e.g., Bridge et al., 2007; Hetrick et al., 2007). The three major symptom categories of PTSD include reexperiencing (the traumatic events are reexperienced through recurrent and/or intrusive thoughts or images, nightmares, and flashbacks), avoidance and numbing (attempts to control or protect against reexperiencing and arousal), and increased arousal (hypervigilance, insomnia, inability to concentrate, and an elevated startle response).

According to a review of prevalence studies, lifetime rates of PTSD in youth were found to range between 1.3% and 6.0%. Therefore, it is a relatively rare event, considering that traumatic events occur to two-thirds of youth (Copeland, Keeler, Angold, & Costello, 2007). In general, prevalence estimates of child PTSD vary depending on the type and intensity of the inciting trauma, the length of time between exposure to the trauma and its professional assessment, the demographic characteristics of study subjects, the sampling techniques used, and the manner in which PTSD is assessed (Saigh, Yasik, Sack, & Koplewicz, 1999).

After the evidence basis is reviewed, it will be appraised in terms of the biopsychosocial risk and protective influences for the development and course of PTSD. From this review, recommendations for expanding the research basis of treatment will be advanced. The case that follow will be used to illustrate the application of evidence-based treatment for PTSD.

STATE OF THE EVIDENCE

PSYCHOSOCIAL TREATMENT

Most of the research conducted for the treatment of youth PTSD involves cognitive–behavioral therapy (CBT) with key intervention strategies that involve exposure and cognitive restructuring (Fao et al., 2000). Exposure is widely accepted as the primary appropriate intervention for reducing a client's symptoms of reexperiencing the event. Contingency management strategies should also be implemented, however, to manage a client's avoidance and other behavioral problems.

Exposure typically begins with the development of an anxiety hierarchy in which the client lists aspects of the feared situation that initiate different degrees of anxiety. In some forms of exposure (such as flooding), intervention sessions begin with the practitioner initiating a client's exposure to the highest-rated item on the hierarchy. Other forms of exposure begin with items rated by the client as provoking moderate anxiety. All exposure methods, however, share a common feature: the client confronts threatening stimuli until the anxiety is reduced. By continued exposure to a threatening stimulus, the client develops mastery of the situation and anxiety diminishes. This leads to a decrease in escape and avoidance behaviors that were previously maintained through negative reinforcement.

Cognitive interventions aim to modify a client's problematic cognitions, such as self-blame, frustrating attempts to mentally "undo" the traumatic event, lack of safety, inability to trust, powerlessness, and loss of control. The process for adjusting these beliefs occurs in steps whereby clients are taught with the practitioner's help to identify their dysfunctional thoughts, challenge those that are evaluated as inaccurate or unhelpful, and replace them with more logical or beneficial thoughts (Rothbaum et al., 2000).

Other psychotherapies used for PTSD involve play therapy, art therapy, and psychodynamic therapy. Play therapy involves approaches that use "play as the principal means for facilitating the expression, understanding, and control of experiences" (Wethington et al., 2008). A survey of 460 therapists indicated that nondirective play therapy was a popular treatment approach (Cohen, Mannarino, & Rogal, 2001). Art therapy allows for the representation of the traumatic experience through visual medium as a way to understand and process the trauma. Psychodynamic therapy allows the child "to release unconscious thoughts and emotions and to integrate the traumatic event into his or her understanding of life and self-concept" (Wethington et al., 2008). The therapist provides reflection, empathy, encouragement, support, and limited interpretation when clinically advantageous, allowing the child to decide how he or she will address the trauma rather than dictating its discussion (Cohen., 2005).

Psychological debriefing is used as a preventive rather than a treatment approach. A group meeting is arranged soon after the traumatic event so that those involved can discuss the event. Group facilitators normalize common stress reactions and provide education about coping strategies and where people can go to get further assistance, if necessary (Wethington et al., 2008).

Systematic Reviews/Meta-Analyses

In a meta-analysis of treatments targeting youth who experienced traumatic events, different psychosocial treatments, including both individual and group CBT, art therapy, play therapy, and psychodynamic therapy, were examined separately (Wethington et al., 2008). For individual CBT (N = 11 studies), statistically significant reductions were found for PTSD symptoms and anxiety but not for externalizing, depression, or internalizing symptoms (see Table 6.1). Furthermore, when youth were being treated for exposure to traumatic events other than sexual abuse, they tended to do better. Not surprisingly, effect sizes were higher when the experimental treatment was compared to a no-treatment control group rather than an alternative treatment. For group CBT, statistically significant reductions resulted for PTSD, anxiety, and depression at small to moderate effects.

Only two studies were found for play therapy, so results could not be synthesized, although both showed positive and statistically significant findings. However, nondirective play therapy has not stood up well to CBT in the few studies in which it was used as a control condition (e.g., Cohen & Mannarino, 1996, 1998).

Few studies in the Wethington et al. (2008) meta-analysis were also found for art therapy (N = 1), psychodynamic therapy (N = 1), and psychological debriefing (N = 1). Therefore results of these studies could not be synthesized. It must be noted that treatment outcome studies tended to exclude youth who were too disruptive or suicidal. Therefore, applicability to children with greater disturbance might be uncertain.

Other systematic reviews and meta-analyses have been organized around traumatic events, most often sexual abuse. A Cochrane Collaboration review sought to determine the efficacy of CBT in addressing the immediate and longer-term sequelae on children who have been sexually abused (Macdonald, Higgins, & Ramchandani, 2006). From the 10 studies that were located, the evidence suggests that CBT may have a positive impact, but most effect sizes were statistically nonsignificant. For PTSD, in particular, six studies assessed symptoms at posttest, resulting in a small to moderate effect (0.43), favoring CBT. At follow-up, there were only two studies, but the average effect increased at this point to 0.56., a moderate effect (see Table 6.1).

Corcoran and Pillai (2008) focused their meta-analysis on only the English language published literature with the purpose of determining whether parent

TABLE 6.1 SUMMARIES OF SYSTEMATIC REVIEWS AND META-ANALYSES:

Author and Purpose	Inclusion Criteria	Main Findings
Corcoran and Pillai (2008)	**Participants** Youth under 17 **Intervention** Parent-involved treatment of child sexual abuse **Studies** English-language, published studies of experimental or quasi experimental designs **Outcomes** Internalizing, externalizing, sexual behaviors, and PTSD	Seven studies Internalizing symptoms Posttest: 0.41 (6 studies) Follow-up: 0.36 (3 studies) Externalizing symptoms Posttest: 0.32 (6 studies) Follow-up: 0.12 (1 study) Child sexual behaviors Posttest: 0.31 (4 studies) Follow-up: 0.45 (1 study) Posttraumatic stress disorder (PTSD) Posttest: 0.37 (5 studies) Follow-up: 0.25 (3 studies)
Macdonald, Higgins, and Ramchandani (2006) To assess the efficacy of cognitive–behavioral therapy (CBT) approaches in addressing the immediate and longer-term sequelae on children who have been sexually abused	**Participants** Children and adolescents up to age 18 years who had experienced sexual abuse **Intervention** CBT	Ten studies Psychological functioning of child: Depression Posttest (5 studies): an average decrease of 1.8 points on the Child Depression Inventory Follow-up (3 studies): an average decrease of 1.9 points PTSD

Studies

Randomized or quasirandomized controlled trials comparing treatment to treatment as usual or no-treatment control

No language restrictions

Outcomes

Psychological functioning of child:

Depression

PTSD

Anxiety

Child behavior problems:

Sexualized behavior

Externalizing behavior (e.g., aggression, "acting out")

Participants

Youth with a median age of less than or equal to 21 years

Intervention

CBT, play therapy, art therapy, crisis debriefing, medication

Wethingron et al. (2008)

To determine the effectiveness of treatments to target children who have suffered traumatic events

Posttest (6 studies): an average decrease of 0.43 standard deviations on various child PTSD scales

Follow-up (2 studies): a decrease of 0.50 standard deviations

Anxiety

Posttest (5 studies): an average decrease of 0.21 standard deviations on various child anxiety scales follow-up (2 studies): a decrease of 0.28 standard deviations

Child behavior problems

Sexualized behavior

Posttest (5 studies): no effect

Follow-up (3 studies): no effect

Externalizing behavior (e.g., aggression)

Posttest (7 studies): did not provide evidence according to the Child Behavior Checklist (CBCL) externalizing behavior scale of an effect

Follow-up (4 studies): lack of evidence of an average effect

Individual CBT (N = 11)

Significant results for PTSD: SMD, −0.63

Anxiety: SMD, −0.31

Nonsignificant results for

Externalizing: SMD, −0.23

Depression: SMD, −0.19

Internalizing: 0.13

(continued)

TABLE 6.1 SUMMARIES OF SYSTEMATIC REVIEWS AND META-ANALYSES (CONT'D)

Author and Purpose	Inclusion Criteria	Main Findings
	Studies Studies published before 2007, including journal articles, government reports, and book chapters, and conducted in high-income economies **Outcomes** Assessed the following disorders and symptoms: PTSD; other anxiety; depressive, externalizing; internalizing; suicidal ideation and behavior; and substance abuse	Traumatic events other than sexual abuse resulted in better outcomes Effect sizes were higher when a control group was used rather than an alternative treatment Group CBT (N = 10 studies) PTSD: SMD, −0.56 Anxiety: 0.37 Depression: 0.40 Play therapy (N = 2) Although studies found benefit, it is difficult to synthesize the results Art therapy (N = 1) Insufficient evidence Psychodynamic (N = 1) Insufficient evidence Medication (N = 2) Insufficient evidence Psychological debriefing Based on a single qualifying study that provided no evidence of beneficial effects; the evidence was insufficient

[a] The study of Skowron and Reinemann (2005) was not included because PTSD was not an area of outcome. The study of Silverman et al. (2008) was not included because conventional meta-analytic techniques were not used.

involvement in the treatment of a sexually abused child would confer benefit. Several reasons have been offered as to why nonoffending caregivers should participate in treatment for their child (Corcoran, 1998). First, maternal support is a predictor of child adjustment after disclosure, and a parent's level of supportiveness could be bolstered by attending treatment. Mothers may also suffer a great deal of distress at learning of their children's sexual abuse, and their negative reactions may impede children's recovery. Intervention may help caregivers cope with stressors associated with their children's sexual victimization, such as separation from a partner, loss of social support, and being involved in legal proceedings. Learning about abuse dynamics can also reduce distress (Deblinger & Heflin, 1996). For instance, caregivers are often upset because they did not learn of the abuse sooner, but they can be told that perpetrators often involve their victims through secrecy. In addition, treatment can assist mothers in learning about how to identify and handle symptoms in their children and to respond appropriately to children's questions and concerns.

In Corcoran and Pillai (2007), the mean effect size for the outcome of PTSD based on five studies was 0.37, a small effect, which was similar to the effect size found for MacDonald et al. (2006). At follow-up, PTSD symptoms had diminished slightly but only two studies assessed outcome at that point. Effect sizes were similar for the other symptom domains studied as sexual abuse is a risk factor not only for PTSD, but also other problems such as depression, behavioral problems, and anxiety other than PTSD (see Table 6.1).

Note that there was substantial overlap between the Corcoran and Pillai (2007) meta-analysis and the MacDonald et al. (2006) systematic review. Although the emphasis of the reviews was different (CBT in one, parent-involved treatment in the other), most of the parent-involved treatments involved CBT. It is noteworthy that parent-involved treatment conferred additional benefits for reduction of PTSD over comparison conditions, which most often was represented by child treatment only and suggests that the nonoffending caregiver be a focus of treatment for child sexual victimization.

APA Division 12 Task Force Review

Silverman, Ortiz, and Viswesvaran (2008) conducted a review according to the Psychological Division 12 Task Force. The most frequently researched intervention has been Trauma-Focused CBT (the focus of the above reviews). Although referred to by different names, common elements include the following:

- brief treatment (around 12 sessions)
- psychoeducation
- coping skills training

- gradual exposure tasks via narratives, drawings, or other imaginal methods
- cognitive processing of the abuse experience
- parent management training.

Although some treatments involve only the child, others include parents in either individual meetings (Cohen et al., 2004; Cohen & Mannarino, 1996, 1998; Deblinger, Lippman, & Steer, 1996; Kolko, 1996) or conjoint sessions in addition to individual child and individual parent meetings (Cohen et al., 2004; Deblinger et al., 1996). When these studies were aggregated together, Silverman et al. (2008) concluded that Trauma-Focused CBT was the only treatment to be classified as "well-established."

Other treatments in the Silverman et al. (2008) review were categorized as "probably efficacious," including School-Based Group CBT for children who had been exposed to community violence and were experiencing trauma symptoms (Kataoka et al., 2003; Stein et al., 2003). A brief intervention (10 weekly sessions), the emphasis here is on psychoeducation, graded exposures (e.g., writing and/or drawing), cognitive and coping skills training (e.g., thought stopping, relaxation), and social skills training.

MEDICATION AND COMBINATION TREATMENT

Although physicians prescribe a variety of medications for children with the disorder, typically the selective serotonin reuptake inhibitors (SSRIs), little research has been conducted. In the Wethington et al. (2008) meta-analysis, only two studies were found that met inclusion criteria, and the differences in studies and results led to the conclusion that there was "insufficient evidence" for medication for PTSD.

Only one study has compared the addition of medication to CBT and it is hampered by small sample size ($N = 24$) (Cohen, Mannarino, Perel, & Staron, 2007). Females aged 10–17 years old and their primary caretakers were randomly assigned to one of two conditions: Trauma-Focused CBT and sertraline or Trauma-Focused CBT and placebo. Few advantages were found for adding medication to CBT. Although replication is necessary, this study suggestions that treatment should start with an initial trial of CBT before adding medication.

BIOPSYCHOSOCIAL INFLUENCES FOR THE DEVELOPMENT OF PTSD

ONSET

Biological Processes

Some dysregulation in biological systems appears to be associated with PTSD (Silva & Kessler, 2004). Specifically, increased activity in the catecholaminergic system has been found in children, even when there is subthreshold PTSD and hypothalamic-pituitary-adrenal axis dysfunction (Kowalik, 2004). Furthermore, brain volume in children is reduced in abused children with PTSD. It is not known to what extent these processes are risk factors for PTSD or result from the person's experiencing certain types of traumatic events. Additionally, the extent to which a genetic component may be responsible is unknown. Children with parents with PTSD often develop PTSD themselves, but whether this is due to environmental factors or genetic factors is not well understood. Finally, females are at greater risk than males for PTSD.

Psychology

INTELLIGENCE. A connection between low IQ and PTSD has been found. On the protective side for intelligence, Storr, Ialongo, Anthony, and Breslau (2007) followed children prospectively from first grade to young adulthood. Those in the highest quartile on reading scores were less likely to be exposed to trauma and therefore to develop PTSD. If causal, it may be that children of lower intelligence are unable to cognitively process through the trauma and/or do not have the coping methods to deal with the event and their symptoms (Silva & Kessler, 2004). Alternatively, IQ could be a confounded variable, occurring with other events, such as brain damage and maternal deprivation, which could result in both lower IQ and PTSD (Silva & Kessler, 2004).

PRIOR MENTAL HEALTH PROBLEMS. Prior mental health problems, particularly internalizing problems, appear to place children at risk for developing PTSD. In the Storr et al. (2007) prospective study, children who were more anxious and depressed in first grade, when later exposed to trauma, were more likely to suffer from PTSD. Preexisting anxiety was also a risk factor in another recent study of trauma response (Copeland et al., 2007).

COPING STRATEGIES. Dissociation has been named as a problematic coping strategy in the aftermath of trauma, increasing the risk for the development of PTSD in youth (Silva & Kessler, 2004) as it has been for adults (Ozer et al., 2003).

CONDITIONING. Conditioning is a process of developing patterns of behavior through responses to environmental stimuli or specific behavioral consequences (Kazdin, 2001). An initially neutral stimulus comes to produce a conditioned response after being paired repeatedly with a conditioned stimulus. In Pavlov's famous research, food (the conditioned stimulus) naturally produced salivation (a nonvoluntary response) in dogs. A bell (the unconditioned stimulus) initially failed to evoke salivation. However, after the bell was paired with the food, over time, the dogs started to salivate when presented with the bell alone. The bell at this point attained the status of a conditioned stimulus as it was capable of producing a response by itself.

Classical conditioning is theorized to play a role in the way PTSD develops. For example, an event of sexual abuse may evoke overwhelming anxiety when the survivor becomes sexually intimate with a first boyfriend. Although a client's initial symptoms may be directly caused by the trauma, many of the ongoing symptoms result from avoiding the conditioned response and the resultant distress. In this way, repeated negative reinforcement in which the avoidance leads to a decrease in symptoms makes the response resistant to extinction (Foa et al., 2000).

Social Environmental factors include the traumatic events on which the diagnosis of PTSD is based. These include the following types of events (Rojas & Pappagogallo, 2004; Silva & Kessler, 2004):

1. physical or sexual abuse
2. witnessing domestic violence of one's parents or other injury to a parent
3. being a victim of or a witness to violent crime
4. migration and exile experiences
5. war-related events
6. hostage scenarios
7. sustaining physical injury, such as burns
8. undergoing life-saving medical procedures
9. natural disasters, such as earthquakes and hurricanes
10. man-made disasters, such as airplane crashes or dam collapses

In PTSD treatment outcome studies, the most common problem, which involved over 50% of the research (11 of 21) reviewed by Silverman et al. (2008), involved sexual abuse. Physical abuse was a target of three of the studies (14%), and three involved community violence. The other studies were represented by only one type of trauma exposure each: major hurricane, marital violence, motor vehicle accidents, and any single event trauma.

As in meta-analyses of risk factors for PTSD in adults (Brewin, Andrews, & Valentine, 2000; Ozer, Best, Lipsey, & Weiss, 2003), trauma severity is associated with PTSD in children (Rojas & Pappagallo, 2004). Having experienced multiple traumatic events is also related to the development of PTSD (Copeland et al., 2007; Silva & Kessler, 2004).

Living in an adverse family environment predisposes youth with traumatic events to be diagnosed with PTSD. Furthermore, children with parents with PTSD often develop PTSD themselves, and this may be due to genetic predisposition; exposure to violence that is directed toward a parent, such as community or domestic violence; and/or that PTSD may hamper parenting abilities (Linares & Cloitre, 2004). For children of all ages, threat to a caregiver is a risk factor for the development of PTSD (Scheeringa et al., 2006).

Finally, the process of immigration may bring with it traumatization either because of strife in the country of origin that led to the person leaving or during the process of immigration itself (U.S. DHHS, 2001). A review according to APA Division 12 Task Force Criteria was conducted on the efficacy of tested interventions with ethnic minority youth (Huey & Polo, 2008). Trauma-focused CBT (described above) earned the categorization of "probably efficacious" for ethnic minority youth with PTSD because it was found to be equally effective for ethnic minority (mostly African-American) youth as for white participants (Cohen et al., 2004 as cited in Huey & Polo, 2008).

TREATMENT AND RECOVERY

Few factors have been identified as protective for recovery from PTSD. Specific to sexual abuse, maternal support is associated with better outcomes (see Corcoran, 1998, for a review). Comorbidity patterns, particularly anger, may play a role in future adjustment. This chapter's case study shows how difficult Terri's family and school personnel found her oppositional and aggressive behaviors, and the consequences these had on her school performance. Indeed, part of the "arousal" criterion in the DSM diagnosis involves "irritability" and "anger outbursts" as symptoms. Saigh, Yasik, Oberfield, Halamandaris, and Bremner (2007) conducted a review and indicated the high comorbidity between PTSD and disruptive behavior disorders, namely ADHD and conduct disorder, and substance use disorders. But even when controlling for comorbid disorders, Saigh et al. (2007) found inflated rates of anger among those with PTSD compared to those who did not have PTSD and who had been traumatized. There is no guidance on how to integrate, sequence, or otherwise address anger problems within the context of anxiety-based exposure treatments. Furthermore, in the systematic review on CBT for sexual abuse, MacDonald et al. (2006) found a negligible effect on externalizing problems from treatment.

RESEARCH RECOMMENDATIONS

Many research recommendations emerge from this review. Some of these involve whether a categorical approach, such as the DSM, for the problem of PTSD is appropriate. Indeed, PTSD has been mathematically assessed as being better described by a dimensional rather than a categorical phenomenon (Broman-Fulks, Ruggiero, Green, et al., 2006). These findings suggest that standardized measures of PTSD may make a more appropriate method of assessment than the DSM system (recall the case of Kay in Chapter 4 who suffered from subthreshold symptoms).

In a related vein, the DSM diagnostic criteria has been criticized for lacking validity for children (Scheeringa et al., 1995). Suggested modifications include making the criteria more inclusive; specifically, Scheeringa, Wright, Hunt, and Zeanah (2006) have proposed reducing the required number of symptoms in the numbing/avoidance and the hyperarousal criteria to one each. As a result of lack of validity, cases falling short of full criteria (subthreshold cases) should be treated.

In the treatment outcome studies on youth PTSD, a great deal of variability exists in the way PTSD is defined. The diagnosis of PTSD is sometimes required, but other times only some symptoms are necessary; in others, having experienced trauma and having psychological adjustment problems are the only criteria (Kowalik, 2004). At a minimum, it seems that participants should be above clinical cut-off scores on standardized measures of PTSD and/or represent at least partial criteria.

Another recommendation is the best time to intervene when trauma has occurred. Because trauma often results in immediate distress that tends to dissipate over time, future research could discover the predictors of transient and more enduring symptoms (Wethington et al., 2008). In this way, better screening of children who have undergone trauma could occur, and resources could be allocated more efficiently. For any treatment, the optimal timing of intervention following the exposure and the onset of the diagnosis should be known so that treatment can be delivered in a targeted way.

Although CBT has been the main focus of research attention, approaches other than CBT are commonly used in practice, and these have received little research focus. Therefore, well-controlled studies of play therapy, art therapy, psychodynamic therapy, and medication are needed. Interventions with ethnic minority populations also need further study. As noted, there are no well-established treatments for youth with ethnic minority backgrounds.

In the treatment outcome literature, sexual abuse as a trauma has received the most attention. In addition to more methodologically rigorous study in this area, research on other traumas that occur to children and that may lead to PTSD is necessary. A final area for future research is how to optimally treat PTSD and behavioral problems when they exist together as illustrated in the case study.

CONCLUSIONS

The state of the research for PTSD in children and adolescents has recently improved but needs further expansion and refinement. Child welfare, in particular, is a system of care that needs to be conversant with evidence-based treatments for PTSD as traumatic events, such as abandonment, physical abuse, and sexual abuse is often the basis for Child Protective Systems involvement. Sexual abuse, in particular, has received the most attention of all the different traumas that may lead to PTSD. Another system of care, the schools, needs to be knowledgeable of the current evidence, especially related to the finding that although subject to little research, crisis debriefings may offer little benefit to youth, and may even demonstrate negative effects.

CASE STUDY

Terri, a 15-year-old, 4-month pregnant white female, has lived in a group home for unwed teenage mothers and their children for the past month. The court placed Terri in the custody of Department of Social Services (DSS) due to truancy (she missed 50 days of school in the past school year), physically violent and verbally abusive behaviors with teachers and classmates, staying out overnight, and being a threat to her own safety and the safety of others. Terri's older cousin is working with DSS to have Terri and her expectant baby placed with her and her husband and their two children.

A year and a half ago Terri described how her mother, who had seldom seen her since giving her up for adoption when she was 3 months old, abducted Terri as she was walking her dog. Terri's mother broke the dog's neck and then tied Terri up in the back of her van and drove to her house in another state. While initially terrified, Terri said that she couldn't remember anything about this drive. In her mother's house Terri was held against her will for almost a month. During this time her mother forced her to have sex with men for money. Terri said she could not remember any of the specifics of these incidents.

Eventually Terri's brother discovered where her mother was living and located Terri in a back room where her mother had kept her tied. The police became involved at this point, but when they went to arrest Terri's mother, she had fled.

Terri made multiple excuses for her truancy, such as having to attend doctor's appointments. She admitted to "smacking" her teacher because this teacher would not "get out of my face" and blamed this teacher for "picking on" her. On the day she hit her teacher, Terri ran from the school building, cursing her teacher and saying she was going to kill herself just to make this teacher happy. She said she did not mean this and had acted only out of anger. Terri resisted going back into the school and police had to physically return her to her classroom. She was currently on court probation for truancy and failure to report to court. In all, there were numerous incidents of anger outbursts at classmates and teachers.

Two months after her return to her grandfather's house, Terri's grades went down. Early childhood testing revealed the presence of mild mental retardation—her IQ is 70—and she has been placed in a special education class since the second grade. At this point, she will have to repeat the ninth grade because of failing grades.

During the past 9 months, Terri experienced difficulty falling asleep. She was frightened unless her bed was positioned away from windows, and she refused to stay in a first-floor bedroom. She had "frightening" dreams, although she did not recount their content. She said when the group home goes on "field trips" she could not sit in the last seat of the van because she felt as if she was back in the seat of her mother's van and became terrified. She said that only recently has she been able to tell anyone about what happened to her while she was with her mother.

She described not being able to look at a dog because of what happened to her dog, and she avoided walking on the streets around her grandfather's house, the area from which she was abducted. About 2 months after the abduction, Terri started hanging around older men and became sexually active. She expressed a desire to become pregnant and when she did, she said that she did not know who the father was. Terri planned to have DNA testing to determine paternity so that she could receive child support payments.

Terri said she had three aunts, an uncle, and several cousins to whom she felt close. She said she knows one of these aunts or cousins would let her live with them if the state would allow them to become foster parents. She currently does not know the whereabouts of her brother. She said she does not like other females though and preferred the company of males.

Terri said she "hated" the group home and "couldn't stand" the other girls at the home. However, she understood that if she obeyed the rules of the group home and demonstrated control of her physically and verbally abusive behaviors, she would be allowed to return to her grandfather's home or live with one of her relatives. Terri said she would like to become a mason or a nurse's aide in a nursing home. She received prenatal care and took her prenatal vitamins. She denied ever using alcohol or drugs.

When Terri was 3 years old, her unmarried parents gave her and her siblings up. Terri's paternal grandfather and grandmother adopted Terri and her older brother to whom she is close. Both her mother and father have long drug histories. Terri's father was in federal prison for drug-related convictions for most of her 15 years, and her mother had been imprisoned for drug-related charges for the past 5 to 6 years. Terri's grandmother died from natural causes when she was 5 years old. Her grandfather, aged 69 years, was her primary caregiver since that time. Terri has a strong emotional attachment to her grandfather who remains in close contact with her, visiting her whenever possible. Her other relatives also visit Terri regularly.

HOW THE EVIDENCE FITS AND APPLICATION

Because of the available evidence when considering treatment in Terri's case, CBT, featuring exposure, would be the intervention of choice. Exposure typically begins with the development of an anxiety hierarchy in which the client lists aspects of the feared situation that initiate different degrees of anxiety. Terri, for example, might list parts of the kidnapping that would be less threatening to talk about, moving to the experiences that were more distressing. She could also rank order the triggers for the abuse, such as small dogs and the back seat of vans, and the therapist would help expose her to these feared stimuli in a gradated fashion. Coping skills, such as relaxation and breathing retraining, would be taught so that she could manage the anxiety that surfaced as she discussed and faced these topics. By continued exposure to these threatening stimuli, Terri will develop mastery of the situation and her anxiety will diminish.

The problematic cognitions that Terri may have formulated from the traumatic experience are unclear from the case study, but lack of safety, inability to trust, powerlessness, and loss of control may certainly be present. Such beliefs would be identified, challenged for their inaccuracy or unhelpfulness, and replaced with more logical or beneficial thoughts as part of CBT (Rothbaum et al., 2000).

HOW THE EVIDENCE DOES NOT FIT

Characteristics of Youth

Terri's presentation of PTSD involves a great degree of oppositional and aggressive behaviors. Part of the "arousal" criterion in the DSM diagnosis involves "irritability" and "anger outbursts" as symptoms. Despite the prominence of anger symptoms, there is no guidance on how to integrate, sequence, or otherwise address anger problems within the context of anxiety-based exposure treatments. Furthermore, in the systematic review on CBT for sexual abuse, MacDonald et al. (2006) found a negligible effect on externalizing problems from treatment. Therefore, it appears that PTSD treatment may not impact externalizing problems well.

Another characteristic of Terri that may inhibit the intervention is her impending pregnancy and, with it, her current placement out of the home. Indeed, the pregnancy may have arisen as a complication of her PTSD. Part of the reexperiencing of the trauma seems to have been Terri's sexual involvement with older men. The impending pregnancy and her stay out of her grandfather's home might currently be absorbing her attention, and CBT treatment and exposure may pale in terms of Terri's priorities.

Characteristics of the Context

A problem with Terri's current placement is the probable lack of trained clinical providers who are knowledgeable and skilled with the use of CBT featuring exposure. Also, her school setting may not have been expected to be able to treat the PTSD, but the school counselor or social worker could possibly have made a referral for appropriate treatment. Then again, there tends to be a dearth of providers trained in the model, so practitioners may not have been available.

DOES THE EVIDENCE-BASED TREATMENT TAKE ADVANTAGE OF STRENGTHS

Trauma-focused CBT for youth often involves parents in the treatment, so that they know how to manage the youth's problems and behaviors, as well as helping them cope with their own reactions. One of Terri's protective factors, despite the fact that her parents are incapable of fulfilling their role, is the presence of supportive relatives, such as her grandfather and cousins. If they would be willing to participate in treatment with her, they could help her process her experiences and practice techniques that would assist in improved coping. They would also be trained to manage any potentially difficult behavior problems she shows.

7

DEPRESSIVE DISORDERS

This chapter covers depressive disorders in youth. A *major depression* is a period of 2 weeks or longer during which a person experiences a depressed mood or loss of interest in nearly all life activities. *Dysthymic disorder* represents a general personality style featuring symptoms that are similar to, but less intense than, those of major depression. The prevalence of depressive disorders in children is 2.8% and in adolescents is 5.7% (Costello, Erkanli, & Angold, 2006).

Discussion of the treatment outcome literature is organized around the available systematic reviews/meta-analyses and the APA Psychological 12 Task Force Criteria reviews that have been conducted and appraised through the biopsychosocial risk and resilience framework. A case, threaded throughout the chapter, will illustrate some of the challenges in applying evidence-based practice.

STATE OF THE EVIDENCE

PSYCHOSOCIAL

Most of the research in the area of child and adolescent depression has focused on *cognitive–behavioral therapies* (CBT), which comprise *behavioral and cognitive* models. Behavioral models focus on the development of coping skills, especially in the domain of social skills and choosing pleasant daily activities, so that the youth receive more reinforcement from their environments. *Cognitive* models include assessing and changing the distorted thinking that people with depression exhibit, in which they cast everyday experiences in a negative light.

For younger children, a representative cognitive-behavioral model is Self-Control Therapy, a school-based intervention with an emphasis on self-management (Stark, Reynolds, & Kaslow, 1987; Stark, Rouse, & Livingston, 1991). Self-management includes self-monitoring, self-evaluating, self-reinforcement, and making appropriate attributions for events. A representative cognitive–behavioral model for teens involves The Coping with Depression for Adolescents (Clark, Hawkins, Murphy, Sheeber, Lewinsohn, & Seeley, 1995; Lewinsohn, Clarke, Hops, & Andrews, 1990). Although modified over time, versions include the following components delivered over 15–16 sessions: (1) cognitive restructuring, (2) social skills training (how to make and maintain friendships), (3) communication and social problem solving (how to share feelings and resolve conflict without alienating others), (4) progressive relaxation training (to ease stress and tension), and (5) structuring mood-boosting activities into daily life. Some versions involve concurrent parent groups that involve sharing information about the topics and skills being taught in the adolescent group.

For slightly younger youth, another representative CBT intervention is the Penn Prevention Program (Gillham & Reivich, 1999; Gillham, Reivich, et al., 2006; Gillham et al., 1995; Jaycox et al., 1994; Roberts et al., 2003), also called the Penn Resiliency Program, and its Chinese adaptation, the Penn Optimism Program (Yu & Seligman, 2002). The Penn Prevention Program is a school-based group intervention but for slightly older children (10–15 year olds). The two main components of the intervention are cognitive (cognitive restructuring and attribution retraining) and social problem solving (problem solving as well as teaching coping strategies for family conflict and other stressors)

Another theoretical treatment model for adolescent depression, although less well studied than CBT, is *interpersonal therapy* (IPT). IPT is a brief (12 session), psychodynamic intervention focusing on how current interpersonal relationships have contributed to depression and helping clients repair these conflicts. Originally designed for adults with depression, this intervention has been adapted for use with adolescents (Mufson, Dorta, Moreau, & Weissman, 2005). The general goals of IPT are to decrease depressive symptoms and to improve interpersonal functioning in the areas of role transitions, grief processes, interpersonal disputes, and interpersonal deficits. For elaboration on the treatment components, see Table 7.1.

Systematic Reviews/Meta-Analyses

Several meta-analyses have been conducted on the youth depression treatment outcome studies. The focus here will be on those published by Weisz et al. (2006), Watanabe, Hunot, Omori, Churchill, and Furukawa (2007), and Brunwasser, Gilham, and Kim (2009) because earlier meta-analyses (Lewinsohn & Clarke, 1999; Michael & Crowley, 2002; Reinecke, Ryan, & DuBois, 1998) possessed certain limitations (Weisz et al., 2006). First, they had included only published studies and

TABLE 7.1 INTERPERSONAL THERAPY DOMAINS

Interpersonal Problem	Goal
Role transitions: Adolescents experience many role transitions that may pose difficulty: "(a) passage into puberty; (b) shift from group to dyadic relationships; (c) initiation of sexual relationships or desires; (d) separation from parents and family; and (e) work, college, or career planning" (Mufson et al., 2005, p. 174).	Clarification about the meaning of the role transition and the nature of the loss Learn new skills to experience success in new roles
Grief processes	Teen mourns the loss and then reestablishes relationships and interests that can compensate for it
Interpersonal disputes, most often parent–child conflict	To change communication and expectations to resolve the dispute (or deficits)
Interpersonal deficits: a person lacks the requisite social skills to establish and maintain appropriate relationships within and outside the family	To improve social skills, increase self-confidence; strengthen current relationships and build new relationships

their search strategies were noncomprehensive. Second, they did not limit their analysis to randomized trials. Third, their meta-analysis relied on fixed effect rather than random effect estimates of effect sizes, and they failed to use other methodologies that are now more conventional (Weisz et al., 2006). Finally, other studies had been conducted since the earlier meta-analyses were carried out.

The Weisz et al. (2006) meta-analysis targeted psychotherapy of child and adolescent depression and included dissertations, along with the published research (see Table 7.2). Weisz et al. (2006) located 35 studies, and found an overall effect size of 0.34 with regard to improvement of depression. The authors note that this effect is less than that obtained for the treatment of other child problems. At follow-up, the effects diminished still further. However, benefits of treatment held up across variations in intervention characteristics. Namely, both group and individual modalities, treatments that focused on cognitive therapy (cognitive restructuring and so forth) versus noncognitive treatment, and treatments of varying lengths of treatments performed as well as each other. A related meta-analysis on CBT for adolescent depression analyzed the effect of programs on the specific outcome of self-esteem and found that they did not influence this outcome (Taylor & Montgomery, 2007) (see Table 7.2).

A meta-analytic review was also conducted on a particular CBT program described above, the Penn Resiliency program (Brunwasser et al., 2009).

TABLE 7.2 SUMMARIES OF META-ANALYSES AND SYSTEMATIC REVIEW RESULTS OF PSYCHOSOCIAL TREATMENT ON YOUTH DEPRESSION

Author and Purpose	Inclusion Criteria	Main Findings
Brunwasser et al. (2009) To evaluate the effectiveness of the Penn Resiliency Program for depression in youth	**Participants** Children and adolescents with depression **Intervention** Penn Resiliency Program **Studies** Published and unpublished studies from 1990 (when the program was developed) to 2009, including quasiexperimental and experimental designs in which Penn Resiliency program was compared to a control group **Outcome** Not delineated but assumed depression symptoms and diagnosis of depression	$N=17$ Comparing Penn Resilience Program to no treatment control on depression symptoms: Posttest: $d = 0.11$ (statistically significant) Follow-up (6-8 months): $d = 0.21$ (statistically significant) Follow-up (12 months): $d = 0.20$ (statistically significant) Comparing Penn Resilience Program to no treatment control on diagnosis of depression at posttest: Program participants 11% less likely to receive diagnosis at posttest (not statistically significant) Comparing Penn Resilience Program to active control: Posttest: $d = -0.02$ (not statistically significant) Follow-up (6-8 months): $d = 0.00$ (not statistically significant)
Watanabe, Hunot, Omori, Churchill, and Furukawa (2007) (used Cochrane methodology) To determine the benefit of psychotherapy over control conditions, any adverse effects, and cost-effectiveness	**Participants** Youth 6–18 years old diagnosed with major depressive disorder, dysthymia, or minor depression, or rated as depressed on the depression inventory **Intervention** Psychotherapy that focused on depression (excluding art therapy, family therapy, and psychodrama) **Studies** Randomized trials of manualized treatment versus no treatment, waiting-list control, attention-placebo or treatment-as-usual	$N = 27$ Psychotherapy was significantly superior to wait-list or attention-placebo (RR = 1.39), but not to treatment as usual

Study	Details	N	Findings
Weisz et al. (2006) To determine the effects of psychotherapy on children and adolescents with depression	**Outcome** "Response" defined as a score below the depression or remittance from a diagnosis **Participants** Youth younger than 19 years old and diagnosed with major depressive disorder, dysthymia, or minor depression or rated as depressed on the depression inventory **Intervention** Psychotherapy for depression **Studies** Published studies and dissertations that targeted depression in youth; randomized studies with treatment and control (untreated, wait-list, active placebo) or minimal treatment **Outcome** Not delineated	N = 35	At posttest, an effect size of 0.34, which at follow-up was reduced still further to a negligible effect
Taylor and Montgomery (2007) To evaluate the impact of cognitive–behavioral therapy (CBT) on self-esteem on adolescents with depression	**Participants** A mean age from 13 to 18 years **Intervention** CBT **Studies** Published randomized controlled and quasirandomized trials **Outcomes** Standardized measures of self-esteem and depression	N = 2	Self-esteem did not reach statistically significant improvement at either posttest or follow-up for the CBT conditions over control

Quasiexperimental and experimental designs were considered, and altogether 17 studies (representing 2,498 youth) were found to meet inclusion criteria. The overall effect size was statistically significant at posttest when the Penn Resilience program was compared to no-treatment control but at a negligible level. The effect size increased at 12 month follow-up to a small level. When the Penn Resilience program was compared to active control groups, the effect size was not at a statistically significant level at either posttest or follow-up. On the outcome of diagnosis, Penn Resiliency participants were 10 percent less likely to receive a diagnosis of depression than no treatment control groups after intervention.

Another systematic review was published on child and adolescent psychotherapy treatment of depression (Watanabe, Hunot, Omori, Churchill, & Furukawa, 2007) (see Table 7.2). Because Watanabe et al. (2007) followed Cochrane Collaboration methodology (but did not register their review with the Cochrane Collaboration), they presumably conducted a more comprehensive search of the worldwide and unpublished literature. These researchers also required the studies to center on manualized treatment. A particular theoretical framework was not specified, although family therapy was excluded because the authors believed it did not have a specific focus on decreasing depressive symptoms. Twenty-seven studies were included, and psychotherapy was found to be significantly superior to wait-list or attention-placebo, but not to treatment as usual.

In sum, these three reviews indicate that treatment appears to result in a small effect on depression symptom. Although this translates into a benefit for depressed youth, the results do not indicate overwhelming support for psychotherapy over active controls.

APA Task Force 12 Criteria

Two APA Division 12 Criteria reviews have recently been conducted (David-Ferdon & Kaslow, 2008; Verdeli et al., 2006). In the Verdeli et al. (2006) review, 16 studies on adolescent treatment and six studies on child treatment were identified. A review according to the Task Force Criteria was also carried out on studies published after 1998 (David-Ferdon & Kaslow, 2008), which posed an update of the previous APA review (Kaslow & Thompson, 1998). Results will be provided separately for children and adolescents.

CHILDREN. For children (grades three to eight), Stark and colleagues' Self-Control Therapy (Stark, Reynolds, & Kaslow, 1987) merited the standard of a "probably efficacious treatment" (David-Ferdon & Kaslow, 2008; Verdeli et al., 2006). In the two studies that have reported results (Stark, Reynolds, & Kaslow, 1987; Stark, Rouse, & Livingston, 1991), Self-Control Therapy performed better than treatment as usual for reducing depression. One limitation is that the self-control program in the two studies did not cover the same material; nor were they the same length. Additionally, only one research team has evaluated the intervention (David-Ferdon & Kaslow, 2008).

The David-Ferdon and Kaslow (2008) review additionally found that the Penn Prevention Program (e.g., Gillham & Reivich, 1999) met criteria for "probably efficacious." Like Self Control Therapy, the Penn Prevention Program is a school-based group intervention but for slightly older children (10–15 year olds). It was categorized as "probably efficacious" because client characteristics were described, treatment was manualized, and more than two group design studies with different research teams showed that the intervention performed better than comparison groups. It fell short of being categorized as "well-established" because although most of the studies found it performed better than no-treatment control groups, only one study showed that the treatment did better than alternative treatment, rather than the required two (David-Ferdon & Kaslow, 2008).

ADOLESCENTS. For adolescents, if all the different CBT manuals offered for adolescent depression are considered as an aggregate, then they meet the criteria for "well-established" (Verdeli et al., 2006). However, when the manualized treatments are covered separately, only the work of the research team of Lewinsohn and colleagues, Coping with Depression for Adolescents (Clark, Hawkins, Murphy, Sheeber, Lewinsohn, & Seeley, 1995; Lewinsohn, Clarke, Hops, & Andrews, 1990), merited the standard of "probably efficacious treatment" for adolescents. In studies, client characteristics were provided, treatment was manualized, and more than two group design studies performed better than alternative treatment or no-treatment control for reducing depression. It is prevented from having the status of "well-established" because only one research team has been involved in its study (David-Ferdon & Kaslow, 2008).

Interpersonal Therapy

Although many fewer studies have been conducted on *interpersonal therapy* compared to CBT, interpersonal therapy has gained the status of a "well-established treatment" for adolescent depression, according to the Verdeli et al. (2006) review. One limitation of the primary studies is that they lack follow-up data. On the positive side, the effectiveness (versus efficacy) was demonstrated by community clinicians in an agency setting (Rossello & Bernal, 1999).

David-Ferdon and Kaslow (2008) reached a different conclusion when surveying the results of interpersonal therapy outcome studies, deeming interpersonal therapy as "probably efficacious" because it was investigated by only one research team. They viewed the cultural adaptation of interpersonal therapy with Puerto Rican adolescents (Rossello & Bernal, 1999) as a different protocol. In this latter study, CBT and interpersonal therapy were compared and no significant differences between the treatments emerged. The results show that no one treatment is more effective for teens with depression (David-Ferdon & Kaslow, 2008).

Although the issue has not been studied empirically, the authors of interpersonal therapy for adolescent depression provide some clinical guidelines as to when interpersonal therapy might be most successful (Mufson, Dorta, Moreau, & Weissman, 2005):

1. The family is willing to be involved in treatment and to try out new communication strategies.
2. Teens have experienced an identifiable interpersonal event that triggered or exacerbated a depressive episode rather than people who have long-standing interpersonal problems.
3. Teens are motivated to be in treatment or to feel better.
4. Teens are not actively suicidal, psychotic, bipolar, or substance abusing.

These guidelines may limit the sample of teens deemed appropriate for this treatment.

Promising Psychosocial Treatments

Two promising treatments will be discussed here: family therapy and self-guided CBT. Family therapy for depression has not been well-studied, although family influences may play a role in the development of depression for adolescents (see the biopsychosocial risk and resilience section). Brent et al. (1996) tested CBT against systemic family therapy and nondirective supportive therapy, and all conditions produced improvements in psychological adjustment and suicidality, although remission was more common in the CBT group (60%) than in either the family therapy or nonsupportive therapy. Reductions in suicidality and improvements in general psychosocial adjustment were not different across groups. At 2-year follow-up, different conditions affected different areas of functioning (Kolko, Brent, Baughter, Bridge, & Birmaher, 2000). Not surprisingly, given its emphasis on family relationships, family therapy positively influenced family conflict and parent–child relationship problems. But interestingly, both supportive therapy and CBT significantly reduced anxiety over the family therapy group.

Another study evaluated family psychoeducation with all family members living in the adolescent's home present for the intervention (Sanford et al., 2006). Significant changes in depressive symptoms among adolescent participants relative to the control condition did not occur, although improvements in the adolescent's social functioning and the adolescent–parent relationship were found. Studies seem to indicate that family approaches may help family functioning, which often plays a role in the development and maintenance of depression.

Because research treatments discussed here may not be available in many communities, one promising treatment is self-directed bibliotherapy using *Feeling Good* (Burns, 1980), which is based on Beck's (1970) cognitive theory of depression. This treatment may be particularly helpful when youth are reluctant to engage in treatment but are motivated to feel better. Ackerson et al. (1998) tested the benefits of bibliotherapy with a small sample of youth (N = 22) using a delayed treatment group as a control. Improvements were found for teens' self-report of depression.

MEDICATION

Although the tricyclic medications have been studied in relation to depression, the available evidence is that they are not effective for children and show very little benefit for adolescents (see Brown et al., 2007 for a review of the reviews and meta-analyses). Despite the rise in popularity in the selective serotonin reuptake inhibitors (SSRIs), a recent downturn has occurred in prescribing rates due to concerns about increased suicidal risk in youth taking antidepressants. Indeed, the UK has now banned the SSRIs for youth 18 years old and younger, and in 2004, The Food and Drug Advisory Administration issued a "black box" warning label on SSRIs about this risk (Food and Drug Administration, 2004). As a result of these concerns, recent reviews on the SSRIs concentrate not only on outcome but also on suicide risk. The Hetrick et al. (2007) and the Bridge et al. (2007) meta-analyses will be a focus here because of their comprehensiveness in inclusion of studies and otherwise strong methodology (see Table 7.3).

In examining the SSRI treatment outcome studies in youth overall, Hetrick et al. (2007) found significant improvement in depression compared to placebo but also an 80% greater risk of a suicide event. The risk of suicide-related behavior was a total of 63 events in 1167 participants in the SSRI group and a total of 32 events in 1073 participants in the placebo group. Reasons for increased suicidality potential with medication are unknown and do not seem related to the efficacy of antidepressants (Bridge et al., 2007).

As far as the different antidepressants are concerned, Prozac and Zoloft have shown sufficient efficacy for adolescents, but only Prozac has received sufficient support for children (Bridge et al., 2007; Usala, Clavenna, Zuddas, & Bonati, 2008; Whittington, Kendall, Fonagy, et al., 2004). The reason why depressed children respond better to fluoxetine compared with other agents is unclear but could be due to study quality, location, or properties of the medication itself, such as its "long half-life" (Bridge et al., 2007). In the Bridge, Iyengar, Salary, et al. (2007) meta-analysis of all available randomized clinical trials of antidepressant treatment of pediatric major depressive disorder (MDD), obsessive compulsive disorder (OCD), and non-OCD anxiety disorders, antidepressant effects were strongest

TABLE 7.3 SUMMARIES OF SYSTEMATIC REVIEWS OF MEDICATION TREATMENT OUTCOME STUDIES ON ADOLESCENT DEPRESSION

Author and Purpose	Inclusion Criteria	Main Findings
Hetrick et al. (2007) (Cochrane review)	**Participants**	Review of 12 trials
To determine whether selective serotonin reuptake inhibitors (SSRIs) are more effective than placebo in the treatment of depression in children and adolescents	Youth ages 6–18 years who were diagnosed with a DSM or International Classification of Disease (ICD) primary diagnosis of depressive disorder	Overall significant increase in depression symptom improvement based on SSRI treatment compared to placebo, but also 80% greater risk of a suicide event (RR 1.80, 95% CI 1.19–2.72).
To determine if the effectiveness of SSRIs differs between children and adolescents	**Intervention** SSRIs compared to placebo	
To determine whether there is an increased risk of adverse outcomes and suicide-related outcomes (including suicide-related behavior and suicidal ideation as defined in the FDA review) in children and adolescents treated with an SSRI	**Studies** Published and nonpublished randomized controlled trials; no language restriction **Outcomes** Depressive disorder according to DSM or ICD criteria Suicide completion	

Bridge et al. (2007)
To assess the efficacy and risk of reported suicidal ideation/suicide attempt of antidepressants for treatment of pediatric major depressive disorder (MDD), obsessive–compulsive disorder (OCD), and non-OCD anxiety disorders

Depression symptoms (on standardized, validated, reliable depression rating scales)

Suicide related outcomes (including suicide-related behavior and suicidal ideation)

Children's functioning

Completion of trial protocol (as a proxy measure for treatment acceptability)

Adverse outcomes

Participants
Children and adolescents (<19 years) with MDD, OCD, or non-OCD anxiety disorders

Intervention
SSRIs as well as other second-generation agents

Studies
Randomized, placebo-controlled trials

Outcome
Primary risk outcome was suicidal ideation/suicide attempt; treatment response

Based on data from 13 trials and 2910 participants. Pooled absolute rates of response were 61% in participants treated with antidepressants and 50% in those treated with placebo, yielding a pooled risk difference of 11%. Pooled absolute rates of suicidal ideation/suicide attempt were 3% in antidepressant-treated participants and 2% in those receiving placebo. The pooled risk difference was 1%.

for non-OCD anxiety disorders, intermediate for OCD, and more modest for MDD. Because of the stronger effects on anxiety, the results of this meta-analysis raises concerns about the degree to which antidepressants target specific neurobiological factors (Luyten, Blatt, & Van Houdenhove, 2006).

From the findings on the risk of suicide with SSRIs, practitioners should educate the youth and the family on the potential benefits and risks of SSRIs and help them consider the various options for treatment. The risk of suicide should be assessed and, if medication is used, it should be monitored regularly.

As a final point under medication, antipsychotics are increasingly being provided to a significant number of youth, although there are no controlled studies on the use of antipsychotic medication or its combination with antidepressants for the treatment of depression in youth (Olfson, Blanco, Liu, Moreno, & Laje, 2006).

COMBINED MEDICATION AND CBT

The research has recently burgeoned on combination treatments (medication and CBT). The largest treatment outcome study on adolescent depression (major depressive disorder) offered in multisites throughout the United States offered four randomized conditions: CBT alone for 12 weeks, fluoxetine (Prozac) alone, combining CBT and Prozac, and placebo (TADS Team, 2007). After 36 weeks follow-up, Prozac seemed particularly effective for the treatment of depression; however, a concern was a greater risk of suicidality with medication. Although CBT did not produce as much improvement as medication, it sped up recovery when offered in combination. Offering CBT along with medication also seemed to protect against suicidal problems that emerged with treatment of Prozac. In the most recent publication of the TADS, the overall conclusion is to offer a combination of both CBT and medication for the treatment of moderate-to-severe depression in adolescents (March & Vitiello, 2009).

A similar study to the TADS, the Time for a Future Adolescent Depression Program, using randomization, compared CBT alone, sertraline (Celexa) alone, and a combination of CBT and medication for teens with DSM-defined depressive disorders (Melvin et al., 2006). In contrast to the results of the TADS, combined treatment was not generally superior to either CBT alone or medication alone. However, adolescents in the CBT condition had a better response than adolescents in the medication-alone condition on rates of depressive disorders at the end of the intervention (David-Ferdon & Kaslow, 2008).

Three other studies on combination treatments will be reviewed, although they target slightly different populations: adolescents nonresponsive to an initial trial of treatment (Brent, Emslie, Clark, et al., 2008; Goodyer, Dubicka, Wilckinson, et al., 2008) and adolescents with comorbid depression and substance use (Riggs, Mikulich-Gilbertson, Davies, et al., 2007). In Brent et al. (2008), the Treatment of

Resistant Depression in Adolescents (TORDIA) study, participants who were initially unresponsive to a trial of medication (N = 334) in six different sites were randomly assigned to either (1) a change to another SSRI, (2) change to another SSRI and add CBT, (3) switch to venlafaxine [Effexor, a serotonin- norepinephrine reuptake inhibitor (SNRI)], or (4) switch to venlafaxine and CBT. The most efficacious condition was a change to another SSRI and CBT. The two different medication conditions (another SSRI or venlafaxine) were not different in terms of statistical significance, but venlafaxine was associated with more adverse events.

In a British study, the ADAPT trial, 208 teenagers who were nonresponsive to a brief psychosocial intervention were randomized to either SSRI and CBT or SSRI alone (Goodyer et al., 2008). The addition of CBT did not confer additional benefits over SSRI in the moderately to severely depressed sample over the 28-week study period; both groups were effective in reducing depression. The CBT addition further did not protect against adverse events and was more expensive to administer. Researchers from the TADS account for the differences in results from their study by explaining that participants in ADAPT may have had greater severity of depression (since to be included they were initially not responsive to treatment (March & Vitiello, 2009). Also, the psychotherapy that all participants received in ADAPT may have contained elements of CBT.

One recent randomized controlled trial of CBT, fluoxetine, and its combination targeted adolescents with both a depressive disorder and a substance use disorder (Riggs, Mikulich-Gilbertson, Davies, et al., 2007). Adolescents were randomized to either medication and CBT or placebo and CBT. After the 16 weeks of treatment, results indicated that the combined medication and CBT performed better on one but not another depression measure and did not greater reduce substance use or conduct disorder (CD) symptoms. There was a high level of treatment response in both groups for depression (fluoxetine and CBT, 84%; placebo and CBT, 78%) but differences between the groups were not statistically significant. Decreases in self-reported drug use and CD symptoms did not differ between the two groups.

Results of these large-scale studies are difficult to interpret together because of the differences in research design and study participants. TADS and TORDIA study came to a similar conclusion about the importance of combining CBT and antidepressant medication, although these results were not supported in all the studies described here.

BIOPSYCHOSOCIAL RISK AND RESILIENCE

The development of depression is linked to biological (pubertal hormones), psychological (negative cognitions), and environmental factors (stressful life events). These levels will be discussed separately, although risk factors are often shared across system levels. For instance, the fact that parental depression is a major risk for depression in youth may partly be explained by genetics (a biological factor), but it can also be explained by parenting and the family environment (a social influence).

BIOLOGICAL

Although heritability accounts for a moderate amount (about 40%) of the variance explained for depression (Boomsma, van Beijsterveldt, & Hudziak, 2005; Kendler, Kuhn, Vittum, et al., 2005), other factors comprise a majority of the variance (about 60%). Some environmental influences, such as stressful life events, may also be moderated by genetic make-up. This may explain why stress leads to depression in some individuals but not others (Kendler et al., 2005). In addition to risk for depression, genetic factors may also protect an individual from being depressed. The long allele of 5-HTTLPR, for example, may reduce the reactivity of a person's neurobiology to stressful events in the environment (Silk et al., 2007).

Biological risks other than genetics may be present. A recent longitudinal study of youth showed that prenatal marijuana exposure was associated with the development of early depression and anxiety (at age 10 years) (Leech, Larkby, Day, & Day, 2006). In this same study, lower IQ, attention problems, and early childhood injuries were also linked to depression and anxiety.

PSYCHOLOGICAL

One risk factor for the development of a depressive disorder, according to a review, is having had a previous anxiety disorder (Rutter, Kim-Cohen, & Maughan, 2006). Unknown are the mechanisms explaining this pattern. It could be that common psychological traits such as low self-esteem, pessimism, and a ruminative thinking style act as risk factors for both depression (Nolen-Hoeksema, 2002) and anxiety. *Rumination* is defined as the proclivity to focus on the symptoms of a distressed mood, mulling over the reasons for its occurrence in an incessant and passive way, rather than in an active, problem-solving manner or by obtaining relief through distraction.

Another personality factor, assumed to be an inherited trait that is also shaped by the environment, is called behavioral inhibition, involving timidity, shyness, emotional restraint, and withdrawal when introduced to unfamiliar situations (Kagan, Reznick, & Snodman, 1987). It also includes emotional reactions that tend toward negativity, including fear, worry, sadness, self-dissatisfaction, and hostility.

According to cognitive theories of depression, depressed individuals have more negative beliefs about themselves, the world, and their future (Beck, 1967). Another type of cognitive theory of depression involves the attributions people make for the events in their lives. Specifically, they attribute global, stable, and internal reasons for negative events (Abramson, Metalsky, & Alloy, 1989). For instance, a person might decide that she did not do well on a paper because she is stupid. Meta-analyses of studies reporting on attributional style and depression have demonstrated moderate to large effect sizes in cross-sectional studies suggesting a strong concurrent association between negative attributional style and higher levels of depressive symptoms in children and adolescents (Gladstone & Kaslow, 1995; Joiner & Wagner, 1995).

Because of the cognitive development that happens in adolescence, youth at this age are at heightened risk for depression. Adolescence is a time of life when the capacity for personal reflection, abstract reasoning, and formal operational thought develop. At this stage, youth can first consider *causality* for the events in their lives, and they may develop a negative bias, such as "Nothing ever works out for me." Adolescence is also a time in development when a *future orientation* develops; with this ability, the adolescent may experience hopelessness about the future (Abela, Brozina, & Haigh, 2002). At the same time, formal operational thinking may help adolescents (ages 12–18 years) benefit more from psychotherapy when compared to children (Watanabe et al., 2007).

SOCIAL

Family factors can influence the development and maintenance of depression in youth (Diamond, Reis, Diamond, Siqueland, & Isaacs, 2002). Parental psychopathology in general, and more specifically depression in mothers, is a particular risk mechanism for youth (Pilowsky, Wickramaratne, Rush, et al., 2006). The association of maternal depression and increased rates of depression in their children may be accounted for by genetics, impaired parenting, modeling, and its link to marital problems (Goodman & Gotlib, 1999). Although most of the research has centered on maternal depression, Kane and Garber (2004) recently conducted a meta-analysis of paternal factors in youth psychopathology. Fathers' depression was related to both youth depression and greater family conflict levels.

Sander and McCarty (2005) conducted a review of family factors and their association with youth depression and concluded that lack of parental warmth and availability was a consistent risk for youth depression. Stress, depression, marital conflict, and social support, in turn, influence parental warmth and availability. A recent meta-analysis of 45 studies also looked at the link between parenting behaviors and youth depression and found that parenting behaviors contributed in a moderate way to depression ($r = 0.28$) (McLeod, Weisz, & Wood, 2007). Hostility from parents correlated in particular with child depression. The direction of causality is, of course, at question as child depression may elicit negative parental reactions or hostility in parents can give rise to depression in children.

A number of studies have indicated a significant relationship between depression and childhood physical abuse and sexual abuse (Paolucci, Genuis, & Violato, 2001; Penza, Heim, & Nemeroff, 2006), which often arise within family circumstances. Of all types of maltreatment, sexual abuse poses the greatest risk for depression and suicide attempts (Fergusson, Beautrais, & Horwood, 2003).

Females are at greater risk of being diagnosed with depression. In epidemiological, community, and clinical youth samples, depression is much more prevalent in females than males (Kovacs, 2001). This gender gap, which emerges by age 14 years, is found internationally—across Canada, Great Britain, and the United States (Wade, Cairney, & Pevalin, 2002)—and persists across the lifespan (Kessler, 2003). It does not appear related to either reporting bias or help-seeking behaviors (Kessler, 2003).

Various reasons, including the biological and the psychosocial, have been hypothesized for the gender gap in depression. Biological theories involve the hormonal shifts females experience during menses, pregnancy, postpartum, and menopause (Desai & Jann, 2000), although the specific mechanisms by which hormones exert their influence have not been delineated (Le, Munoz, Ippen, & Stoddard, 2003). Another hypothesis is that hormonal changes interact with the psychosocial. Role changes associated with reproductive events in societies that devalue women's roles may result in depression.

Social reasons for depression may involve the fact that the rate of sexual abuse is higher in females than in males (Bolen & Scannepeico, 1996). Although, in general, having positive peers is associated with less depression in adolescence (Gutman & Sameroff, 2004), for teen girls interpersonal stress may contribute to the onset of depression. Adolescent girls invest more than boys in relationships and therefore, may be more reactive to the opinions of others and more dependent on their approval (Girgus & Nolen-Hoeksema, 2006).

For these reasons, gender-specific interventions may be warranted (David-Ferdon & Kaslow, 2008), and one such program, ACTION, is currently being evaluated (Stark et al., 2006). Interventions may help girls more competently navigate relationships, to attack distorted thinking ("I have to be popular, otherwise I'm nobody"), and to develop active coping skills rather than ruminating. When they are 12 years old, males and females diverge in their use of rumination, with girls showing higher rumination, and depression differences emerge about a year later (Jose & Brown, 2008).

Because a recent longitudinal study found that poor emotional control predicted depression in females (Patton, Olsson, Bond, et al., 2008), programs for depression in girls could also focus on helping them manage difficult feelings. Persistence of depression in girls was related to family conflict and reports of being bullied, so programs could further focus on reducing interpersonal stress.

Beyond personal and familial characteristics, larger systems may play a role in a teen becoming depressed. High levels of neighborhood adversity, even in the presence of family stability, may be associated with depression in low socioeconomic status (SES) boys (Silk et al., 2007). Neighborhood problems also pose risks for girls, whereas neighborhood cohesiveness acts as a protective influence (Gutman & Sameroff, 2004).

Low SES may be linked to depression. In a systematic review on anxiety and depression for youth aged 10–15 years, lower compared to higher SES youth had a higher prevalence of depression and anxiety (Lemstra, Neudof, D'Arcy, et al., 2008). Twenge and Nolan-Hoesksema (2002) studied the link between SES and depression in a different way. They meta-analyzed all studies that measured both SES and used a specific measure to assess depression, the Children's Depression Inventory, and found no relationship.

In the Twenge and Nolan-Hoesksema (2002) meta-analysis, Latino youth had elevated scores compared to either white or African-American samples. According to the Centers for Disease Control and Prevention (2008), rates of suicide attempts and plans among adolescent Latinas are significantly higher than their Caucasian and African-American counterparts. Additionally, disparities exist between Latinos and Caucasians in terms of receipt of adequate mental health care for depression (Alexandre, Martins, & Richard, 2009). Adequate mental health is defined as receiving medication as well as at least four visits to a doctor or eight visits to a mental health professional. In a study of risk and protective factors for Latino adolescent depression, Umana-Taylor and Updegraff (2007) found that males showing a strong orientation toward white, mainstream culture may be at more risk for the deleterious impact of discrimination. Conversely, high identification with Latino culture may act as a protective influence in the face of discrimination and does not negatively affect their self-worth and contribute to depression. Relatedly, acculturation was the subject in a recent study (Cespedes & Huey, 2008). Specifically, a discrepancy between gender role expectations among Latino teenagers and their parents was associated with depression, particularly among girls.

Unfortunately, there are few treatment outcome studies focusing on Latinos or youth from other ethnic minorities, with the exception of Rossello and Bernal (1999) (described below) and Yu and Seligman (2002) (in China). Of note is the lack of studies on American Indians and Alaskan Natives, who have the highest rate of suicide in the 15- to 24-year-old age group (Centers for Disease Control and Prevention, 2004 as cited in David-Ferdon & Kaslow, 2008).

Huey and Polo (2008) used the APA Task Force criteria to evaluate the efficacy of treatments for ethnic minority youth. In a randomized trial conducted in Puerto Rico with depressed youth, Rossello and Bernal (1999) found that both the CBT and IPT groups showed reductions in depressive symptoms and increases in self-esteem in comparison with the wait-list control group. Clinical significance indicated that 82% of the participants in IPT and 59% of those in CBT were in the functional range at posttest. Despite the efforts of researchers to incorporate and equalize cultural content for both treatments, IPT had positive outcomes on self-concept and social adaptation over the wait-list control, whereas CBT had not. No such changes were evident for CBT. With its focus on relationships, IPT may have a greater degree of compatibility of IPT with Puerto Rican cultural values of *personalismo* ("personalism"; i.e., the preference for personal contacts in social situations) and *familismo* ("familism"; i.e., the tendency to place the interest of the family over the interests of the individual) shared by most Latino groups.

However, in a subsequent study in which Puerto Rican youth with depression were randomized to CBT or IPT, CBT led to greater reductions in depression than IPT (Rossello, Bernal, & Rivera-Medina, 2008). Thus, CBT meets criteria for probably efficacious in treating Latino youth with depression, whereas IPT meets criteria for possibly efficacious (David-Ferdon & Kaslow, 2008). Given the mixed findings and the increased risk of depression in Latinos, future study by independent investigators could help to determine effective treatments.

TABLE 7.4 BIOPSYCHOSOCIAL RISK AND PROTECTIVE FACTORS FOR ONSET OF DEPRESSION TO ADDRESS IN INTERVENTIONS

Factors	Evidence-Based Treatment	Other Factors to Address
Biological		
Gender	Medication	Specialized treatment for females
Gay/lesbian		Gay and lesbian-sensitive treatment
Adolescence		Target screening and referral at the 13- to 15-year-old age group
Psychological		
Cognitive distortions and negative affectivity	Cognitive–behavioral therapy (CBT)	
Poor coping skills, such as rumination		
Social		
Parental hostility	Family therapy	Address the problems of hostility and/or depression in treatment manuals
Parental depression		
Neighborhood crime		Help family attain safe housing
Discrimination		Culturally sensitive treatment for ethnic minorities
School failure		Address school performance
Socioeconomic status		Make sure an individualized education plan (IEP) is in place at the school system
		Screening at school for depression and effective services available or by referral
		Amelioration of environmental stressors

TABLE 7.5 BIOPSYCHOSOCIAL RISK AND PROTECTIVE FACTORS FOR TREATMENT AND RECOVERY OF DEPRESSION TO ADDRESS IN INTERVENTIONS

Biopsychosocial Risk	Evidence-Based Treatment	Factors Left Unaddressed
Features of the depression		
Early onset		Screening for depression in primary care settings and schools
Biological		
Poor physical health/ disability		Screening for depression in primary care and hospital settings
		Treatment sensitive to physical health problems (incapacity, disability, pain)
Psychological		
Suicidal ideation, hopelessness, and negative thoughts	Cognitive–behavioral therapy (CBT)	Work on enhancing optimism and motivation, perhaps through motivational interviewing
Comorbid diagnoses [anxiety, attention deficit hyperactivity disorder (ADHD)]	CBT and medication addresses anxiety	Treatment manuals to address comorbidity, especially for disruptive behavior disorders
Social		
Family problems	Family therapy/family-involved treatment	
Chronic stress		Address coping/ameliorating stress

Source: Kaminski & Garber, 2002; Rushton, Forcier, & Schectman, 2002; Rao, Hammen, & Poland, 2010

Tables 7.4 and 7.5 will indicate how current evidence-based treatments address biopsychosocial risk and protective influences for the onset and for the recovery of depression in youth, respectively. They will also list, when gaps are left unaddressed, the intervention implications that may be posed.

RESEARCH RECOMMENDATIONS

THEORY BASIS

Research recommendations are discussed in terms of both theory and methodology. The first recommendation for theory involves the fact that treatment outcome studies on youth depression focus on CBT. One-third of the studies in the Weisz et al. 2006 meta-analysis concerned CBT. However, researchers should also undertake other theoretically oriented treatments, such as psychodynamic therapy and the eclectic treatments that are often used in clinical settings.

Additionally, family therapy has not been fully explored, although aspects of family functioning—parental mental illness, stressful family life events, as well as actual parenting behavior, such as hostility and rejection—play a role in the onset and maintenance of depression, and these, for the most part, have not been addressed in the available interventions (McLeod et al., 2007). Future investigation could identify the level of family involvement (ranging from none to having the whole family present in sessions) necessary for certain qualities of depressed youth and their parents (Sander & McCarty, 2005). Furthermore, researchers must consistently report the specifics of family involvement, including the frequency, intensity, and types of contact, so that readers of this research can understand the potential benefits of this modality (David-Ferdon & Kaslow, 2008).

Other recommendations involve the theory basis of CBT. A meta-analysis indicated that CBT did not necessarily impact the measures that were consistent with the theory (Luyten et al., 2006). For example, CBT did not affect cognitive measures of change more than other types of therapies. Therefore, future research in this area should concern itself with the processes of therapeutic change rather than just treatment outcome research.

CBT comprises many different components, including cognitive, behavioral, and coping training techniques. Therefore, another recommendation is that dismantling studies, ones that compare various components of treatment to one another, are needed to help specify change factors (Chu & Harrison, 2007). In the TORDIA study, CBT participants who received social skills training and problem-solving skills training were 2.3 and 2.6 times, respectively, to have a positive treatment response (Kennard, Clarke, Weersing, Asarnow, Shamseddeen et al., 2009). These results suggest that these two training components may represent key elements of CBT, and therefore, might be offered initially in treatment. However, this finding needs to be replicated and studied more systematically as these two components were confounded with length of intervention (i.e., the longer people were in treatment, the more likely they were to receive these two skills-based trainings).

A further question for investigation is how best to impact comorbid disorders when they are present. Recall that in Weisz et al. (2006) externalizing disorders were not affected by treatment for depression. Another comorbid condition is sexual or physical maltreatment. If they are part of the youth's background, how can treatment for depression concurrently address abuse or trauma issues? How can two treatment foci—depression and abuse history, for example—be integrated under one theoretical framework? CBT by itself did not fare well in the TADS study for youth who had suffered maltreatment (Lewis, Simons, Nguyen et al., 2010). Would interpersonal therapy (which discusses interpersonal losses or ruptures) or family therapy (which may help repair family dynamics conducive to maltreatment) lend itself better for this subpopulation of depressed youth? These questions may be posed for future research.

METHODOLOGY

Many recommendations for research involve methodological aspects of studies. First, treatments tested for depression may not outperform conditions that control for attention and support as the placebo effect for improvement in depression is high (Vitiello, 2009). Many of the CBT studies relied on wait-list controls. In the future, researchers could rely on conditions that control for attention and support. In particular, Brown et al. (2007) suggest that psychoeducation, currently a component of many depression treatments, could be used as an information control condition. Psychoeducation involves educating youth and families on the symptoms of depression, its potential course, and the available treatments and their potential costs and benefits.

A further problem with wait-list control conditions is that participants cannot remain untreated through follow-up. In the Weisz et al. (2006) meta-analysis, one-third of studies included did not report follow-up data. Because depression can reoccur and is related to a host of potentially negative outcomes, future research must strive to include follow-up periods to consider the impact of treatment. A related recommendation is to test the utility of booster sessions to prevent future episodes of depression.

Another methodological recommendation for future treatment outcome studies is to report intent-to-treat analysis in treatment outcome studies targeting youth depression. Weisz et al. (2006) acknowledged that their meta-analytic effects could have been positively biased upward; only about a third of studies (11) reported intent-to-treat analysis. Including only people who complete treatment in the analysis of program effects may overestimate effect sizes.

At the most basic level, future researchers should report demographic information on their participants so readers can understand the generalizability of the particular treatment to other populations. Furthermore, for meta-analytic purposes, to perform moderator analysis, participant characteristics, such as SES and ethnicity, need to be identified. However, only 37% of the 35 outcome studies reviewed by Weisz et al. (2006) reported information on ethnicity (Sander & McCarty, 2005).

An additional aspect of concern for future research is the impact of teen depression programs on suicidality. Weisz et al. (2006) found in their meta-analysis that programs had a negligible impact on suicidality. Additionally, the studies that have directly targeted teen suicidality have also had disappointing results (Corcoran, Dattalo, Grindle, Brown, 2010). Future studies on adolescent depression must continue to assess suicidality in youth, and manuals should provide guidance to clinicians on the management of suicidal crises should they emerge.

This also relates to a limitation of the pharmacological treatment outcome studies, which typically recruit through advertisement, excluding youth who are at risk of suicide or have serious comorbidity. However, the latter are often seen in clinic-referred youth with depression. This means that participants in random-ized, controlled trials are not similar to typical clinic referrals and generalizability is therefore limited (Hetrick et al., 2007).

The reviews that were conducted according to APA Psychological Task Force criteria indicate that one re-occurring barrier for gaining sufficient support for "well-established" treatments is that more than one research team has not investi-gated the particular program. "The potential problems of allegiance effects (i.e., intervention effects tend to be larger when evaluated by the group of researchers who prefer and developed the intervention protocol) . . . Replication is necessary to demonstrate that the treatment protocol is contributing to change, and that change is not only the result of expertise. In addition, replication is required to demonstrate that the positive impact of an intervention will generalize to different therapists, settings, and patients" (David-Ferdon & Kaslow, 2008). A related issue is that community settings will treat youth for depression even if they do not meet DSM criteria, whereas treatment outcome studies, particularly those for medica-tion, will often rely on DSM criteria for inclusion into the study. However, sub-threshold cases (those in which youth do not meet full criteria for a depressive disorder) may produce as much impairment as those that meet full criteria (Gonzalez-Tejara, Canino, Ramirez, et al., 2005; Keenan et al., 2008).

CONCLUSIONS

This chapter presents a review of the state of the evidence for the treatment of depression in children and adolescents. Although CBT and IPT have met criteria for "well-established" psychosocial interventions according to the APA Psychological Task Force Division 12 criteria, treatment, recent systematic reviews and meta-analyses indicate that psychotherapy may only have a small effect on outcomes, particularly when compared to active control conditions. Antidepres-sants can be effective, particularly with adolescents, although they may also bring with it increased risk of suicidality. Psychotherapy combined with medication may protect against any suicidality that may emerge. More research is clearly needed to determine effective treatments for community youth, such as the case study described and incorporated throughout this chapter.

CASE STUDY

Blanca Garcia is a 15-year-old Latina female in eighth grade. She is 5 months preg-nant. Felipe, the father of the baby, broke off the relationship shortly after Blanca discovered she was pregnant. Blanca wants to give the baby up for adoption. However, both her mother and Felipe's mother are pressuring her to keep the baby so that Blanca and her mother can raise the baby together. At the time of this assessment, Blanca was hospitalized for a suicide attempt, which included drinking a bottle of rubbing alcohol, swallowing prescription pills, and deeply cutting both arms. She is currently still at the psychiatric hospital and will remain there until she stabilizes.

Blanca was brought to the attention of the school social worker during seventh grade because she ran away from home. She hid at Felipe's house for 5 days until her mother went to the house and demanded that she return home; Blanca's mother did not report her missing to the authorities.

After returning, Blanca reported to the school social worker that she ran away after a heated argument with her mother Maria regarding her relationship with Felipe. She said that during the argument, Maria grabbed a belt and began to hit her, leaving marks. At this report, Child Protective Services (CPS) went to the house to investigate, but Blanca feared her mother would get into trouble and decided not to cooperate with CPS. Although CPS did not take up the case, the worker secured home-based counseling for the family through the state department of mental health. The in-home counseling lasted for 4 months, but after that time the mother kept rescheduling and canceling sessions until they were terminated from the agency. Blanca also continued to see the school social worker for individual counseling. Both the in-home counselor and the school social worker described Blanca as "quiet," and "depressed" with "flat affect."

Blanca is the oldest of five children. Her mother Maria immigrated to the United States 10 years ago, leaving Blanca and her younger sister in El Salvador with Blanca's maternal grandparents. Blanca's father left the family when Blanca was 2 years old and since she left El Salvador, she has had no contact with him. After 4 years in the states, Maria sent for Blanca and her sister. Blanca moved to the United States at the age of 7 years. The transition to the United States was difficult for her; she missed her grandparents and had difficulty adjusting to her mother in a new environment. They had no extended family in the area, but Blanca's mother had found an enclave of other Salvadoreans with whom she associated. Blanca and her family identify as Catholic, but they do not attend services. Blanca's mother works in a sandwich eatery chain full-time; the wage is low, but she does have health insurance through her employment. Blanca's mother denied that she had ever suffered from a mental disorder or that anyone in her family had.

Blanca spoke no English when she moved to the states and learned English in her elementary school's ESL program. She remembers that time as being really "hard and confusing." She stated during counseling, "Living in El Salvador was the happiest time of my life."

Around the age of 9 years, Blanca began to take on a lot of responsibilities for her younger siblings. She often stayed home from school to provide childcare for younger siblings, wash clothes, and cook meals for the family. Because she missed so much school, she was retained in fifth grade.

Blanca presents with a flat affect and responds slowly to questions. She reports that she does not care about school and describes it as "boring" and "a waste." Her grades are below average. She states that most of her friends are older girls from the neighborhood. She says she cries daily about her plight and feels little relief. She watches television, listens to music, and sleeps to cope with her problems, but "nothing helps." She feels tired and attributes it to the pregnancy. Weight gain since the start of the pregnancy has only been 5 pounds. She has received two prenatal care visits from the local health clinic, but missed her last few appointments because she didn't have a way to get there. See Box 7.1 for the DSM diagnosis for this case.

BOX 7.1   *DSM-IV* DIAGNOSIS

Axis I: 296.23 Major Depressive Disorder, single episode, and severe without
       psychotic features

[Rationale: For the more than a 2-week period, Blanca has experienced many of the criteria of major depressive disorder such as (1) depressed mood almost everyday (daily crying), (2) a disinterest in all or most activities (school is "boring" and "a waste"; "nothing helps," (3) failure to gain weight appropriate for her age or circumstances, such as pregnancy, (4) possible hypersomnia (sleeping to cope), (5) feelings of worthlessness, (6) psychomotor retardation, which is observable by her slow response to questions, (7) fatigue (although this could be due to pregnancy), and (8) a suicide attempt. Blanca was given the severe specifier because she had eight symptoms of depression (five are required) and one of the symptoms included a serious suicide attempt. The symptoms have impaired Blanca's functioning as evidenced by her suicidal episode. To our knowledge, this is Blanca's first major depressive episode.]

300.4 Dysthymic Disorder, Early Onset

[Rationale: Dysthmic Disorder was also assigned because during the past year Blanca has been experiencing an almost continuous depressed mood including low self-esteem and feelings of hopelessness. She could possibly have met other symptoms of dysthmia, although neither the in-home counselor nor the school social worker revealed other information. However, only two symptoms are required of several that connote depressed mood.]

V61.20 Parent–Child Relational Problem (the conflict-laden relationship Blanca has with
       her mother)

V62.3 Academic Problems (Blanca has a history of absences from school, has below
       average grades, and has little desire to be at school. Although the depression might
       be the reason for her apathy and low motivation, it appears that her educational
       problems preceded the depression).

V15.81 Noncompliance with Treatment (Blanca does not receive adequate prenatal care)

(continued)

BOX 7.1 *DSM-IV* DIAGNOSIS (CONT'D)

Axis II: V71.09 No Diagnosis

Axis III: Pregnancy (5 months)

Axis IV: Problems with the primary support group—neglect and abuse

Problems related to the social environment—break-up with boyfriend, inadequate social support, and acculturation problems

Educational problems—below average grades

Economic problems—Blanca's mother's wages are low, and the family lives in poverty

Problems with access to health care services—lack of transportation to a health clinic for prenatal care

Axis V: GAF = 20 (the serious suicide attempt and the risk to both herself and her fetus)

HOW THE EVIDENCE FITS

In considering the evidence-based treatments available for Blanca, interpersonal therapy might be the intervention of choice given that many of Blanca's stressors arose out of an interpersonal context. Interpersonal stress involves four main areas: loss, conflict, role transitions, and interpersonal deficits (Mufson, Dorta, Moreau, & Weissman, 2005). Blanca has struggled with at least three of these areas. First, she has suffered many losses, including the loss of her father, grandparents, and other relatives and friends when she left El Salvador. More recently, she has experienced a break-up from her boyfriend. The second area of interpersonal stress for Blanca involves the conflictual relationship she has with her mother. A third area involves role transitions. Although adolescence is in itself a role change, Blanca seemed to have struggled more recently with the role change that descended on her with pregnancy. She was also prevented from enjoying her adolescence previous to this because of the role she has as caretaker of her siblings while her mother worked.

APPLICATION

Interpersonal therapy is a brief treatment model divided into three phases (Mufson et al., 2005). In the initial phase (sessions one through four), the interpersonal therapist would perform a diagnostic assessment with Blanca, provide education about depression, conduct an interpersonal inventory, and draw up a treatment contract. The interpersonal inventory would provide the basis for the goals that are the focus of work in the middle phase. For the relationship losses Blanca has suffered, the goal is for her to mourn and discuss her feelings so that understanding and acceptance can take place and new relationships and interests can be built. For the conflictual relationship with her mother, a goal is to help Blanca and her mother communicate their expectations to bring about resolution. For the role transitions, the goals are to help her process the role transitions and the demands that have been thrust on her. The therapist can then assist Blanca in learning new skills so that she can enjoy success in these new roles. Since some of the role transitions involve her family, the therapist may include Blanca's mother to support Blanca and to help her adjust to the normative role transition, such as adolescence as it is experienced by an acculturated female in the United States.

HOW THE EVIDENCE DOES NOT FIT

Characteristics of Youth

Although interpersonal therapy has been tested with Latino youth, these were living in Puerto Rico (Rosello & Bernal, 1999); therefore, the applicability of interpersonal therapy to a Salvadorean female is unknown. In Blanca's country of origin, it is not unusual for girls to stay home and forego their education to help the household; a baby born to a teenager out of wedlock is raised by the family. In contrast, in mainstream U.S. culture, the importance of education is emphasized; teenagers are allowed certain freedoms (rather than having to assume adult responsibilities, such as staying home from school to take care of siblings), and pregnant females (even teenagers) are sometimes given a choice of how they will handle their pregnancy.

In addition to Blanca's ethnicity, the authors of the interpersonal treatment manual have named a number of client parameters that they see as important for people to be appropriate candidates (Mufson, Dorta, Moreau, & Weissman, 2005). Blanca, as well as her mother, would have to be motivated to participate in treatment. Although Blanca may be willing to attend, her mother in the past has not been compliant with the home-based services; this is at least partly due to the fact that she is the primary provider for her family.

Additionally, Blanca would have to be stabilized as far as suicidal risk in order to meet the guidelines the authors of the model created. Treatment manuals for depression tend not to delineate the therapist's role in the care of a suicidal crisis. For most research trials, being suicidal rules out inclusion in the study. However, in real-world cases, suicidal crises and other stressful life events have to be navigated by practitioners.

Pregnancy is generally a rule out for treatment outcome studies, but Blanca's pregnancy is a major stressful life event she is undergoing. She wants to give the child up for adoption, but her mother and mother's boyfriend have disagreed. In an interpersonal context, the relationships with her mother will be addressed, but not the crisis of the pregnancy per se. Obviously, this crisis will be an important aspect of any future intervention for Blanca.

Characteristics of the Context

Although the immediate relationships in Blanca's life will be addressed by interpersonal therapy, Blanca's mother needs additional support, such as child support, government benefits, and information about attaining documented status. Interpersonal therapy per se will not address these contextual factors that have influenced the development of Blanca's depression.

Another problem related to context with this evidence-based treatment is that training for interpersonal therapy is not readily available in most communities; therefore, providers are not conversant in the model. At this point, the treatment setting to which Blanca will be referred after she leaves the psychiatric hospital is unknown. Interpersonal therapy has been tested only in outpatient settings to date and not in inpatient facilities.

As can be seen from Blanca's previous treatment experiences—school counseling and home-based counseling—knowledge of and skill in evidence-based treatment are scant among community providers. In neither of these two settings did Blanca receive evidence-based treatment. At this point, it is not clear if receipt of evidence-based treatment at these earlier points of time would have prevented the crisis that has led to Blanca's suicide attempt.

DOES THE EVIDENCE-BASED TREATMENT TAKE INTO ACCOUNT STRENGTHS

Interpersonal therapy takes into account strengths in terms of strengthening and repairing existing relationships and building new relationships. It may also be a fit for Blanca's Latina cultural background in which a central value is the importance of relationships. However, interpersonal therapy may not be able to address all the risks to which Blanca is being subjected at this time in her life.

III

EATING DISORDERS

8

ANOREXIA NERVOSA AND BULIMIA NERVOSA

Eating disorders are characterized by disturbances in a person's eating behaviors and perceptions of body weight and shape (APA, 2000). The pathological fear of becoming overweight leads those with eating disorders to enact extreme, potentially damaging behaviors to lose weight and keep it off. *Anorexia nervosa* (AN) and *bulimia nervosa* (BN) are the two primary eating disorders. This chapter incorporates a case study to show how multidimensional risk influences may lead to the development of eating disorders. Also explored are the contextual factors that affect the treatment and recovery process, followed by corresponding research recommendations.

SCOPE OF THE PROBLEM

The prevalence rates for the DSM-defined eating disorders, AN and BN, are low. BN, purging type, is 1–3% of females aged 11–20 years (Gowers & Bryant-Waugh, 2004). The prevalence of anorexia among females is approximately 0.3% (Hoek & van Hoeken, 2003) to 0.5% (Gowers & Bryant-Waugh, 2004). Despite these low rates, the majority of teens seeking treatment (80%) qualify for Eating Disorder Not Otherwise Specified (Eddy, Doyle, Hoste, et al., 2008) because DSM criteria are not typically applicable to adolescents. Eating disorders must be successfully identified and treated, for even low-level eating disorder symptoms (fasting, dieting, using a weight loss drink or powder, skipping meals, smoking more cigarettes), as well as higher-level eating disorder symptoms (diet pill usage, vomiting, laxative use), are associated with suicidal behavior in adolescents (Crow, Eisenberg, Story, & Neumark-Sztainer, 2008) and physical and mental health problems in adults (Wilson et al., 2007). Suicide is the major cause of death for people with AN (Berkman et al., 2007), and suicide rates for those with AN are greater than in the normal population (Pompili, Mancinelli, Girardi, et al., 2004).

STATE OF THE EVIDENCE

The majority of studies for eating disorders are conducted with adult women; therefore, little evidence is available to guide effective treatment for adolescents. Unfortunately, adolescence is when eating disorders commonly arise (Gowers & Bryan-Waugh, 2004). Because of the lack of research, studies on adult women will be drawn on, recognizing both the advantages and disadvantages of this practice (see Box 8.1). This discussion will be organized according to AN and BN.

ANOREXIA NERVOSA

Psychosocial Treatment

Most striking about the treatment outcome studies for AN is the lack of research that has been conducted. In their review, Wilson, Grilo, Vitousek, et al. (2007) found only 15 randomized or quasirandomized studies in the past 20 years, and most were conducted with adult women and did not include adolescents.

BOX 8.1 ARGUMENTS FOR AND AGAINST APPLYING EATING DISORDER STUDIES WITH ADULTS TO ADOLESCENTS

Arguments for Extrapolating Results of Studies with Adults to Teenagers

1. Features of eating disorders remain the same across people of different ages.
2. Studies have included both adolescents and adults, although results have not been reported separately.
3. Similar disorders, namely depression and anxiety, have been used for both adults and adolescents with similar efficacy.

Arguments against Extrapolating Results of Studies with Adults to Teenagers

1. Youth are even more likely than adult women to receive a diagnosis of EDNOS, and treatment of EDNOS does not have an evidence basis in adults, much less teens.
2. In adolescence, treatment may have to attend to physical growth and development. Recovery in adolescents may be defined by adjusting to a new physical state rather than the premordid physical status of adults.
3. Parents are usually involved in their children's treatment, and from a practical standpoint are responsible for shopping, meal planning, and preparation.
4. For *pharmacotherapy*, children and adolescents may require higher doses to attain similar blood levels and therapeutic effect because of the child's more rapid liver metabolism and more efficient clearance by the kidney. Furthermore, many psychotropic drugs are not licensed for use in children.

TABLE 8.1 SUMMARIES OF COCHRANE COLLABORATION SYSTEMATIC REVIEWS AND META-ANALYSES: PSYCHOSOCIAL TREATMENT

Author and Purpose	Inclusion Criteria	Main Findings
Hay et al. (2003) To evaluate the evidence from randomized controlled trials for the efficacy of outpatient psychotherapies used in the treatment of older adolescents and adults with Anorexia Nervosa	**Participants** Older adolescents and adults diagnosed with Anorexia Nervosa **Interventions** Individual outpatient psychotherapy **Studies** Randomized controlled trials that have evaluated any form of individual psychotherapy for outpatients with anorexia nervosa **Outcomes** A range of outcomes including eating disorder attitudes and beliefs, interpersonal functioning, mental health symptoms, and physical functioning (weight, menstruation, etc.)	$N = 7$ Specific psychotherapies were more efficacious than treatment as usual or no treatment, but there was little difference between specific psychotherapies other than dietary advice, which had a 100% noncompletion rate in one small trial. Because of study limitations, no specific approach was recommended.
Perkins et al. (2006) To evaluate the evidence of the efficacy of pure Self Help/Guided Self Help with respect to eating disorder symptoms, compared with wait-list or placebo/attention control, other psychological or pharmacological treatments (or combinations/augmentations) in people with eating disorders	**Participants** People with a diagnosis of Anorexia Nervosa, Bulimia Nervosa, Binge Eating Disorder, or Eating Disorder Not Otherwise Specified **Interventions** Self-help interventions: "Pure" self-help Guided self-help **Studies** Randomized controlled trials/controlled clinical trials **Outcomes** A range of outcomes including bingeing, purging, and psychosocial adjustment	$N = 13$ Compared to other psychological therapies at the end of treatment and follow-up, self-help did not differ in a statistically significant way in improvement on bingeing and purging, other eating disorder symptoms, level of interpersonal functioning, depression, or dropout. Compared to no treatment, self-help did not significantly differ from wait-list in abstinence from bingeing or purging, or depression, although self-help produced greater improvement on other eating disorder symptoms, psychiatric symptomatology, and interpersonal functioning.

Furthermore, a systematic review of outpatient psychotherapies for AN found only seven studies, and authors discovered little evidence to support any particular intervention (Hay et al., 2003) (see Table 8.1).

The most attention has centered on the Maudsley model, a family intervention that has been used with adolescents as well as adults. Developed by Dare and Eisler at London's Maudsley Hospital in the 1980s, it has recently been manualized by Lock et al. (Lock, Le Grange, Agras, & Dare, 2001). Influenced by Minuchin's family systems therapy (Minuchin, Rosman, & Baker, 1978), there are some key differences. In family systems therapy, the family is viewed as the patient and therapy is designed to alter disturbed family processes that gave rise to the problems in the identified patient (i.e., the adolescent with the eating disorder). In the Maudsley model of family therapy, the family is not seen as the source of pathology and instead is incorporated into the treatment team. The main approach is to get the parents to unite to stand up to an externalized illness and refeed their adolescent until a healthy weight is resumed. Family treatment may include therapeutic techniques from traditional family therapy or other schools of psychotherapy.

Keel and Haedt (2008) determined, from their review according to APA Task Force criteria, that the Maudsley model of family therapy earned the categorization of a "well-established" treatment. They centered on two studies, which showed that the Maudsley model was advantageous compared to individual therapy [psychoanalytically oriented individual therapy (Robin et al., 1999) and eclectic individual therapy (Russell et al., 1987)]. However, several other reviewers have noted the confound in these studies of modality of treatment (family versus individual) and target of treatment (weight and eating issues vs. no emphasis), meaning that the results of these studies are uninterpretable and cannot be synthesized (Agras et al., 2004; Commission on Adolescent Eating Disorders, 2005).

Subsequent research has focused on examining different formats and intensities of the Maudsley approach (Eisler et al., 2000; Le Grange et al., 1992; Lock et al., 2005) rather than testing it against alternative models of treatment. For instance, the Maudsley model was designed as a conjoint family treatment (with parents and the child with the eating disorder present), but it has been tested against a condition in which parents were seen separately from the child (Le Grange et al., 1992). The latter condition was actually more effective for those whose families were high in expressed emotion (critical comments toward the person with the eating disorder), even at 5-year follow-up (Eisler et al., 2000). This study suggests that conjoint family therapy and separated family therapy may be helpful for AN, but the latter is more appropriate for families with high levels of expressed emotion. Given the accumulated evidence, the decision to brand the Maudsley model as "well-established" does not seem warranted. Additionally, there are some controversies with the Maudsley model Some families find the process of forcing the child to eat as required by the approach as too onerous a process to undertake; therefore, it may be unacceptable to youth and their families.

At the same time, the Maudsley model has influenced other family interventions for adolescents and young adults (Ball & Mitchell, 2004; Robin et al., 1994), but family therapy has not established itself as more helpful than individual therapy in these studies.

Medication

A range of medications has been offered for anorexia nervosa, but most typically involve the selective serotonin reuptake inhibitors (SSRIs). A systematic review of antidepressant medication treatment outcome studies for adult women with AN found few randomized controlled trials to include (N = 6) (Claudino, Hay, Lima, et al., 2006). In all, medication did little to improve symptoms (see Table 8.2). Medication may be more appropriate when anxiety or depression is also present, and, in general, people with anorexia report that psychosocial interventions are more helpful than medication (Bell, 2003).

BULIMIA NERVOSA

Like AN, BN initiates in adolescence, but no controlled trials with adolescents have been conducted (Commission on Adolescent Eating Disorders, 2005;

TABLE 8.2 SUMMARIES OF COCHRANE COLLABORATION SYSTEMATIC REVIEWS AND META-ANALYSES: MEDICATION STUDIES

Author and Purpose	Inclusion Criteria	Main Findings
Claudino et al. (2006) To evaluate the efficacy and acceptability of antidepressant drugs in the treatment of Anorexia Nervosa	**Participants** Adult women diagnosed with Anorexia Nervosa **Interventions** Antidepressant treatment **Studies** Published and unpublished studies before 2004–2005, randomized, controlled trials **Outcome** Primary outcome was weight change with secondary outcomes of severity of eating disorder, depression symptoms, anxiety symptoms, global clinical state, and acceptability of treatment (noncompletion rates)	N = 7 clinical trials Results were hard to meta-analyze because of different outcome variables in the studies. Four studies did not find results favoring antidepressants in improving weight gain, eating disorder, or related symptoms.

Gowers & Bryant-Waugh, 2004; Wilson et al., 2007). Additionally, when adolescents have been included in research, differential outcome by age has not been explored (Shapiro et al., 2007). A review of psychotherapy studies showed that about 40% of women with bulimia who complete treatment recover, although this percentage drops to 32.6% when including those who drop out from treatment (Thompson-Brenner, Glass, & Westen, 2003). Psychosocial treatment outcome studies typically involve cognitive–behavioral therapy (CBT) and interpersonal therapy.

Cognitive–Behavioral Therapy

CBT is based on the premise that negative overconcern with weight and shape results in unhealthy dieting and other weight-control behaviors, which, in turn, trigger binge eating (Fairburn, Marcus, & Wilson, 1993). The treatment consists of cognitive and behavioral procedures designed to do the following:

- enhance the motivation for change
- replace dysfunctional dieting with a regular and flexible pattern of eating
- decrease undue concern with body shape and weight
- prevent relapse.

Treatment typically has consisted of 16–20 sessions of individual therapy over 4–5 months, although it has also been offered as group therapy (Chen et al., 2003; Nevonen & Broberg, 2006). Authors have described adaptations of CBT that take account of the specific developmental features of adolescence, mainly lack of motivation to change and including family members into treatment as parents are responsible for meal preparation, planning, and grocery shopping (Lock, 2005; Schmidt, 2009; Wilson & Sysko, 2006).

To build motivation, motivational interviewing techniques have been encompassed in CBT for teenagers (Wilson & Sysko, 2006). Motivational interviewing is a collaborative, client-centered but directive method in which the client's ambivalence to change is explored with the goal of increasing motivation to change (Miller & Rollnick, 2002). Wilson and Sysko (2006) discuss the decisional balance technique from motivational interviewing in which the teenager is asked to explore the advantages and disadvantages of having the eating disorder and the advantages and disadvantages of making change.

Several systematic reviews and meta-analyses have been conducted on the use of CBT with BN. However, the focus here will be on those conducted by the Cochrane Collaboration as they have the most rigorous methodology (see Table 8.1).

The main purpose of Hay, Bacaltchuk, and Stefano (2004) was to review psychotherapies for bingeing in BN and binge-eating disorder. CBT held certain advantages: it performed better than wait-list control for bulimic symptoms and depression and it was more beneficial for binging abstinence compared to other psychotherapies. Group CBT was found to be as effective as individual CBT in the symptoms of bulimia and binge-eating. However, CBT was not any better than other psychotherapies for other bulimic symptoms or depression. In other words, it is yet to be established whether CBT is consistently better than other psychotherapy because other psychotherapies, too, are advantageous over control groups.

One study on CBT for teens with BN has been conducted. Schmidt, Lee, Beecham, et al. (2007) compared a self-help version of CBT with therapist facilitation to a Maudsley-style family therapy in a randomized, controlled trial. The CBT condition produced greater reductions in bingeing at 6 months but not 12 months, with no other differences on other outcomes, which included behavioral and attitudinal eating disorder symptoms. However, adolescents found the CBT treatment more acceptable, and it was less expensive than family therapy. One problem with the study is the confounding of modality (family versus self-help) and theoretical orientation (Maudsley-style family therapy versus CBT).

Interpersonal Therapy

Interpersonal therapy (IPT) has also been used with adults with BN. Recall from Chapter 7 that IPT was originally developed for adults with depression and then used with adolescents for this disorder. IPT targets interpersonal problems and not the eating pathology (Commission on Adolescent Eating Disorders, 2005). Two studies have compared IPT and CBT and discovered that IPT does not achieve as many benefits until follow-up (Fairburn, Jones, Peveler, et al., 1991; Fairburn, Norman, Welch, et al., 1995). Because IPT seems to work more slowly, Shapiro et al. (2007) recommend that CBT be used before IPT, unless the consumer preference is for IPT.

Family Therapy

Family therapy (a modified version of the Maudsley model) for BN has been examined in two recent studies (Le Grange et al., 2007; Schmidt et al., 2007). From these studies, Keel and Haedt (2008) determined that family therapy was possibly efficacious for younger adolescents but not for older adolescents; CBT-guided self-care emerged as possibly efficacious when it was compared with family therapy. Again, these conclusions need careful assessment. In the Le Grange et al. (2007) study, family therapy produced greater reductions in binging, vomiting, and food restraint at posttest but not at 6 months follow-up compared to supportive psychotherapy in their randomized, controlled trial. CBT had certain advantages over family therapy in Schmidt et al. (2007) as discussed above, although outcomes were generally similar to family therapy at 12 months. At this point, it is difficult to see many differences between family therapy and other types of treatments, including supportive therapy.

Medication and Combination Treatment

Some Cochrane systematic reviews have concerned themselves with the use of antidepressants as treatment for BN. Bacaltchuk and Hay (2003) examined antidepressants compared to placebo. Nineteen trials were located with few including adolescents. The authors found that the likelihood of short-term remission from binge episodes was increased more with the use of antidepressants (70% reduction) than placebo (50% reduction). No statistically significant difference in acceptability of treatment was indicated between antidepressants and placebo. Although no differential efficacy emerged among the three different classes of antidepressants [SSRIs, tricyclic antidepressants (TCAs), or monoamine oxidases (MAOs)], fluoxetine (an SSRI) was subject to the most research and was considered more acceptable to participants than other antidepressant agents. Like others (e.g., Shapiro et al., 2007), Bacaltchuk and Hay (2003) noted that doses of fluvoxamine (Prozac) are often higher (60 mg) than they are when used to treat depression (20 mg). They cautioned that the results of their review should be generalized only to young adults with BN who did not show severe comorbidity.

Bacaltchuk, Hay, and Trefiglio (2001) looked at medication compared to psychotherapy and their combination. Remission rates were 20% for antidepressants compared to 39% for psychotherapy (N = 5 studies), and dropout rates were higher for antidepressants (40% for participants in the medication group and 18% for CBT). However, there were no statistically significant differences in mean binge frequency and depression between people taking antidepressants and those using psychotherapy. Remission rates were 23% for antidepressants versus the combination of antidepressants and psychotherapy (42%) (N = 5 studies). Remission rates were 36% for psychotherapy versus the combination of antidepressants and psychotherapy (49%) (N = 7). Psychotherapy appeared to be more acceptable to subjects. When antidepressants were combined with psychological treatments, acceptability of the latter was significantly reduced. Combination therapy appears to produce few consistent gains over psychotherapy alone when considering other outcomes, including depression and mean binge frequency.

PROMISING TREATMENTS

Several treatments have emerged as promising. First, Fairburn (2008) developed an enhanced manual-based treatment for the full range of eating disorders, rather than just focusing on BN. This treatment was tested in England with a sample of 154 adults who were diagnosed with either BN or Eating Disorder Not Otherwise Specified (NOS); people with AN were screened out of the study (Fairburn, Cooper, Doll, O'Connor, Bohn, et al., 2009). Participants were involved in 20 sessions of 50-minute weekly treatment, and were randomly assigned to a basic treatment, an enhanced treatment, or a waiting-list control. Clinicians received 6 months of training on this model. The basic treatment focused on eating pathology only whereas the enhanced treatment also targeted low self-esteem, interpersonal difficulties, mood regulation, and perfectionism, features believed to maintain eating disorders and complicate treatment (see recovery and adjustment factors below). Using the standard for successful treatment as eating disorder pathology one standard deviation less than the community mean, a little over 50% of the sample in the treatment groups were successfully treated whereas the control group did not show improvement; these results were maintained at follow-up. No statistically significant differences emerged between the two groups except for a trend toward those that showed greater pathology in terms of the clinical features named above to respond better to the enhanced treatment. The authors concluded that the basic treatment, which required less training, should be the default treatment unless clinically indicated. Whether adolescents would also benefit from this treatment is unknown and needs to be tested.

A second promising treatment involves motivational interviewing as resistance and ambivalence are hallmarks of the eating disorders and clients may not be motivated for action-oriented methods, such as CBT. As discussed, motivational interviewing techniques have been encompassed into CBT for the treatment of eating disorders in teenagers (Wilson & Sysko, 2006). However, motivational interviewing should also be tested on its own in randomized, controlled trials for teenagers. One group design study has been conducted on motivational interviewing. Treasure et al. (1999) randomly assigned women with BN to four sessions of CBT or motivational interviewing. Both groups significantly reduced binge eating and purging over the 4-week period, and there were no differences between groups. The results of this study imply that motivational interviewing may perform as well in CBT in reducing BN symptoms, at least initially, although longer-term outcomes are needed (Kotler, Boudreau, & Devlin, 2003). Motivational interviewing was also tested in a pretest, posttest design (Feld et al., 2001). By the end of treatment, motivation to change had increased, and 6 weeks later, 17 (90%) were engaged in treatment. The results suggest that motivational interviewing may be helpful for engaging people in treatment, but randomly controlled studies are needed (Kotler et al., 2003).

Dialectical behavior therapy (DBT) is an intensive, 1-year outpatient intervention originally devised for people with borderline personality disorder. The purpose as applied to eating disorders is to increase coping in the areas of emotional regulation and distress tolerance. Salbach, Klinkowski, Pfeiffer, Lehmkuhl, and Korte (2007) describe the use of DBT with 31 adolescents with either BN or AN in a German inpatient facility, although results have not yet been reported.

Perkins et al. (2006) looked at self-help interventions for BN. At the end of treatment, self-help did not significantly differ from waiting-list in abstinence from binging or purging, or depression, although self-help produced greater improvement on other eating disorder symptoms, psychiatric symptomatology, and interpersonal functioning. Compared to other psychological therapies, self-help did not differ significantly at end of treatment or follow-up in improvement on binging and purging, other eating disorder symptoms, level of interpersonal functioning, depression, or dropout. In sum, self-help approaches may be a promising first-line intervention or may be appropriate for those living in rural areas, in areas in which CBT or IPT is unavailable such as rural areas, or when transportation or money is a problem. Web-based interventions, or text message interventions, also need development and testing and may have a role, particularly with treatment of adolescents.

BIOPSYCHOSOCIAL RISK AND RESILIENCE

ONSET

For an examination of the risk and protective mechanisms for the onset of eating disorders, anorexia and bulimia will be considered together, as they share overlapping risk factors, symptoms, and causes (White, 2000).

Biology

Biological influences on eating disorders include heritability. A recent meta-analysis found that AN is moderately heritable (Bulik, Sullivan, Tozzi, et al., 2006). Other biological influences include preterm birth and pregnancy complications (Favaro et al., 2006). Picky eating in childhood further presents risk for thin body preoccupation and possibly anorexia (Agras et al., 2007).

Adolescence is clearly a developmental stage that makes females vulnerable to eating disorders. There is a tension between the cultural ideal of female beauty and the physical reality of the female body after puberty. Interpersonal relationships are valued more by females than males, and much of the basis of social success has to do with an emphasis on physical attractiveness (Striegel-Moore, 1993).

Early onset of puberty (prior to age 11 years) particularly confers risk for the development of eating disorders; conversely, later-onset menarche (age 14 years and over) is protective. Early-maturing females tend to be shorter and heavier; therefore, their body type strays further from the current body ideal

(Mizes & Palmero, 1997; Striegel-Moore, 1993). In fact, a lean body build presents protection from eating disorders because this body type matches the contemporary standard. People often tease early-maturing girls for their development; they may also be exposed to experiences for which they are not psychologically prepared, such as dating and sexual pressure.

Childhood obesity poses risk for bulimia (Stice, 2002), as does dieting (Lowe & Timko, 2004; Patton, Selzer, Coffey, Carlin, & Wolfe, 1999). The restraint and deprivation associated with dieting may leave some vulnerable to binging (Lowe, 2002). At the same time, because dieting is fairly normative among adolescent and adult women, it is the more disturbed eating habits and attitudes that are associated with the development of eating disorders (Fairburn, Cooper, Doll, & Davies, 2005).

Psychology

Body dissatisfaction and distortion, negative affect, perfectionism, impulsivity, and substance use are risk factors for eating disorders (Stice, 2002). Having a mental disorder, such as depression or anxiety, puts individuals at risk for the development of an eating disorder. Most people with eating disorders have another psychiatric disorder (almost 90%), with most comorbid disorders preceding the eating disorder (Lewinsohn et al., 2000). Depression (50–75%) is particularly common followed by the anxiety disorders, especially social phobia and obsessive compulsive disorder (Fonagy, Target, Cottrell, et al., 2002; Lewinsohn et al., 2000), and then substance use disorders (Franko, Dorer, Keel, et al., 2005). Personality disorders are often present with eating disorders, although estimates of prevalence vary widely (Cassin & von Ranson, 2005). People with bulimia typically suffer from cluster B (borderline) and C personality disorders (avoidant), whereas cluster C (avoidant and obsessive-compulsive) personality disorders are associated with anorexia.

Social Influences

Family influences on eating disorders have been noted, but whether this is due to genetic mechanisms, childhood experiences, family concerns about weight, family psychopathology, or transaction patterns is unknown (Cooper, 1995; Wilson, Heffernan, & Black, 1996). In addition, specific types of problematic patterns have not been delineated. Sexual abuse, often within the context of the family, occurs to 20–50% of people with eating disorders (Yager et al., 2002).

Another family process involves the extent to which parents transmit societal values having to do with weight and appearance (Streigel-Moore & Cachelin, 1999). When parents show excessive focus on their own or their children's shape and size, children may feel pressure to lose weight (Kotler et al., 2001). In a prospective 11-year-old study, father's body dissatisfaction with himself was associated with child thin body preoccupation, as was parental overcontrol of child eating and parental teasing about weight and shape (Agras, Bryson, Hammer, & Kraemer, 2007).

A poor social support system may evolve from social isolation, social anxiety, and public self-consciousness and increase the risk of eating disorders. Peer teasing about weight may also be detrimental (Agras et al., 2007). Certain extracurricular activities, such as involvement in sports and dance that emphasize very low body fat, put an individual at risk for eating disorders. Activities that emphasize health and fitness protect against the development of eating disorders (Kelly, Wall, Eisenberg, et al., 2004), as well as activities that presumably involve other aspects of the individual aside from appearance and weight.

The societal overemphasis on thinness for females has resulted in eating-disordered attitudes and behaviors. Indeed, increased exposure to media, namely magazines and television, was associated with women's body dissatisfaction, the belief that we should attain the thin ideal portrayed, and more anorexic and bulimic symptoms (Grabe, Ward, & Hyde, 2008). Finally, products involving weight and appearance targeted at females are big business, creating strong incentives for their use. Furthermore, corporations boost markets for products involving weight and appearance that target women's supposed flaws.

Unlike many other mental disorders, high socioeconomic status does not confer protection against the development of eating disorders (Striegel-Moore & Cachelin, 1999). Females from middle and upper socioeconomic classes may indeed be more vulnerable due to increased demands in terms of social compliance and perfectionism.

Some epidemiological studies have been done on ethnic factors. Although white women in Western countries do not have higher rates of diagnosable eating disorders than nonwhite women, they do have higher rates of body dissatisfaction and eating disturbance; this latter effect is especially large between whites and African-Americans (O'Neill, 2003). In Western countries, Asians have risks similar to whites, if not higher (Wildes, Emery, & Simons, 2001). There is a lack of existing research on eating disorders as they pertain to Hispanic, Native American, East Indian, and Eastern European women (O'Neill, 2003).

TREATMENT AND RECOVERY

Following the onset of an eating disorder, certain risk and protective mechanisms are thought to maintain the condition or determine whether a person recovers (Gowers & Bryant-Waugh, 2004). Tables 8.3 and 8.4 identify these factors separately for AN and BN with implications for intervention.

TABLE 8.3 RISK AND RESILIENCE FACTORS INFLUENCING THE COURSE OF
ANOREXIA NERVOSA

Risk	Protective	Implications
Features of the disorder		
Initially lower minimum weight	Shorter duration of illness before treatment	Early identification and referral to treatment in health care provider, school, and psychotherapy settings
Longer duration of eating disorder		
Developmental stage		
Adults	Adolescent (younger adolescents have better outcome than older adolescents)	Early identification and referral to treatment
Psychological		
Greater body image disturbance		Focus on body image disturbance in treatment
Psychological disorders [obsessive-compulsive disorder (residual symptoms at the end of treatment) or other anxiety disorders, depression, and substance abuse]		Treat comorbid disorders, especially obsessive-compulsive disorder, so that complete remission is obtained
Resistance and denial		Use motivational interviewing
Sexual problems		
Impulsivity		
Social		
Disturbed family relationships before the onset of the disorder	Support and empathic relationships	Address family functioning
Impaired social functioning		Build interpersonal functioning and support systems
Treatment factors		
Failure to respond to previous treatment		

From Bell (2003), Berkman et al. (2007), Gowers and Bryant-Waugh (2004), Keel, Dorer, Franko, et al. (2005), NICE (2004), and Yager et al. (2002).

SYSTEMS OF CARE

Across systems of care, there is poor recognition of eating disorders. Health care providers, despite routine assessment of patients' weight, are often not aware of eating pathology (Johnston et al., 2007). Even among psychotherapists, recognition of eating disorders and/or the ability to treat them are low. Hudson et al. (2006) found that although many people with eating disorders had undergone psychotherapy for other disorders, their eating disorder went untreated.

TABLE 8.4 RISK AND RESILIENCE FACTORS INFLUENCING THE COURSE OF BULIMIA NERVOSA

Risk	Protective	Implications
Features of the disorder		
High rates of binging and vomiting	Milder symptoms	
Preoccupation and ritualization of eating	Shorter duration of illness	
Long duration of symptoms	Younger age of onset	Early identification and referral to appropriate treatment
Psychological		
Other psychological disorders (substance misuse and depression)		Treat comorbid disorders
Personality disorder, especially borderline		
Impulsivity		
Greater body image disturbance		
A lower motivation for change		Use motivational interviewing
Perfectionism		
Social		
	Support and empathic relationships	Develop social functioning in the adolescent and improve the ability of family members to be supportive.
Treatment factors		
A short abstinence period	Early change in purging frequency	Education to providers and clients indicating that treatment should not be terminated until complete abstinence is obtained for a period of time.
Only a reduction in bulimic behaviors at end of treatment	Complete abstinence at end of treatment	

From Bell (2003), Berkman et al. (2007), Fonagy et al. (2002), Gowers and Bryant-Waugh (2004), Keel, Dorer, Franko, et al. (2005), Keel and Mitchell (1997), NICE (2004), Wilson et al. (1999), and Yager et al. (2002).

Finally, when treatment is procured, providers do not use evidence-based methods (Von Ranson & Robinson, 2006).

A recent survey of mental health professionals providing psychotherapy for eating disorders in Calgary, Alberta, Canada, revealed that 35% of the doctoral-level respondents listed CBT as their primary orientation (Von Ranson & Robinson, 2006). More commonly, CBT techniques were combined with a diverse array of psychological treatments, including addiction-based approaches. Not only is there no empirical support for the latter, but Wilson and Latner (2001) argue that an addiction model of treatment is theoretically and procedurally incompatible with CBT. Wilson et al. (2007) further noted the potential pitfalls of pursuing a "psychotherapy integration" strategy. "Combining cognitive behavioral therapy with a psychotherapy that has no evidence of efficacy is premature at best. Integrating cognitive behavioral therapy with a conceptually incompatible framework of dubious validity cannot be recommended. Finally, combining other approaches with cognitive behavioral therapy carries the risk of undermining the efficacy of cognitive behavioral therapy by diluting the focus on essential mechanisms and targets of change. Care must be taken to ensure that combined treatments are conceptually and clinically consistent" (Wilson et al., 2007).

An implication is that community therapists need to be trained in evidence-based treatment. Less than 50% of the eating disorder practitioners in the Canadian survey had received training in graduate school for the disorder, but most indicated they would attend training in CBT or IPT if it were available (Von Ranson & Robinson, 2006). As indicated in Chapter 7, training for IPT, in particular, is scant, but it is also true of CBT for the eating disorders.

RESEARCH RECOMMENDATIONS

The most striking finding of this review is the lack of studies with participants who are in adolescence, when eating disorders typically arise. Early detection of eating disorder symptoms is critical in adolescents. Perhaps if treatment was applied and tested at this stage, eating disorders would not become so entrenched and chronic. Therefore, a priority is to conduct treatment outcome research with adolescent samples or have sufficient teens in samples to analyze by age. Developmentally appropriate modifications for teenagers, including the appropriate level of parental involvement and the fact that adolescents usually do not choose to be in treatment and, therefore, lack motivation, need further study (Gowers & Bryant-Waugh, 2004). More research could also elucidate the relative merits of individual, family, or combination treatments, and for choice among systems of care—inpatient, day treatment, or outpatient care—for different subgroups of adolescents with eating disorders (Wilson et al., 2007).

Of relevance to future study in this area is that most adolescents (and adults) present with Eating Disorder Not Otherwise Specified (EDNOS) (Gowers & Bryant-Waugh, 2004; Wilfley, Bishop, Wilson, & Agras, 2007). Rather than being a residual category, EDNOS "is the most common disorder given in outpatient clinical settings" (Wiffley, Bishop, Wilson, & Agras, 2007, p. 5124) and for which there are no evidence-based treatments (Gowers & Bryant-Waugh, 2004). There are several reasons why EDNOS accounts for the majority of adolescent cases. First, the DSM criteria for AN lack relevance for prepubescent girls and for males (Franko, Wonderlich, Little, & Herzog, 2004). For example, the required criterion for AN, "amenorrhea," may have yet to occur in prepubescent girls, and does not apply to males. Another criterion for AN that lacks relevance to males and younger adolescents since they may not have the weight to lose is the weight requirement: 85% of ideal body weight (Wiffley, Bishop, Wilson, & Agras, 2007; Anderson, Bowers, & Watson, 2001). As a result of these factors, many researchers recommend more relaxed criteria, which will hopefully be implemented in *DSM-IV* (e.g., Kotler, Cohen, Davies, Pine, & Walsh, 2001; Wiffley et al., 2007). In the meantime, treatments that were developed for AN and BN should be tested with EDNOS so that practitioners will have guidance on evidence-based treatment for this diagnosis (Gowers & Bryant-Waugh, 2004).

There is also a need to test treatment beyond CBT and IPT. More studies on motivational interviewing with teenagers are required, and with long-term follow-up. Additionally, the brief treatments typically tested in randomized, controlled trials may not be appropriate for AN, which, in clinical settings, is typically treated long term with psychodynamic or eclectic therapies. Further research should be conducted on the combination of psychosocial treatment and medication and how to sequence psychosocial and pharmacological interventions (Agras, Brandt, Bulik, et al., 2004).

The methodological quality of the treatment outcome research on AN, in particular, needs to be improved. The methodological and statistical problems have included "poor or unclear randomization procedures, inadequate allocation concealment procedures, inappropriate statistics for repeated measures designs, incomplete statistical reporting . . . inattention to the effects of differential treatment duration, small sample size, nonmanualized treatments, incomplete reporting of data and analyses . . . (and) use of an excessive number of diagnostic and outcome assessment measures" (Commission on Adolescent Eating Disorders, 2005, p. 333). As a result of these problems, studies have been difficult to synthesize. Additionally, given the chronic and frequently relapsing course of eating disorders, future investigators are encouraged to evaluate outcome long term (Bacaltchuk & Hay, 2003).

Further research should also systematically include depression, anxiety, substance abuse, and personality disorders in samples because these comorbid mental health disorders are so common in eating disorders (Bacaltchuk & Hay, 2003). Appropriate treatments also need to address both the eating disorder and the cooccurring disorder, and the integration and sequencing of such treatments deserve further study. For example, versions of CBT and IPT target eating disorders, as well as depression, so how can they be used in a way that tackles these cooccurring disorders?

A final recommendation is the need to gather epidemiological data about the frequency of eating disorders and their presentation among different ethnic groups (Shapiro et al., 2007). Females of ethnic minority backgrounds must also be represented in studies and ethnicity should be a factor tested for its relationship to outcome.

CONCLUSIONS

This chapter has reviewed the state of the empirical evidence for the treatment of eating disorders, namely BN and AN. Unfortunately, there is little to guide the treatment of adolescents, although these disorders typically arise in adolescence. It must be treated then before full-blown disorders and entrenched patterns of dysfunctional attitudes and behaviors result.

CASE STUDY

Jenny, a 16-year-old Asian female, has lived at a residential treatment center for adolescent girls for 3 months. This is her first time in treatment. Jenny was born in a small rural town in Taiwan; her parents immigrated to America from Asia when Jenny was 2 years old in hopes of creating a better life for themselves. Jenny is an only child and has no close relatives in the United States. She reports that her family has always been very poor and has just "scraped by." When Jenny was 12 years old, her father and mother got into a bitter dispute over their economic situation and Jenny's father walked out on her and she hasn't seen him since. Jenny's mother, who speaks little English, began work as a seamstress. She works 12–18 hours a day, 7 days a week.

When Jenny was 14 years old, her mother couldn't afford more than a rental apartment in an impoverished, crime-ridden urban neighborhood. Jenny's mother still worked long hours, which left Jenny alone for many hours of the day. She started hanging out with peers in her neighborhood and began smoking marijuana, drinking alcohol, and taking over-the-counter diet pills or amphetamines she could "score" from her friends. Despite the diet pill use, she gained 20 pounds because she ate mainly "junk food"—cookies, potatoes chips, fast food, and so on. Eventually, she said she was using substances about five to six times a week; she then went from skipping classes to dropping out of school. Some days she was not able to get out of bed for 24 hours at a time because she was so unmotivated and unhappy. Jenny said she was so desperate to obtain alcohol and drugs that she began prostituting herself out to her male peers. She eventually contracted a sexually transmitted disease. This all occurred 6 months after her 14th birthday; 4 months ago she was arrested for drinking when underage and trying to steal a car. Jenny is currently on probation for these crimes. She reported no increased tolerance, withdrawal symptoms, or previous attempts to stop using substances. However, she realized that without treatment she would still be using.

Jenny stated her mother won't even try to learn English, whereas Jenny speaks only English. Jenny and her mother would get in verbal screaming matches when her mother would confront her about her out-of-control ways, weight gain, and drug use. Jenny said she would leave for days at a time without letting her mother know where she was. Since she has been at the residential treatment program, Jenny has had only occasional contact with her mother due to her mother's work schedule and the language division between them.

When asked how she feels, Jenny responded "fat and worthless." She said she cries daily and often thought about committing suicide and has attempted to do so on one occasion by taking about 10 aspirin and drinking. The suicide attempt occurred about 9 months ago.

When given the Beck Depression Inventory at intake, Jenny scored a 21, which represents moderate to severe depression. Because Jenny was not in school for over a year, no teacher reports were available. Jenny's mother completed the Behavior Assessment System for Children (BASC). The score for depression in the BASC was in the high/at-risk range.

Three months after Jenny was admitted to the residential treatment program, one of the other residents at the program came forward and told the staff that Jenny had been purging after meals. When the staff approached Jenny, she became confrontational and denied that she was purging. On further probing, Jenny broke down and said she had been doing this since she arrived at the program because she was depressed and also because of the availability of food in the house, which she has stolen and stashed in her room. Jenny reported that she usually feels as if she can't control how much she eats. She tells herself that she won't eat more than just a salad and some vegetables at a meal, and then always ends up "eating like a pig." After dinner, she would ask the staff if she could take a shower and then when the water was running, she would force herself to vomit in the toilet or in the shower. She did this at least three times a week.

Jenny stated that she feels "better" after she purges her food and that if she was skinny, she would not have any problems. Jenny constantly talked about how fat she is to others and compares herself to her peers. She admitted that she thought about her body weight most of the day. Jenny is about 10 pounds overweight and has not menstruated in the past 3 months.

Jenny had a difficult time waking up in the morning and is often reprimanded for not getting out of bed on time. She refused to go to school most days because she said she was "not interested" or "doesn't care." Jenny stated that she just wishes she would "die," although she doesn't have a specific plan. She reported that there is no reason for her to live because she is "stupid, ugly, and fat."

HOW THE EVIDENCE FITS

Although there is a knowledge base for CBT with adults diagnosed with bulimia nervosa, only one study has been conducted with an adolescent sample and this was carried out in a self-help format. However, CBT has also been researched for the treatment of adolescent depression, substance use disorders, and conduct disorder, comorbid disorders with which Jenny struggles. Therefore, CBT may act as the treatment of choice for her at this time.

APPLICATION

Several authors have described adaptations of CBT that take into account the specific developmental features of adolescents (Lock, 2005; Schmidt, 2009; Wilson & Sysko, 2006). An initial motivational component may be necessary as teens rarely present voluntarily for treatment. Motivational interviewing would allow Jenny to describe what she likes about her eating disorder and how it works for her and then the disadvantages of her behaviors. She could also weigh the pros and cons of changing her behavior as part of the decisional balance technique of motivational interviewing. In this way, both sides of Jenny's ambivalence would be allowed free exploration, and she could be allowed to make a decision about her treatment goals. After Jenny has reached a sufficient level of motivation (motivational interviewing is usually conducted in a one- to four-session format), she would begin CBT techniques.

As part of CBT treatment, she would first monitor her eating disorder symptoms—her binges and her vomiting—to establish her pattern of behavior and triggers. Second, she would learn assertiveness and communication strategies so that she is able to communicate more effectively with her mother and to set boundaries with others without using food as a way to do this. Third, social skills training would enable her to develop healthy friendships that are not based on substance use. Fourth, problem-solving skills would be taught so that she is empowered to handle the stressors that afflict her and to reduce her sense of hopelessness and helplessness about her life. Finally, cognitive restructuring would be an important aspect of the treatment because Jenny states that "if she were skinny, she would be happy." She would be helped to identify the extent to which these beliefs are dysfunctional and to replace them with more adaptive thoughts.

CBT for adolescents usually includes a greater level of family involvement because parents structure the teen's home environment and are responsible for grocery shopping and meal planning and preparation. However, in this case, Jenny lives in residential treatment where these activities are handled by the facility. Placement staff can also control the availability of binge food, help Jenny refrain from binging and purging by encouraging her involvement in alternative activities, and reinforce Jenny for sticking to a regular meal plan and refraining from binging and purging.

Additionally, Jenny's mother is not easily engaged in the treatment services, given her heavy work schedule and language barriers. Therefore, Jenny may be able to make progress in individual therapy before her mother is included. Also, Jenny's mother can be seen separately at first (with a translator) so that information about eating disorders and the CBT treatment can be explained to her, and she can start work on the communication skills that will be necessary for an improved relationship with her daughter.

HOW THE EVIDENCE DOES NOT FIT

Characteristics of Youth

Because our knowledge draws mainly from the treatment of BN in adults, it is still not clear how well CBT addresses eating disorders in youth, such as Jenny. Furthermore, comorbid disorders, particularly substance use disorders, have typically been screened out of the eating disorder treatment outcome research. It is not known, therefore, how CBT for the cooccurring disorders in Jenny's case—depression, substance use, and conduct disorders—may be integrated to either concurrently or sequentially address the problems she faces (see Box 8.2).

Furthermore, treatment outcome studies on eating disorders have mostly been conducted with whites. Therefore, the research provides little guidance as to the responsiveness of psychotherapy for teens of ethnic minorities, such as Jenny and her largely unacculturated mother.

Characteristics of the Client's Context

CBT focuses on the individual. Although it may help the person with relationship skills, such as communication and social skills, most CBT techniques are focused on change at the individual level. The interface with the environment is mainly on building coping skills to help the person manage environmental stress. However, Jenny has a number of stressors in her environment, such as poverty and living in a single-parent home in a high-crime neighborhood.

Another contextual problem involves the lack of knowledge about evidence-based treatment among treatment providers. Therefore, it is unknown whether practitioners at Jenny's residential program have the necessary expertise and knowledge to deliver effective treatment for her eating disorder as well as her other mental health problems.

DOES THE EVIDENCE-BASED TREATMENT TAKE ADVANTAGE OF STRENGTHS

The cognitive-behavioral treatment of eating disorders assumes that several skill deficits need amelioration (social skills, assertiveness, communication, problem solving, adaptive thinking). Considering this stance, it does not appear to address potential strengths. In terms of the positive reinforcement the facility can provide

BOX 8.2 MULTIAXIAL DIAGNOSIS FOR "JENNY"

Axis I

296.34 Major Depression, severe without psychotic features

[Rationale: Jenny's responses to the Beck Depression Inventory indicate that her depression is moderate to severe. Her mother's report on the Behavior Assessment System for Children (BASC) also corroborates a high level of depression. In clinical interview, she reports feeling sadness, emptiness, or irritability every day. She describes herself as "worthless" and says that food is her only pleasure. She has experienced weight gain as a result. Jenny has a loss of energy as shown by the fact that she remains in bed for long periods of time. She cries excessively and considers suicide. By her own report, Jenny has experienced some of these symptoms before she entered the residential treatment program, although they have intensified since being in treatment. Because she found it difficult to provide specific symptoms and time frames for symptoms, the specifier "recurrent" was not given. Jenny's depression was deemed severe because she meets almost all the criteria and because she is having persistent thoughts of death. Finally, the depression has been listed first because of its severity.]

307.51 Bulimia Nervosa, purging type

[Rationale: Jenny claims she binge eats at least three times a week with food that she has stolen and hoarded. This has been going on for the past 3 months. To compensate for the binges, Jenny prevents weight gain by vomiting. Jenny fits the purging type because she regularly engages in self-induced vomiting. She also has a history of abusing diet pills. Furthermore, Jenny's self-evaluation is unduly influenced by body shape and weight. She thinks about her weight constantly, compares herself unfavorably to others, and feels "worthless" because she says she's fat.]

304.80 Polysubstance Dependence, in a controlled environment

[Rationale: The client used at least three substances (alcohol, marijuana, and diet pills) for over a year and the "overall use of substances significantly impaired" her functioning (APA, 2000, p. 293). Her use interfered with important obligations (i.e., attending school) and contributed to conflict with her mother. Also, to buy and/or get alcohol, marijuana, and diet pills, she prostituted herself and eventually contracted a sexually transmitted disease. Furthermore, the theft of the car was done while she was drinking, so her use contributed to illegal behavior.

Jenny did not meet the criteria for dependence for each of the substances involved (alcohol, marijuana, or amphetamines) as there is no evidence of increased tolerance or symptoms of withdrawal; nor has she participated in detoxification. Although Jenny has remained sober for 3 months, she is open about the fact that if she was not in treatment, she would still be using drugs and alcohol. Therefore, the specifier "In a Controlled Environment" was included.]

312.82 Conduct Disorder, Adolescent-Onset Type, mild

[Rationale: Conduct disorder was indicated because it met at least three of the required criteria; in the area of "theft, she stole a car; she showed "serious violations of rules," including running away from home on more than two occasions for periods of time, and repeated absence from school. Her extreme sexual activity also indicates behavior in which age-appropriate societal norms are violated. These behaviors were apparent over a 12-month period, and the theft occurred 6 months ago. The behaviors began when Jenny was 14 years old; hence, it was labeled "adolescent-onset type." The specifier "mild" was

(continued)

> **BOX 8.2** MULTIAXIAL DIAGNOSIS FOR "JENNY" (CONT'D)
>
> given because she met minimal criteria and her behaviors caused only minor harm to others. The pattern of behaviors contributed to her clinically significant impairment in social (associating with only substance-using peers) and academic (truancy and eventually dropping out of school) functioning.]
>
> **Axis II V71.09**   No Diagnosis
>
> **Axis III**   None
>
> **Axis IV**
>
> Problems with Primary Support—Jenny's father has abandoned the family and she has not had contact with him in 4 years. Jenny's mother has only occasional contact with her since Jenny has been at the residential treatment program; their relationship has been marked by conflict.
>
> Educational Problems—Jenny is 2 years behind in her schooling because of truancy and dropping out.
>
> Legal Problems—Jenny is currently on probation for being arrested for drinking underage and attempting to steal a car.
>
> Problems with the Social Environment —Jenny does not have an extended family available to her, or friends that are nonusing.
> Economic problems (poverty in family)
>
> **Axis V 27**
>
> [Rationale: Major impairment in multiple areas (academic, peers, family, legal) and suicidal ideation with a previous attempt.]

Jenny for refraining from binge and purge behavior, the staff can be oriented toward times when Jenny is able to control her behavior and reinforce her for this through special privileges.

The motivational interviewing that CBT may encapsulate for adolescents with eating disorders can be viewed as a more strengths-based orientation toward treatment. Motivational interviewing assumes that a natural process of change is for individuals to feel ambivalent about their problem and about changing their problem. Techniques are geared toward exploring ambivalence, supporting the individual, and strengthening motivation to change.

CONCLUSION

9

BARRIERS TO EVIDENCE-BASED PRACTICE AND RECOMMENDATIONS

This concluding chapter discusses some of its recurring themes of this book and how these relate to the barriers and facilitators for implementation of evidence-based practice (EBP). One major barrier is the acceptance of EPB by practitioners due to the dissimilarity of research and clinical practice. Assuming that practitioners accept EBP, a second barrier is the standard of evidence they should accept. A third critical barrier is practitioner and administrator accessibility to EBPs. Recommendations for addressing these barriers through program planning, service delivery, and research will be explored (see Tables 9.1, 9.2, and 9.3).

PRACTITIONER AND ADMINISTRATOR ARGUMENTS AGAINST EVIDENCE-BASED PRACTICE

Researchers, academics, and practitioners in support of EBP are convinced of its logic. Why create new interventions for common client problems if considerable resources have already gone into developing precise intervention tools (manuals) and testing them to find positive results over control conditions? Why not use these interventions rather than one that has not been subject to intense formulation and investigation?

Despite the apparent advantages of EBP, concerns have been raised by its critics, and these need to be addressed to strengthen the knowledge base (Weisz et al., 2006). Foremost, before EBP can be implemented, it must be accepted by practitioners and administrators. The arguments against EBP, largely drawn from Norcross et al. (2005), and how these can be addressed will comprise the first section of this chapter.

TABLE 9.1 RESEARCH RECOMMENDATIONS TO REDUCE BARRIERS FOR EVIDENCE-BASED PRACTICE (EBP)

1. Comorbid disorders should be routinely allowed into research samples and the impact of treatment tested on the comorbid disorder.

2. Refine or redesign existing treatment manuals to take into account comorbidity and the social context in order to increase the relevance of EBPs.

3. Study the adaptations that clinicians make to existing treatment manuals to improve their tailoring to individual circumstances of the client.

4. Use moderator analysis in meta-analysis to discover how certain interventions address the individual and contextual factors of the child and family.

5. Test culturally sensitive treatment or the impact of models that have been researched with the mainstream culture on children of ethnic minority backgrounds.

6. Investigate other aspects of EBP as originally conceptualized: the clinician's expertise and the decision-making process; and client values.

7. Test treatment models beyond cognitive–behavioral therapy (CBT), such as family therapy, psychodynamic therapy, constructivist therapies (solution-focused, narrative), motivational interviewing, and eclectic therapy, and for the different lengths of treatments that are provided (ranging from one or two sessions for motivational interviewing and solution-focused therapy) to months-long psychodynamic therapy.

8. Investigate treatment outcome for understudied disorders in youth, namely eating disorders and reactive attachment disorder, and the problem of suicidality.

9. Treatments delivered in settings other than university-based clinics, such as inpatient hospitals, day treatment, and residential placement, should be studied.

10. Conduct clinical effectiveness studies by representative practitioners in community settings.

11. Work toward a consensus of practice guidelines across disciplines.

12. Develop university–agency partnerships to research real-world applications of EBPs.

TABLE 9.2 RECOMMENDATIONS FOR PROGRAM PLANNERS AND ADMINISTRATORS TO REDUCE BARRIERS FOR EVIDENCE-BASED PRACTICE (EBP)

1. Choose publicly available treatments rather than commercially packaged treatments to keep costs down.

2. Allow time and resources for training and supervision in EBPs.

3. Allow staff to select themselves into evidence-based treatment as providers and measure the relationship of group status (evidence-based treatment or treatment as usual) to youth outcomes (e.g., adjustment, behavior, family functioning).

4. Reach out to university departments involved in child treatment so they can conduct research and provide supervision and training.

TABLE 9.3 POLICY RECOMMENDATIONS TO REDUCE BARRIERS FOR EVIDENCE-BASED PRACTICE (EBP)

1. Increase collaboration across federal funding agencies involved in child treatment research.
2. Develop a comprehensive federal plan for financing the treatment of mental health, including provision of EBPs.
3. Dissemination of information related to EBPs could be provided through websites, national advocacy and support organizations involved in child and adolescent mental health, federal government brochures, and video presentations in the waiting rooms of public clinics.
4. Require evaluation of child and family treatment outcomes for agencies as a condition of government or grant funding.
5. Provide funding, incentives, and resources to forge more university and community agency partnerships.
6. Direct more research resources to the school system since a large proportion of children receive mental health services through the school system (Mills, Stephan, Moore, et al., 2006).
7. Require in the academic disciplines involved in mental health treatment—social work, psychology, counseling—clinical knowledge and training of EBPs in both their graduate school curriculum and continuing education.

RESEARCH IS DISSIMILAR TO CLINICAL PRACTICE

One of the central arguments against EBP and a main barrier for proponents of EBP to overcome is the possible irrelevance of results of research-based interventions to the clients seen by practitioners in clinical settings as typically practiced. EBPs differ in critical ways from treatment provided in clinical practice in terms of characteristics of participants, providers, and settings (see Table 9.4).

Characteristic of Participants

One criticism of EBPs and a recurring theme in this book has been their lack of attention to the typical comorbidity patterns of mental health disorders, as well as the social context of youth and their families. Comorbidity often acts as a screen-out criterion for randomized controlled trials. The purpose, of course, is to tightly control experiments so that internal validity emerges as a priority. However, external validity may suffer as a result, and little is known about how youth with comorbid disorders might respond to a treatment that has been designed and tested for a single disorder. As argued throughout this book, future research should accept people with comorbid disorders into studies and assess the impact of such

TABLE 9.4 DIFFERENCES BETWEEN RESEARCH STUDIES AND CLINICAL PRACTICE

Research	Clinical
Diagnostic Practices	
Often limited to a single diagnosis	Diagnosis is structured with an eye to reimbursement for agency services and least restrictive diagnosis.
Standardized diagnostic interviews	Children and families seen may have multiple problems (i.e., divorce, single-parenting, frequent moves, poverty) that are not restricted to a single DSM diagnosis.
Based on the DSM diagnostic system	There is generally a low level of agreement between diagnoses generated in clinical practice and those obtained by standardized diagnostic interviews.
Participant Characteristics	
Receive financial and other incentives for participation and attendance	Complex and severe cases with comorbidity
	Dropout of treatment
Provider Characteristics	
Learn only one specific treatment protocol and treat only one specific type of client	Typically treat a highly diverse clientele (e.g., 5–8 youths with different diagnoses in a single workday) and use a wide range of interventions
Treatment Characteristics	
Length of treatment: typically brief and specific in duration	No specific length
	There are typically only three to five sessions but it may go on for long periods of time or as booster sessions from time to time as needed.

From Silverman and Kurtines (2005) and Weisz, Doss, and Hawley (2006).

disorders on outcome. Research must also determine the type of and the sequencing of treatment that will effectively address comorbid patterns in youth.

Another theme has been the lack of attention of evidence-based interventions to the social context of the child and family (e.g., poverty, minority ethnic status, adverse family environments, and stressful life events). If these factors are left out of the equation, practitioners will find EBPs irrelevant to the circumstances of their clients. They constrain practitioners' ability to determine the best treatment course given the individual needs of the client. Therefore, a continued need for researchers is to refine or redesign existing treatment manuals to take into account the social context of individuals in order to increase the relevance of EBPs. Moderator analysis in meta-analysis can also inform the knowledge base about how certain interventions address contextual factors of the child and family.

Recall from Chapter 1 that the original definition of EBP, formulated by Sackett, Richardson, Rosenberg, & Haynes (1997), involved a decision-making process on the part of the clinician, which involves blending the research evidence, his or her own expertise and available resources, and client values. Although much focus, this book included, has been on the research support for different interventions, very little has gone into investigating the other two aspects of the decision-making process of EBP: the clinician's expertise and the decision-making process and the client values, which may constitute a range of factors, including spiritual and cultural values, expectations, preferences, and motivation (Gilgun, 2005).

Specific to one contextual variable, ethnic minority background, future research could center on testing treatment that has been created for a specific cultural group or adapted from models already tested on youth from mainstream culture (Weisz et al., 2006). It is necessary first to understand how the mental health disorder is typically experienced in a particular culture (in terms of somatic pain or spiritual malaise, for instance) and regarded by the particular community (for instance, as a stigma). Focus groups of people from the community (parents, mental health professionals, and service providers) could assess whether an intervention is compatible with the values and mores of the culture. For instance, interventions that increase the assertiveness of youth may not seem as appropriate as those that guide them toward following the rules of their parents, and cultures vary as to the appropriate expression of emotion. If available, members of the culture can deliver the intervention in the same language as the family. Practitioners must also be aware of their own level of knowledge regarding the ethnic groups with whom they work, as well as their attitudes and biases (Weisz et al., 2006).

An acknowledged difficulty is the recruitment of people from ethnic minority groups to participate in treatment outcome research (Weisz et al., 2006). The reasons are many and include the way ethnic minorities have been treated by the mainstream majority in the past, a lack of cultural match between providers and clients, the acceptability of treatment, and individual barriers, involving transportation to get to treatment and childcare for siblings while parents participate. Recruitment requires researchers to develop collaborative relationships with community agencies and professionals, including the schools, juvenile services, clergy, and mental health and health providers (Weisz et al., 2006).

Of relevance here is that knowledge of EBPs is typically low among family members and youth, especially for nonnative speakers (Cooper, Aratani, Knitzer, et al., 2008). Dissemination of information related to EPBs could be provided through websites, national advocacy and support organizations involved in child and adolescent mental health, federal government brochures, and video presentations in the waiting rooms of service providers and public clinics.

Another argument against EBPs is that they are viewed as being an overly structured approach to intervention due to their use of treatment manuals, a defining feature of EBPs. To address the supposed rigidity of EBP, Nock et al. (2004) argue that although treatment manuals delineate procedures and guidelines, they do not dictate "every word and action." Indeed, modifications may be necessary because of developmental stage, comorbidity, or other concurrent problems afflicting the child or the family.

However, this level of adaptation may detract from the fidelity of the treatment, and fidelity to treatment has been associated with better outcomes (Lipsey, Landenberger, & Wilson, 2007; Wilson et al., 2003). Although clinicians routinely use eclectic approaches to tailor treatment to an individual, "There are no formal or clearly replicable procedures for how to do this, in terms of selecting one or more treatments or components of treatment among all available therapies and deciding in what proportion and sequence they ought to be delivered to patients. [Also,] it is not yet well established that different clinicians would select the same or a similar individualized treatment plan (i.e., reliability) when presented with the same case" (Kazdin, 2008, p. 149).

The lack of flexibility of EBPs is further seen as interfering with rapport building and the development of a good therapeutic relationship and working alliance, which is seen as necessary to maintain attendance and foster good outcomes (Weisz, Doss, & Hawley, 2005). The association between therapist–client relationship factors and outcome was examined through a meta-analysis of 49 child and adolescent treatment outcome studies and was found to be moderate in nature ($r = 0.28$) (Karver, Handelsman, & Fields, 2006). Recall, however, that many of the treatment effect sizes for child mental health disorders have been small (i.e., depression, posttraumatic stress disorder, individual treatment for youth antisocial behavior). The fact that relationship factors are moderately related to outcome signals that they represent key variables of the therapeutic process, perhaps more so than the particular type of treatment (Wampold, 2001).

Characteristics of Interventions

Another argument against EBP is that cognitive–behavioral therapy (CBT) represents much of the research undertaken and is therefore overly represented on lists of EBTs. If clinicians practice outside the framework of CBT, they can easily argue that other treatments might be equally as effective, if not more so, than CBT, although they have yet to be tested. CBT arose out of a research tradition; its skills-based and step-by-step procedures lend themselves to manualization, whereas other psychotherapies often do not.

Furthermore, EBTs have not necessarily proven themselves as more beneficial than other active control conditions when compared (Brown et al., 2007). This issue has been studied empirically through two meta-analyses. Weisz, Doss, and Hawley (2006) compared EBTs to treatment as typically practiced in clinics (treatment as usual). They found that EBT outperformed treatment as usual by a small effect with treatment as usual showing negligible effects on outcome. More recently, Miller, Wampold, and Varhely (2008) examined the differences between active comparison treatments. Although some aspects of their meta-analysis might have been flawed (they argued for the use of combining dependent variables in studies and some of the comparisons in studies were not independent), they reached the same conclusion as Weisz in that EBTs produced a small effect over comparison conditions. They further examined therapist allegiance to treatment and discovered that this reduced the small advantage of EBT to zero.

An implication for future treatment outcome studies is that they must broaden their theoretical perspectives beyond CBT to psychotherapies such as family therapy, psychodynamic therapy (other than interpersonal therapy), constructivist therapies (solution-focused, narrative), and eclectic therapy, models seen in practice more commonly than CBT (Weisz, Doss, & Hawley, 2005). Motivational interviewing is also a promising approach for certain disorders in which motivation can play a key component, such as eating disorders, substance use disorders, and antisocial problems, and deserves further investigation in youth mental health treatment.

As well as diversifying coverage on understudied theoretical orientations, there are certain problems and disorders that deserve more research attention (Weisz, Doss, & Hawley, 2005). As noted in Chapter 8, very little investigation exists on eating disorders in adolescence, a time when most symptoms begin. The research is particularly scant on the treatment of Eating Disorder Not Otherwise Specified, which is the typical diagnosis given to adolescents. Eating disorders often run a chronic course, and risk of premature death (especially for anorexia nervosa) is high. Reactive attachment disorder is another problem with potentially deleterious consequences in terms of personal and family suffering and high costs for the restrictive settings that often serve those afflicted. Such a diagnosis is likely most often seen in Child Protective services settings where knowledge of EBTs is low. A final clinical problem related to depression is suicidality, which so far has remained unaffected by the few available interventions, and is of obvious paramount concern.

An additional way in which research and clinical treatments depart is the length of intervention. Most research trials are brief, involving about 12–18 sessions, but people in clinic settings are often seen for shorter periods of time, such as three to four sessions; additionally, therefore, research needs to reflect these different levels of service usage (Weisz, Doss, & Hawley, 2005).

Characteristics of Settings

Research-based treatment is typically undertaken in university-affiliated outpatient settings. Practitioners working in other settings, such as inpatient hospitals, day treatment, and residential placement, are left without guidance for EBT (Weisz et al., 2005). Armelius and Andreassen's (2007) systematic review on CBT for youth antisocial behavior in residential treatment settings is a notable exception.

The fragmentation of the mental health treatment delivery system in the United States means that often children's mental health needs are served by other systems, such as schools, primary care, particularly for those who receive Medicaid, juvenile justice, and child welfare. Because these other systems have not developed with mental health in mind, levels of unmet needs are often high (American Psychological Association Task Force on Evidence-Based Practice for Children and Adolescents, 2008). Multiple risks, such as poverty, community violence, exposure to drugs and alcohol, and maltreatment, may also be present for youth in such systems (Huang et al., 2005).

One problem specific to the Medicaid system is that such children are more likely to receive medication and, specifically, antipsychotics, than middle-class youth (Crystal, Olfson, Huang, Pincus, & Gerhard, 2009). Evidence-based psychotherapies are underutilized for these youth because medication is reimbursed at a higher rate for providers. An additional risk for receiving treatment in these other systems is that interventions implemented by personnel untrained in mental health counseling may yield poor outcomes. For example, Lipsey, Landenberger, and Wilson (2007) found that when criminal justice personnel administered CBT programs for offenders, outcomes were negatively affected.

Furthermore, a barrier to the implementation of EBT in child welfare and juvenile justice settings is that administrators of state and county systems are not familiar with EBT for mental health disorders. A potential facilitator in these settings would be to mandate conditions for treatment contract providers; to win a contract, in their bids potential agency providers would have to state their knowledge and capacity for the implementation of EBT.

A policy recommendation to reduce the fragmentation of the mental health treatment system is to increase collaboration across federal funding agencies involved in child treatment research (i.e., National Institutes of Mental Health, National Institute of Child Health and Human Development, National Institutes of Natural Sciences, the Agency for Healthcare Research and Quality, the Centers for Disease Control and Prevention, the Substance Abuse and Mental Health Services Administration, and the Institute for Education Science) (Brown et al., 2007). In addition, at the federal level, a comprehensive plan for financing the treatment of mental health must be developed, so that fragmentation of services is reduced (Cooper, Aratani, Knitzer, et al., 2008).

To increase the relevance of EBPs for administrators, practitioners, and other front-line staff, research needs to be conducted in the context they experience. There is general agreement that the next stage of research should involve clinical effectiveness studies by representative practitioners in community settings (Weissman, Verdeli, Gameroff, et al., 2006). This will entail conducting intervention research in collaboration with mental health providers (Weisz, Doss, & Hawley, 2006).

Because some agency staff will likely be resistant to learning and using new treatment models, a specific recommendation for administrators is to allow staff to self-select whether they want to be trained and supervised in a particular EBT. Over time, the impact of the EBT on certain child and adolescent mental health disorders can be evaluated relative to the treatment as usual to determine empirically the relative advantage of either treatment on youth and family outcomes. This may be a way to both set up naturally occurring comparison groups and avoid mandating staff to adopt treatments in which they are not interested.

WHAT STANDARD OF EVIDENCE SHOULD BE CHOSEN?

Assuming that practitioners, administrators, and policymakers accept the notion of EBT, a barrier to its implementation is that no standard of evidence is widely accepted among the different disciplines involved in mental health treatment. Even those who are motivated to pursue EBT and families seeking information will be confused about which guidelines to follow (Weisz, Jensen, & McLeod, 2005). To address this problem, researchers may well need to work toward a "broad consensus across disciplines" (Weisz & Addis, 2006, p. 197).

This book works with two standards of EBT—systematic reviews and meta-analyses with preference given to those conducted with Cochrane methodology and the APA Psychological 12 Task Force Criteria. However, there are other systems for classifying the results of treatment outcome studies (Nathan & Gorman, 2007; California Evidence-Based Clearinghouse for Child Welfare, http://www.cachildwelfareclearinghouse.org/; Roth and Fonagy, 2005; U.S. Health and Human Services Agency for Healthcare Research and Quality, http://www.ahrq.gov/clinic/epcindex.htm#psychiatry).

In general, however, it appears that quantitative syntheses of the literature can better inform the field of mental health than reliance on categorical systems, which involved a cruder level of measurement. Indeed, the medical field now uses systematic reviews and meta-analyses as their standard for synthesizing results of clinical trials of evidence (Littell et al., 2008). Most of the categorical systems rely on the published literature only, limit the time span included (e.g., the updated APA reviews in the recent issue of the *Journal of Clinical Child and Adolescent Psychology* focused only on the past 10 years), and do not include a systematic and comprehensive method for locating relevant studies. Furthermore, research flaws can be more easily concealed (Gambrill, 2007). Littell (2005) described how multisystemic therapy was routinely assessed as an EBT by several federal agencies, including the National Institute on Drug Abuse, National Institute on Mental Health, Surgeon General's office, Center for Substance Abuse Prevention, the Office of Juvenile Justice and Delinquency Prevention, and the Substance Abuse and Mental Health Services Administration. However, when Littell et al. (2005)

applied the Cochrane Collaboration methodology to systematic reviews, she found, when meta-analyzing results of studies into their various outcomes, that none of the average effect sizes was significantly better than the alternative treatment provided. Furthermore, by carefully assessing methodology of the primary studies, Littell et al. (2005) found flaws in study design and randomization procedures that called into question the multisystemic therapy (MST) researchers' claims that they employed experimental designs.

Finally, systematic reviews and meta-analyses, when considering the body of studies in a certain area, can determine, through moderator analysis, the kinds of participants, treatments, settings, or research design characteristics that can account for variation in outcome. As discussed, in making EPBs relevant to practitioners it is critical to take into account the characteristics of participants, interventions, and settings, and this can be achieved through moderator analysis.

For systematic reviews and meta-analyses to be conducted, primary studies have to be methodologically rigorous and conform to reporting standards as prescribed by the CONSORT guidelines (Moher, Schulz, & Altman, 2001; http://www.consort-statement.org/). The CONSORT guidelines have been adopted as the standard for reporting trials in medicine and in journals of the American Psychological Association. Similar statements are available to guide reporting on nonrandomized trials (Caetano, 2004). Additionally, conventional and updated meta-analytic techniques must be used in published studies, including using pooled effect sizes weighting by inverse variance methods, computing effect sizes based on a comparison of between-group differences, maintaining independence, and using newer methods of assessing publication bias. As a result of limitations of meta-analyses, many recent publications unfortunately do not contribute to the state of the evidence basis for child and adolescent mental health treatment. Finally, standards for reporting meta-analyses of randomized controlled trials have been developed. Originally called QUOROM (Quality Of Reporting On Meta-analyses of randomized controlled trials) (Moher et al., 1999), it is now entitled PRISMA (for Primary Reporting Items for Systematic reviews and Meta-Analysis). More standardization of reporting in both primary studies and their syntheses will contribute to improving knowledge accumulation.

LACK OF ACCESSIBILITY OF EVIDENCE-BASED PRACTICE

Other barriers for implementation of EBTs relate to the lack of accessibility of EBT in terms of obtainability, cost, and training. The majority of interventions are described only briefly in the article published on the study, and are not obtainable through manuals or videos (Chorpita et al., 2007).

Specific to CBT, treatments are often represented by different manuals. Because many of these share overlapping strategies, practitioners will have difficulty knowing which ones to choose for certain clients and situations (Kazdin et al., 1990 as cited in Chorpita, Becker, & Daleiden, 2007). Furthermore, CBT is often offered as a package of techniques. Research could address how clinicians can offer more focused treatment by understanding the necessary and sufficient components of such a package (Weisz, Sandler, Durlak, & Anton, 2005).

A facilitator for selection of cost-effective EBTs is the use of manuals that are publicly available rather than commercially based packages. For instance, Lipsey, Landenberger, and Wilson (2007) found that noncommercially based CBT programs were as effective as commercial packages for adults and juveniles who had been in trouble for criminal offending. The important variable in this meta-analysis was a high degree of treatment fidelity.

Another barrier related to accessibility is the ability of the treatment workforce to have adequate training and supervision to implement EBPs. Graduate school education in the professions responsible for supplying the mental health workforce and continuing education requirements as part of licensing for these professions are discussed.

Weissman, Verdeli, Gameroff, et al. (2006) surveyed training directors of psychiatry, psychology, and social work programs in the United States to determine the extent of "gold standard training" present in graduate school education for evidence-based psychotherapy. "Gold standard training" is defined as both a didactic course and supervised clinical work in a particular treatment model. The two disciplines with the largest number of students and the emphasis on training for clinical practice, the PsyD and the MSW, required the lowest percentage of gold standard training in EBP. Social work faculty explained the lack of coursework and clinical supervision for EBPs by the fact that their mandate was not to provide training in psychotherapy. Indeed, the mission of social work is to bring services and resources to oppressed and vulnerable populations to improve quality of life and to bring about social economic and justice (NASW, 1999). This mission may include psychotherapy, but also means the provision of other direct services to people in need, as well as community action and policy advocacy. However, Weissman et al. (2006) reported evidence that social workers are providing psychotherapy annually to 0.5% of the adult population. Additionally, most EBTs grew out of research by psychologists and psychiatrists, whereas social workers have not generally emphasized research as the path to effective treatment" (Weisz, Jensen, & McLeod, 2005).

In the Weissman et al. (2006) survey results, psychiatry had the highest rate of compliance with EBT, likely because accreditation requirements mandated training in EBT. This finding suggests that accreditation requirements, rather than voluntary changes, are effective in changing practice. A recommendation is that, at a minimum, clinical graduate school programs must have one course on CBT and one course on interpersonal therapy with practice-based supervision, the gold standard for training (Mullen, Bellamy, Bledsoe, & Francois, 2007). Additionally, continuing education should require training in EBTs.

CONCLUSIONS

This chapter has focused on barriers to implementation of EBTs and how these can be circumvented. Although there are substantial arguments for the practice of EBT, there are also very sound reasons against its use, which mainly involve the complexities of intervening children and adolescents with multiple needs in typical service delivery systems. These arguments and realities will have to be addressed by their proponents with a greater melding of research with clinical practice to advance the state of EBT.

REFERENCES

CHAPTER 1

American Psychiatric Association. (2000). *Diagnostic and statistical manual of mental disorders* (4th ed., text rev.). Washington, DC: Author.

Arthur, M., Hawkins, J., Pollard, J., Catalano, R., & Baglioni Jr., A. (2002). Measuring risk and protective factors for substance use, delinquency, and other adolescent problem behaviors. *Evaluation Review, 26*(6), 575.

Birmaher, B., Axelson, D., Strober, M., Gill, M., Valeri, S., Chiappetta, L., Ryan, N., Leonard, H., Hunt, J., Iyenger, S., Keller, M. (2006). Clinical course of children and adolescents with bipolar spectrum disorders. *Archives of General Psychiatry, 63*(2), 175–183.

Bogenschneider, K. (1996). An ecological risk/protective theory for building prevention programs, policies, and community capacity to support your. *Family Relations, 45*(2), 127–138.

Burns, B., Phillips, S., Wagner, H., Barth, R., Kolko, D., Campbell, Y., et al. (2004). Mental Health Need and Access to Mental Health Services by Youths Involved With Child Welfare: A National Survey. *Journal of the American Academy of Child & Adolescent Psychiatry, 43*(8), 960–970.

Caplan, P., & Cosgrove, L. (Eds.). (2004). *Bias in psychiatric diagnosis.* Lanham, MD: Jason Aronson.

Chambless, D. L., and Hollon, S. D. (1998). Defining empirically supported therapies. *Journal of Consulting and Clinical Psychology, 66,* 7–18.

Cohen, J. (1969). *Statistical power analysis for the behavioral sciences.* New York: Academic Press.

Cohen, J. (1988). *Statistical power analysis for behavioral sciences,* 2nd ed. Hillsdale, NJ: Lawrence Erlbaum Associates.

Cooper, J., Aratani, Y., Knitzer, J., Douglas-Hall, A., Masi, R., Banghart, P., and Dababnah, S. (2008).*Unclaimed Children Revisited: The Status of Children's Mental Health Policy in the United States.* Retrieved 2010, from http://www.nccp.org/publications/pub_853.html.

Costello, E. J., Egger, H., & Angold, A. (2005). 10-year research update review: The epidemiology of child and adolescent psychiatric disorders: I. Methods and public health burden. *Journal of the American Academy of Child and Adolescent Psychiatry, 44,* 972–986.

Dekovic, M. (1999). Risk and protective factors in the development of problem behavior during adolescence. *Journal of Youth and Adolescence*, 28(6), 667–685.

Dickersin, K. (2005). Publication bias: Recognizing the problem, understanding its origins and scope, and preventing harm. In H. R. Rothstein, A. J. Sutton, & M. Borenstein (Eds.), *Publication bias in meta-analysis: Prevention, assessment, and adjustments* (pp. 11–33). Chichester, UK: John Wiley & Sons.

Doss, A., & Weisz, J. R. (2008). Diagnostic agreement predicts treatment process and outcomes in youth mental health clinics. *Journal of Consulting and Clinical Psychology*, 76(5), 711–722.

Fazel, S., Doll, H., & Långström, N. (2008). Mental disorders among adolescents in juvenile detention and correctional facilities: a systematic review and metaregression analysis of 25 surveys. *Journal of the American Academy of Child and Adolescent Psychiatry*, 47(9), 1010–1019.

Grant, B., Hasin, D., Blanco, C., Stinson, F., Chou, S., Goldstein, R., et al. (2005). The epidemiology of social anxiety disorder in the United States: results from the National Epidemiologic Survey on Alcohol and Related Conditions. *The Journal Of Clinical Psychiatry*, 66(11), 1351–1361.

Harris, G., & Carey, B. (2008). Researchers fail to reveal full drug pay. *New York Times*. Downloaded on January 5, 2009 at http://www.nytimes.com/2008/06/08/us/08conflict.html?_r=1&page wanted=print.

Kessler, R. C., Adler, L. A., Barkley, R., Biederman, J., Conners, C. K., Faraone, S. V., et al. (2005). Patterns and predictors of attention deficit/hyperactivity disorder persistence into adulthood: Results from the National Comorbidity Survey Replication. *Biological Psychiatry*, 57, 1442–1451.

Knitzer, J. (1982). *Unclaimed children: The failure of public responsibility to children and adolescents in need of mental health services*. Washington, DC: Children's Defense Fund.

Kutchins, H., & Kirk, S. (1997). *Making us crazy: DSM: The psychiatric bible and the creation of mental disorders*. New York, NY US: Free Press.

Lemery, K., & Doelger, L. (2005). Genetic Vulnerabilities to the Development of Psychopathology. *Development of psychopathology: A vulnerability-stress perspective* (pp. 161–198). Thousand Oaks, CA US: Sage Publications, Inc.

Lipsey, M. W., & Wilson, D. B. (2001). *Practical meta-analysis*. Thousand Oaks, CA: Sage.

Littell, J. (2005). Lessons from a systematic review of effects of multisystemic therapy. *Children and Youth Services Review*, 27(4), 445–463.

Littel, J., Corcoran, J., & Pillai, V. (2008). *Systematic reviews and meta-analysis*. New York: Oxford University Press.

Mash, E., & Barkley, R. (2007). *Assessment of childhood disorders*, 4th ed. New York: Guilford Publications.

McMillen, J. C., Scott, L., Zima, B., Ollie, M., Munson, M., & Spitznagel, E. (2004). Use of mental health services among older youths in foster care. *Psychiatric Services*, 55, 811–817.

Norcross, J., Beutler, L., & Levant, R. (2005). *Evidence-based practices in mental health: Debate and dialogue on the fundamental questions*. Washington, DC: American Psychological Association.

Pompili, M., Mancinelli, I., Girardi, P., Ruberto, A., & Tatarelli, R. (2004). Suicide in anorexia nervosa: a meta-analysis. *International Journal of Eating Disorders*, 36(1), 99–103.

President's New Freedom Commission on Mental Health. (2003). *Achieving the promise: Transforming mental health care in America. Final Report*. Downloaded on January 21, 2009 from http://www.mentalhealthcommission.gov/reports/FinalReport/downloads/downloads.html.

Proctor, E. K. (2007). Implementing evidence-based practice in social work education: Principles, strategies, and partnerships. *Research on Social Work Practice, 17*(5), 583–591.

Rubin, A., & Parrish, D. (2007). Views of Evidence-Based Practice Among Faculty in Master of Social Work Programs: A National Survey. *Research on Social Work Practice, 17*(1), 110–122.

Rutter, M. (1987). Psychosocial resilience and protective mechanisms. *American Journal of Orthopsychiatry, 57*, 316–331.

Rutter, M., Maugham, N., Mortimore, P., & Ouston, J. (1979). *Fifteen thousand hours.* Cambridge, MA: Harvard University Press.

Sackett, D. L., Richardson, W. S., Rosenberg, W., & Haynes, R. B. (1997). *Evidence-Based Medicine— How to Practice and Teach EBM.* New York: Churchill Livingstone.

Shaffer, D., Schwab-Stone, M., Fisher, P. W., Cohen, P., Piacentini, J., Davies, M., et al. (1993). The Diagnostic Interview Schedule for Children–Revised version (DISC–R): I. Preparation, field testing, interrater reliability, and acceptability. *Journal of the American Academy of Child & Adolescent Psychiatry, 32*(3), 643–650.

U.S. Department of Health and Human Services. (1999). *Mental health: A report of the surgeon general.* Retrieved 2010, from http://www.surgeongeneral.gov/library/mentalhealth/home.html.

Wallerstein, J., & Lewis, J. (1998). The long-term impact of divorce on children: A first report from a 25-year study. *Family & Conciliation Courts Review, 36*(3), 368–383.

Werner, E. (2000). Protective factors and individual resilience. In J. Shonoff & S. Meisels (Eds.), *Handbook of early childhood intervention, 2nd ed.* (pp. 115–133). Cambridge: Cambridge University Press.

Werner, E., & Smith, R. (1982). *Vulnerable but invincible: A longitudinal study of resilient children and youth.* New York: McGraw-Hill.

Werner, E., & Smith, R. (2001). *Journeys from childhood to midlife.* Ithaca, NY: Cornell University Press.

Weisz, J., Jensen, A., & McLeod, B. (2005). *Development and Dissemination of Child and Adolescent Psychotherapies: Milestones, Methods, and a New Deployment-Focused Model. Psychosocial treatments for child and adolescent disorders: Empirically based strategies for clinical practice* (2nd ed.) (pp. 9–39). Washington, DC US: American Psychological Association.

Zlotnik, J. (2007). Evidence-based practice and social work education: A view from Washington. *Research on Social Work Practice, 17*(5), 625–629.

CHAPTER 2

American Academy of Child and Adolescent Psychiatry. (2007). Practice parameter for the assessment and treatment of children and adolescents with attention-deficit/hyperactivity disorder. *Journal of the American Academy of Child and Adolescent Psychiatry, 46*, 894–921.

American Psychiatric Association (2000). *Diagnostic and statistical manual of mental disorders* (4th ed. Text revision). Washington, DC: Author.

Arnold, L. (1996). Sex differences in ADHD. *Journal of Abnormal Child Psychology, 24*, 555–569.

Arnold, L. E., Elliott, M., Sachs, L., Bird, H., Kraemer, H. C., Wells, K. C., Abikoff, H. B., Comarda, A., Conners, C. K., Elliott, G. R., Greenhill, L. L., Hechtman, L., Hinshaw, S. P., Hoza, B., Jensen, P. S., March, J. S., Newcorn, J. H., Pelham, W. E., Severe, J. B., Swanson, J. M., Vitiello, B., & Wigal, T. (2003). Effects of ethnicity on treatment attendance, stimulant response/dose, and 14-month outcome in ADHD. *Journal of Consulting and Clinical Psychology, 71*(4), 713–727.

Bailey, R. K., & Owens, D. L. (2005). Overcoming challenges in the diagnosis and treatment of attention-deficit/hyperactivity disorder in African Americans. *Supplement to the Journal of the National Medical Association, 97*, 5–16.

Barkley, R. A., Fischer, M., Smallish, L., & Fletcher, K. (2004). Young adult follow-up of hyperactive children: Antisocial activities and drug use. *Journal of Child Psychology and Psychiatry, 45*(2), 195–211.

Barkley, R. A., & Murphy, K. R. (2006). *Attention-deficit hyperactivity disorder* (3rd ed.): *A clinical workbook*. New York: Guilford Press.

Bentley, K., & Walsh, J. (2006). *The social worker and psychotropic medication* (3rd ed.). Pacific Grove, CA: Brooks/Cole.

Bhutta, A., Cleves, M., Casey, P., Cradock, M., & Anand, K. (2002). Cognitive and behavioral outcomes of school-aged children who were born preterm: A meta-analysis. *Journal of the American Medical Association, 288*, 728–737.

Biederman J. (2005). Attention-deficit/hyperactivity disorder: A selective overview. *Biological Psychiatry, 57*(11), 1215–1220.

Biederman, J., Ball, S. W., Monuteaux, M. C., Mick E., Spencer, T. J., McCreary, M., Cote, M., & Faraone S. V. (2008). New insights into the comorbidity between ADHD and major depression in adolescent and young adult females. *Journal of the American Academy of Child & Adolescent Psychiatry, 47*(4), 426–434.

Biederman, J., Petty, C. R., Dolan, C., et al. (2008). The long-term longitudinal course of oppositional defiant disorder and conduct disorder in ADHD boys: Findings from a controlled 10-year prospective longitudinal follow-up study. *Psychological Medicine, 38*(7), 1027–1036.

Bjornstad, G., & Montgomery, P. (2005). Family therapy for attention-deficit disorder or attention-deficit/hyperactivity disorder in children and adolescents. *Cochrane Database of Systematic Reviews, 2*, CD005042.

Bloom B., & Dey A. N. (2006). Summary health statistics for U.S. children. *National Health Interview Survey, 2004*, (227), 1–85.

Braun, J., Kahn, R., Froehlich, T., Auginger, P., & Lamphear, B. (2006). Exposures to environmental toxicants and attention deficit hyperactivity disorder in U.S. children. *Environmental Health Perspectives, 114*, 12.

Briscoe-Smith, A. M., & Hinshaw, S. P. (2006). Linkages between child abuse and attention-deficit/hyperactivity disorder in girls: Behavioral and social correlates. *Child Abuse & Neglect, 30*(11), 1239–1255.

Brown, R. T., Antonuccio, D. O., Dupaul, G. J., Fristad, M. A., King, C. A., Leslie, L. K., McCormick, G. S., Pelham, W. E., Piacentini, J. C., & Vitiello, B. (2007). *Childhood mental health disorders: Evidence-base and contextual factors for psychosocial, psychopharmacological, and combined interventions*. Washington, DC: American Psychological Association.

Centers for Disease Control and Prevention. (2005). Mental health in the United States. Prevalence of diagnosis and medication treatment for attention-deficit/hyperactivity disorder—United States, 2003. *Morbidity and Mortality Weekly Report, 54*, 842–847.

Cheng, J. Y., Chen, R. Y., Ko, J. S., & Ng, E. M. (2007). Efficacy and safety of atomoxetine for attention-deficit/hyperactivity disorder in children and adolescents-meta-analysis and meta-regression analysis. *Psychopharmacology, 194*(2), 197–209.

Chronis, A., Jones, H., Lahey, B., Rathouz, P., Pelham, W., Jr., Williams, S., et al. (2007). Maternal depression and early positive parenting predict future conduct problems in young children with attention-deficit/hyperactivity disorder. *Developmental Psychology, 43*(1), 70–82.

Chronis, A. M., Gamble, S. A., Roberts, J. E., & Pelham, W. E. (2006). Cognitive-behavioral depression treatment for mothers of children with attention-deficit/hyperactivity disorder. *Behavior Therapy, 37,* 143–158.

Conners, C. K., Epstein, J. N., March, J. S., et al (2001) Multimodal treatment of ADHD in the MTA: An alternative outcome analysis. *Journal of the American Academy of Child and Adolescent Psychiatry, 40*(2), 159–167.

Connor, D., Glatt, S., Lopez, I., Jackson, D., & Melloni, R. (2002). Psychopharmacology and aggression; I. A meta-analysis of stimulant effects on overt/covert aggression-related behaviors in ADHD. *Journal of the American Academy of Child and Adolescent Psychiatry, 41,* 253–262.

Corcoran, J., & Dattalo, P. (2006). Parent involvement in treatment for ADHD: A meta-analysis of the published studies. *Research in Social Work Practice, 16,* 561–570.

Counts, C. A., Nigg, J. T., Stawicki, J. A., Rappley, M. D., & von Eye, A. (2005). Family adversity in DMS-IV ADHD combined and inattentive subtypes and associated disruptive behavior problems. *Journal of the American Academy of Child Adolescent Psychiatry, 44*(7), 690–698.

Cuffe, S. P., McKeown, R. E., Jackson, K. L., Addy, C. L., Abramson, R., & Garrison, C. Z. (2001). Prevalence of attention-deficit/hyperactivity disorder in a community sample of older adolescents. *Journal of the American Academy of Child and Adolescent Psychiatry, 40*(9), 1037–1044.

Derks, E. M., Dolan, C. V., Hudziak, J. J., Neale, M. C., & Boomsma, D. I. (2007). Assessment and etiology of attention deficit hyperactivity disorder and oppositional defiant disorder in boys and girls. *Behavior and Genetics, 37*(4), 559–566.

DuPaul, G. J., & Power, T. J. (2000). Educational interventions for students with attention-deficit disorders. In T. Brown (Ed.), *Attention-deficit disorders and comorbidities in children, adolescents, and adults* (pp. 607–634). Washington, DC: American Psychiatric Press, Inc.

Fabiano, G. (2007). Father participation in behavioral parent training for ADHD: Review and recommendations for increasing inclusion and engagement. *Journal of Family Psychology, 21*(4), 683–693.

Faraone, S. V., & Biederman, J. (2002). Efficacy of adderall for attention-deficit/hyperactivity disorder: A meta-analysis. *Journal of Attention Disorders, 6*(2), 69–75.

Faraone, S. V., Biederman, J., Morley, C. P., & Spencer, T. J. (2008). Effect of stimulants on height and weight: A review of the literature. *Journal of the American Academy of Child and Adolescent Psychiatry, 47*(9), 994–1009.

Faraone, S. V., & Khan, S. A. (2006). Candidate gene studies of attention-deficit/hyperactivity disorder. *Journal of Clinical Psychiatry, 67*(8), 13–20.

Faraone, S. V., Perlis, R. H., Doyle, A. E., et al. (2005). Molecular genetics of attention-deficit/hyperactivity disorder. *Biology and Psychiatry, 57,* 1313–1323.

Ford, T., Goodman, R., & Meltzer, H. (2004). The relative importance of child, family, school and neighborhood correlates of childhood psychiatric disorder. *Social Psychiatry and Psychiatric Epidemiology, 39*(6), 487–496.

Hinshaw, S. P. (2007). Moderators and mediators of treatment outcome for youth with ADHD: Understanding for whom and how interventions work. *Journal of Pediatric Psychology, 32,* 664–675.

Hinshaw, S. P., Owens, E. B., & Sami, N. (2006). Prospective follow-up of girls with attention-deficit/hyperactivity disorder into adolescence: Evidence for continuing cross-domain impairment. *Journal of Consulting and Clinical Psychology, 74*(3), 489–499.

Huey, S. J., & Polo, A J. (2008). Evidence-based psychosocial treatments for ethnic minority youth. *Journal of Clinical Child and Adolescent Psychology, 37*, 262–301.

Jacobvitz, D., Hazen, N., Curran, M., & Hitchens, K. (2004). Observations of early triadic family interactions: Boundary disturbances in the family predict symptoms of depression, anxiety, and attention-deficit/hyperactivity disorder in middle childhood. *Development and Psychopathology, 16*, 577–592.

Jensen, P. S., Arnold, L. E., Swanson, J. M., Vitiello, B., Abikoff, H. B., Greenhill, L.L., Hechtman, L., Hinshaw, S. P., Pelham, W. E., Wells, K. C., Conners, C. K., Elliott, G. R., Epstein, J. N., Hoza, B., March, J. S., Molina, B. S. G., Newcorn, J. H., Severe, J. B., Wigal, T., Gibbons, R. D., & Hur, K. (2007). Three-year follow-up of the NIMH MTA study. *Journal of the American Academy of Child & Adolescent Psychiatry, 46*(8), 989–1002.

Jensen, P., & Hinshaw, S. (2001). ADHD comorbidity findings from the MTA study: Comparing comorbid subgroups. *Journal of the American Academy of Child & Adolescent Psychiatry, 40*(2), 147.

Kahn, R. S., Khoury, J., Nichols, W. C., & Lanphear, B. P. (2003). Role of dopamine transporter genotype and maternal prenatal smoking in childhood hyperactive-impulsive, inattentive, and oppositional behaviors. *Journal of Pediatrics, 143*(1), 104–110.

Kessler, R. C., Adler, L. A., Barkley, R., Biederman, J., Conners, C. K., & Faraone, S. V., et al. (2005). Pattererns and predictors of attention deficit/hyperactivity disorder persistence into adulthood: Results from the National Comorbidity Survey Replication. *Biological Psychiatry, 57*, 1442–1451.

King, S., Griffin, S., Hodges, Z., Weatherly, H., Asseburg, C., Richardson, G., Golder, S., Taylor, E., Drummond, M., & Riemsma, R. (2006). A systematic review and economic model of the effectiveness and cost-effectiveness of methylphenidate, dexamfetamine and atomoxetine for the treatment of attention deficit hyperactivity disorder in children and adolescents. *Health Technology Assessment, 10*, 125.

Kreppner, J., O'Connor, T., & Rutter, M. (2001). Can inattention/overactivity be an institutional deprivation syndrome? *Journal of Abnormal Child Psychology, 29*, 513–529.

Lahey, B., Hartung, C., Loney, J., Pelham, W., Chronis, A., & Lee, S. (2007). Empirical articles: Are there sex differences in the predictive validity of DSM–IV ADHD among younger children? *Journal of Clinical Child & Adolescent Psychology, 36*(2), 113–126.

Laucht, M., Skowronek, M. H., Becker, K., et al. (2007). Interacting effects of the dopamine transporter gene and psychosocial adversity on attention-deficit/hyperactivity disorder symptoms among 15-year-olds from a high-risk community sample. *Archives of General Psychiatry, 64*(5), 585–590.

Levy, F., Hay, D. A., & Bennett, K. S. (2006). Genetics of attention deficit hyperactivity disorder: A current review and future prospects. *International Journal of Disability, Development and Education, 53*(1).

Lundahl, B., Tollefson, D., Risser, H., & Lovejoy, M. (2008). A meta-analysis of father involvement in parent training. *Research on Social Work Practice, 18*(2), 97–106.

Mannuzza, S., & Klein, R. (1999). Adolescent and adult outcomes in attention-deficit/hyperactivity disorder. In H. Quay & A. Hogan (Eds.), *Handbook of disruptive behavior disorders* (pp. 279–294). New York: Plenum Publishers.

McClellan, J., & Werry, J.S. (2003). Evidence-based treatments in child and adolescent psychiatry: An inventory. *Journal of the American Academy of Child and Adolescent Psychiatry, 42*, 1388–1400.

Miller C. J., Flory J. D., Miller S. R., Harty S. C., et al. (2008). Childhood attention-deficit/hyperactivity disorder and the emergence of personality disorders in adolescence: A prospective follow-up study. *Journal of Clinical Psychiatry, 69*(9), 1477–1484.

Miller, T., Nigg, J., & Miller, R. (2009). Attention deficit hyperactivity disorder in African American children: What can be concluded from the past ten years? *Clinical Psychology Review, 29*, 77–86.

Monuteaux, M. C., Faraone, S. V., Michelle Gross, L., et al. (2007). Predictors, clinical characteristics, and outcome of conduct disorder in girls with attention-deficit/hyperactivity disorder: A longitudinal study. *Psychological Medicine, 37*(12), 1731–1741.

MTA (Multi-Modal Treatment Study of Children with Attention-Deficit/Hyperactivity Disorder Cooperative Group). (1999). A 14-month randomized clinical trial of treatment strategies for attention-deficit/hyperactivity disorder. *Archives of General Psychiatry, 56*, 1073–1086.

Nigg, J., Nikolas, M., Friderici, K., Park, L., & Zucker, R. A. (2007). Genotype and neuropsychological response inhibition as resilience promoters for attention-deficit/hyperactivity disorder, oppositional defiant disorder, and conduct disorder under conditions of psychosocial adversity. *Developmental Psychopathology, 19*(3), 767–86.

Ohan, J., & Johnston, C. (2005). Gender appropriateness of symptom criteria for attention-deficit/hyperactivity disorder, oppositional-defiant disorder, and conduct disorder. *Child Psychiatry and Human Development, 35*, 359–381.

Olfson, M., Marcus, S., & Wan, G. (2009). Stimulant dosing for children with ADHD: A medical claims analysis. *Journal of the American Academy of Child & Adolescent Psychiatry, 48*(1), 51–59.

Owens, E. B., Hinshaw, S. P., Kraemer, H. C., Arnold, L. E., Abikoff, H. B., Cantwell, D. P., Conners, C. K., Elliott, G., Greenhill, L. L., Hechtman, L., Hoza, B., Jensen, P. S., March, J. S., Newcorn, J. H., Pelham, W. E., Severe, J. B., Swanson, J. M., Vitiello, B., Wells, K. C., & Wigal, T. (2003). Which treatment for whom for ADHD? Moderators of treatment response in the MTA. *Journal of Consulting and Clinical Psychology, 71*(3), 540–552.

Pelham, W. E., & Fabiano, G. A. (2008). Evidence-based psychosocial treatments for attention-deficit/hyperactivity disorder. *Journal of Clinical Child and Adolescent Psychology, 37*(1), 184–214.

Pelham, W., Jr., Wheeler, T., & Chronis, A. (1998). Empirically supported psychosocial treatments for attention deficit hyperactivity disorder. *Journal of Clinical Child Psychology, 27*(2), 190.

Pfiffner, L. J., Yee Mikami, A., Huang-Pollock, C., Easterlin, B., Zalecki, C., & McBurnett, K. (2007). A randomized, controlled trial of integrated home-school behavioral treatment for ADHD, predominantly inattentive type. *Journal of American Academy of Child and Adolescent Psychiatry, 46*(8), 1041–1050.

Pliszka, S. (2000). Patterns of psychiatric comorbidity with attention-deficit/hyperactivity disorder. *Child and Adolescent Psychiatric Clinics of North America, 9*, 525–540.

Polanczyk, G., de Lima, M. S., Horta, B. L., Biederman, J., & Rohde, L. (2007). The worldwide prevalence of ADHD: A systematic review and metaregression analysis. *The American Journal of Psychiatry, 164*(6), 942–948.

Polderman, T. J., Derks, E. M., Hudziak, J. J., Verhulst, F. C., Posthuma, D., & Boomsma, D. I. (2007). Across the continuum of attention skills: A twin study of the SWAN ADHD rating scale. *Journal of Child Psychology and Psychiatry, 48*(11), 1080–1087.

Rothe, E. M. (2005). Considering cultural diversity in the management of ADHD in Hispanic patients. *Journal of the National Medical Association, 97*(10 Suppl), 17S–23S.

Rucklidge, J. J., & Tannock, R. (2001). Psychiatric, psychosocial, and cognitive functioning of female adolescents with ADHD. *Journal of the American Academy of Child and Adolescent Psychiatry, 40*(5), 530–540.

Schachter, H., Pham, B., King, J., Langford, S., & Moher, D. (2001). How efficacious and safe is short-acting methylphenidate for the treatment of attention-deficit disorder in children and adolescents? A meta-analysis. *CMAJ: Canadian Medical Association Journal, 165*(11), 1475–1488.

Sonuga-Barke, E. J., Lasky-Su, J., Neale, B.M., Oades, R., Chen, W., Franke, B., Buitelaar, J., Banaschewski, T., Ebstein, R., Gill, M., Anney, R., Miranda, A., Mulas, F., Roeyers, H., Rothenberger, A., Sergeant, J., Steinhausen, H.C., Thompson, M., Asherson, P., & Faraone, S. V. (2008). Does parental expressed emotion moderate genetic effects in ADHD? An exploration using a genome wide association scan. *American Journal of Medical Genetics. Neuropsychiatric Genetics, 147B*(8), 1359–1368.

Stein, M., Sarampote, C., Waldman, I., Robb, A., Conlon, C., Pearl, P., et al. (2003). A dose-response study of OROS methylphenidate in children with attention-deficit/hyperactivity disorder. *Pediatrics, 112*(5), e404–e413.

Swanson, J., Arnold, L., Kraemer, H., Hechtman, L., Molina, B., Hinshaw, S., et al. (2008). Evidence, interpretation, and qualification from multiple reports of long-term outcomes in the multimodal treatment study of children with ADHD (MTA): Part I: Executive summary. *Journal of Attention Disorders, 12*(1), 4–14.

Vedantam, S. (2009). *Debate over drugs for ADHD reignites.* Retrieved on March 27, 2009 from http://www.washingtonpost.com/wp-dyn/content/article/2009/3/26.

Weiss, G., & Trokenberg-Hechtman, L. (1993). *Hyperactive children grown up: ADHD in children, adolescents, and adults.* New York: The Guilford Press.

Weisz, J., & Hawley, K. (1998). Finding, evaluating, refining, and applying empirically supported treatments for children. *Journal of Clinical Child Psychology, 27*(2), 206.

Willcutt, E. G., Doyle, A. E., Nigg, J. T., Faraone, S. V., & Pennington, B. F. (2005). Validity of the executive function theory of attention-deficit/ hyperactivity disorder: a meta-analytic review. *Biology and Psychiatry, 57*, 1336–1346.

Wolraich, M. L., Wibbelsman, C. J., Brown, T. E., Evans, S. W., Gotlieb, E. M., & Knight, J. R., et al. (2005). Attention-deficit/hyperactivity disorder among adolescents: A review of the diagnosis, treatment, and clinical implications. *Pediatrics, 115*, 1734–1747.

Wymbs, B. T., Pelham, W. E., Molina, B. S. G., Gnagy, E. M., Wilson, T. K., & Greenhouse, J. B (2008). Rate and predictors of divorce among parents of youths with ADHD. *Journal of Consulting and Clinical Psychology, 76*(5), 735–744.

CHAPTER 3

Aman, M. G., Binder, C., & Turgay, A. (2004). Risperidone effects in the presence/absence of psychostimulant medicine in children with ADHD, other disruptive behavior disorders, and subaverage IQ. *Journal of Child and Adolescent Psychopharmacology, 14*(2), 243–254.

American Psychiatric Association. (2000). *Diagnostic and statistical manual of mental disorders* (4th ed., text rev.). Washington, DC: Author.

Angold, A., Costello, E., Farmer, E., et al. (1999). Impaired but undiagnosed. *Journal of the American Academy of Child and Adolescent Psychiatry, 38*, 129–137.

Baker, L., & Scarth, K. (2002). Cognitive behavioural approaches to treating children and adolescents with conduct disorder. Downloaded 2009 from http://www.lfcc.on.ca/conduct_disorder_manual_CMHO.pdf.

Bassarath, L. (2003). Medication strategies in childhood aggression: A review. *Canadian Journal of Psychiatry. Revue Canadienne De Psychiatrie, 48*(6), 367–373.

Bender, K., Springer, D. W., & Kim, J. S. (2006). Treatment effectiveness with dually diagnosed adolescents: A systematic review. *Brief Treatment and Crisis Intervention, 6*(3), 177–205.

Bernal, M.E., Klinnert, M.D., Schultz, L.A. (1980). Outcome evaluation of behavioral parent training and client-centered parent counseling for children with conduct problems. *Journal of Applied Behavior Analysis, 13*(4), 677–691.

Bradley, M. C., & Mandell, D. (2005). Oppositional defiant disorder: A systematic review of evidence of intervention effectiveness. *Journal of Experimental Criminology, 1*(3), 343–365.

Brestan, E., & Eyberg, S. (1998). Effective psychosocial treatments of conduct-disordered children and adolescents: 29 years, 82 studies, and 5272 kids. *Journal of Clinical Child Psychology, 27*(2), 180–189.

Burke, J., Loeber, R., & Birmaher, B. (2002). Oppositional defiant disorder and conduct disorder: A review of the past 10 years, part II. *Journal of the American Academy of Child and Adolescent Psychiatry, 41*, 1275–1294.

Christman, A. K., Fermo, J. D., & Markowitz, J. S. (2004). Atomoxetine, a novel treatment for attention-deficit-hyperactivity disorder. *Pharmacotherapy, 24*(8), 1020–1036.

Connor, D. F., Fletcher, K. E., & Wood, J. S. (2001). Neuroleptic-related dyskinesias in children and adolescents. *Journal of Clinical Psychiatry, 62*(12), 967–974.

Crick, N., & Dodge, K. (1994). A review and reformulation of social information-processing mechanisms in children's social adjustment. *Psychological Bulletin, 115*(1), 74–101.

Dekovic, M. (1999). Parent-adolescent conflict: Possible determinants and consequences. *International Journal of Behavioral Development, 23*(4), 977–1000.

Derzon, J. (2006). How effective are school-based violence prevention programs in preventing and reducing violence and other antisocial behaviors? A meta-analysis. In S. R. Jimerson & M. J. Furlong (Eds.), *Handbook of school violence and school safety: From research to practice* (pp. 429–441). Mahwah, NJ: Erlbaum.

Dickersin, K. (2005). Publication bias: Recognizing the problem, understanding its origins and scope, and preventing harm. In H. R. Rothstein, A. J. Sutton, & M. Borenstein (Eds.), *Publication bias in meta-analysis: Prevention, assessment, and adjustments* (pp. 11–33). Chichester, UK: John Wiley & Sons.

Dinkmeyer, D., & McKay, G. (1976). *Systematic training for effective parenting.* Circle Pines, MN: American Guidance Service.

Dodge, K. A. (1986). A social information processing model of social competence in children. In M. Perlmutter (Ed.), *Minnesota symposium on child psychology* (Vol. 18, pp. 77–125). Hillsdale, NJ: Erlbaum.

Dretzke, J., Davenport, C., Frew, E., Barlow, J., Stewart-Brown, S., Bayliss, S., Taylor, R., Sandercock, J., & Hyde, C. (2009). The clinical effectiveness of different parenting programmes for children with conduct problems: A systematic review of randomized controlled trials. *Child and Adolescent Psychiatry and Mental Health, 3,* 7. Doi: 10.1186/1753-2000-3-7.

Egger, H., & Angold, A. (2006). Common emotional and behavioral disorders in preschool children: Presentation, nosology, and epidemiology. *Journal of Child Psychology & Psychiatry, 47*(3/4), 313–337.

Ehrensaft, M. K. (2005). Interpersonal relationships and sex differences in the development of conduct problems. *Clinical Child and Family Psychology Review, 8*(1), 39–63.

Eyberg, S. M., Boggs, S., & Algina, J. (1995). Patent-child interaction therapy: A psychosocial model for the treatment of young children with conduct problem behavior and their families. *Psycopharmacology Bulletin, 31,* 83–91.

Eyberg, S. M., Nelson, M. M., & Boggs, S. R. (2008). Evidence-based psychosocial treatments for children and adolescents with disruptive behavior. *Journal of Clinical Child and Adolescent Psychology, 37*(1), 215–237.

Forehand, R., & McMahon, R. J. (1981). *Helping the noncompliant child: A clinician's guide to parent training.* New York: Guilford.

Frick, P. J. (2006). Developmental pathways to conduct disorder. *Child and Adolescent Psychiatric Clinics of North America, 15*(2), 311–331.

Gansle, K. A. (2005). The effectiveness of school-based anger interventions and programs: A meta-analysis. *Journal of School Psychology, 43,* 321–341.

Garza, Y., & Bratton, S. C. (2005). School-based child-centered play therapy with Hispanic children: Outcomes and cultural considerations. *International Journal of Play Therapy, 14*(1), 51–79.

Gelhorn, H., Stallings, M., Young, S., Corley, R., Rhee, S. H., Christian, H., & Hewitt, J. (2006). Common and specific genetic influences on aggressive and nonaggressive conduct disorder domains. *Journal of the American Academy of Child and Adolescent Psychiatry, 45,* 570–577.

Gordon, T. (1970). *Parent effectiveness training.* New York: Wyden.

Hankin, B. L., Abela, J. R., Auerbach, R. P., McWhinnie, C. M., & Skitch, S. A. (2005). Development of behavioral problems over the life course: A vulnerability and stress perspective. In B. L. Hankin, J. Abela, & R. Z. John (Eds.), *Development of psychopathology: A vulnerability-stress perspective* (pp. 385–416). Thousand Oaks, CA: Sage Publications.

Hill, J. (2002). Biological, psychological and social processes in conduct disorders. *Journal of Child Psychology and Psychiatry, 43*(1), 133–164.

Hudley, C., & Graham, S. (1993). An attributional intervention to reduce peer-directed aggression among African Americans boys. *Child Development, 64,* 124–138.

Huey, S., & Polo, A. (2008). Evidence-based psychosocial treatments for ethnic minority youth. *Journal of Clinical Child & Adolescent Psychology, 37*(1), 262–301.

Ipser, J., & Stein, D. J. (2007). Systematic review of pharmacotherapy of disruptive behavior disorders in children and adolescents. *Psychopharmacology, 191,* 127–140.

Jaffee, S., Caspi, A., Moffitt, T., Dodge, K., Rutter, M., Taylor, A., & Tully, L. (2005). Nature × nurture: Genetic vulnerabilities interact with physical maltreatment to promote conduct problems. *Development and Psychopathology, 17*(1), 67–84.

Kazdin, A. (2001). Treatment of conduct disorders. In J. Hill & B. Maughan (Eds.), *Conduct disorders in childhood and adolescence* (pp. 408–448). New York: Cambridge University Press.

Kazdin, A. (2003). Psychotherapy for children and adolescents. *Annual Review of Psychology*, *54*(1), 253.

Lahey, B. B., & Waldman, I. D. (2003). A developmental propensity model of the origins of conduct problems during childhood and adolescence. In B. B.Lahey, T. E. Moffitt, & A.Caspi (Eds.), *Causes of conduct disorder and juvenile delinquency* (pp. 76–117). New York: Guilford Press.

Ledingham, J. (1999). Children and adolescents with oppositional defiant disorder and conduct disorder in the community: Experiences at school and with peers. In H. Quay & A. Hogan (Eds.), *Handbook of disruptive behavior disorders* (pp. 353–370). New York: Kluwer Academic/ Plenum.

Legrand, L. N., Keyes, M., McGue, M., Iacono, W. G., & Krueger, R. F. (2008). Rural environments reduce the genetic influence on adolescent substance use and rule-breaking behavior. *Psychological Medicine, 38*, 1341–1350.

Lochman, J., Barry, T., & Pardini, D. (2003). Anger control training for aggressive youth. In *Evidence-based psychotherapies for children and adolescents* (pp. 263–281). New York: Guilford Press.

Lochman, J. E., Coie, J. D., Underwood, M. K., & Terry, R. (1993). Effectiveness of a social relations intervention program for aggressive and nonaggressive, rejected children. *Journal of Consulting & Clinical Psychology, 61*(6), 1053–1058.

Lochman, J. E., Curry, J. F., Dane, H., & Ellis, M. (2001). The Anger Coping Program: An empirically-supported treatment for aggressive children. *Residential Treatment for Children and Youth, 18*, 63–73.

Lochman, J. E., & Wells, K. C. (2003). Effectiveness of the coping power program and of classroom intervention with aggressive children: Outcomes at a 1-year follow-up. *Behavior Therapy, 34*, 493–515.

Lochman, J. E., & Wells, K. C. (2004). The Coping Power Program for preadolescent aggressive boys and their parents: Outcome effects at the 1-year follow-up. *Journal of Consulting & Clinical Psychology, 72*, 571–578.

Loeber, R., Burke, J. D., Lagey, B. B., Winters, A., & Zera, M. (2000). Oppositional defiant and conduct disorder: A review of the past 10 years, part I. *Journal of the American Academy of Child and Adolescent Psychiatry, 39*(12), 1468–1484.

Loeber, R., Burke, J., & Lahey, B. (2002). What are adolescent antecedents to antisocial personality disorder? *Criminal Behaviour & Mental Health, 12*(1), 24.

Loeber, R., Farrington, D., Stouthamer-Loeber, M., Moffitt, T., & Caspi, A. (1998). The development of male offending: Key findings from the first decade of the Pittsburgh Youth Study. *Studies on Crime & Crime Prevention, 7*(2), 141–171.

Lundahl, B., Risser, H., & Lovejoy, M. (2006). A meta-analysis of parent training: Moderators and follow-up effects. *Clinical Psychology Review, 26*(1), 86–104.

Macdonald, G., Higgins, J. P. T., & Ramchandani, P. (2006). Cognitive-behavioural interventions for children who have been sexually abused. *Cochrane Database of Systematic Reviews*, Issue 4, CD001930.

MacDonald, G. M., & Turner, W. (2008). Treatment foster care for improving outcomes in children and young people (review). *The Cochrane Library, 2008* (1).

McCart, M. R., Priester, P. E., Davies, W. H., & Azen, R. (2006). Differential effectiveness of behavioral parent-training and cognitive-behavioral therapy for antisocial youth: A meta-analysis. *Journal of Abnormal Child Psychology, 34*(4), 527–543.

McCart, M., Priester, P., & Davies, W. (2007). Review: Effects of behavioural parent training and cognitive-behavioural therapy on antisocial behaviour in children remain unclear. *Evidence-Based Mental Health*, 10(2), 54.

McGee, R., & Williams, S. (1999). Environmental risk factors in oppositional-defiant disorder and conduct disorder. In H. Quay, C. Herbert, & A. Hogan (Eds.), *Handbook of disruptive behavior disorders* (pp. 419–440). Dordrecht, Netherlands: Kluwer Academic Publishers.

Meichenbaum, D., & Cameron, R. (1973). *Stress inoculation: A skills training approach to anxiety management.* Waterloo, Ontario, Canada: University of Waterloo.

Minuchin, S., & Fishman, H. C. (1981). *Family therapy techniques.* Cambridge, MA: Harvard University Press.

Miranda, J., Bernal, G., Lau, A., Kohn, L., Hwang, W. C., & LaFromboise, T. (2005). State of the science on psychosocial interventions for ethnic minorities. *Annual Review of Clinical Psychology*, 1(1), 113–142.

Moffitt, T., Caspi, A., Rutter, M., & Silva, P. (2001). *Sex differences in antisocial behavior: Conduct disorder, delinquency, and violence in the Dunedin longitudinal study.* Cambridge: Cambridge University Press.

Mytton, J., DiGuiseppi, C., Gough, D., Taylor, R., & Logan, S. (2006). School-base secondary prevention programmes for preventing violence. *Cochrane Database Systems Review*, 3, CD004606.

Nguyen, L., Huang, L. N., Arganza, G. F., & Liao, Q. (2007). The influence of race and ethnicity on psychiatric diagnoses and clinical characteristics of children and adolescents in children's services. *Cultural Diversity and Ethnic Minority Psychology*, 13(1), 18–25.

Nigg, J., & Huang-Pollock, C. (2003). An early-onset model of the role of executive functions and intelligence in conduct disorder/delinquency. *Causes of conduct disorder and juvenile delinquency* (pp. 227–253). New York: Guilford Press.

Nock, M. K., Kazdin, A. E., Hiripi, E., & Kessler, R. C. (2007). Lifetime prevalence, correlates, and persistence of oppositional defiant disorder: Results from the National Comorbidity Survey Replication. *Journal of Child Psychology and Psychiatry*, 48(7), 703–713.

Ohan, J., & Johnston, C. (2005). Gender appropriateness of symptom criteria for attention-deficit/hyperactivity disorder, oppositional-defiant disorder, and conduct disorder. *Child Psychiatry & Human Development*, 35(4), 359–381.

Pappadopulos, E., Jensen, P. S., Schur, S. B., MacIntyre, J. C., 2nd, Ketner, S., Van Orden, K., et al. (2002). "Real world" atypical antipsychotic prescribing practices in public child and adolescent inpatient settings. *Schizophrenia Bulletin*, 28(1), 111–121.

Pappadopulos, E., Woolston, S., Chait, A., Perkins, M., Connor, D. F., & Jensen, P. S. (2006). Pharmacotherapy of aggression in children and adolescents: Efficacy and effect size. *Journal of Canadian Academy of Child and Adolescent Psychiatry*, 15(1), 27–36.

Patterson, G., Chamberlain, P., & Reid, J. (1982). A comparative evaluation of a parent-training program. *Behavior Therapy*, 13(5), 638–650.

Patterson, G. R., & Gulljon, M. E. (1968). *Living with children: New methods for parents and teachers.* Champaign, IL: Research Press.

Patterson, G. R., Reid, J. B., Jones, R. R., & Conger, R. E. (1975). *A social learning approach to family intervention: Families with aggressive children* (Vol. 1). Eugene, OR: Castalia.

Porter, A., Timmer, S., Klisanac, L., Urquiza, A. J., Zebell, N., & McGrath, J. (2009). Dissemination of parent-child interaction therapy: Out of the University and into the community.

Downloaded 2009 from http://cmtc.tv/absolutenm/articlefiles/15-2006.pdf%20Florida%20 poster01.06.pdf.

Porter, A., Timmer, S., Urquiza, A. J., Zebell, N., & McGrath, J. (2009). Disseminating PCIT to child maltreatment agencies: A snapshot in time. Downloaded 2009 from http://cmtc.tv/ absolutenm/articlefiles/159.06.pdf%20CAN%20CONF%20FINAL%20Outcome%20poste r.pdf.

Reyno, S. M., & McGrath, P. J. (2006). Predictors of parent training efficacy for child externalizing behavior problem—a meta-analytic review. *Journal of Child Psychology and Psychiatry, 47*(1), 99–111.

Robinson, T., Smith, S., & Miller, M. (2002). Effect of a cognitive-behavioral intervention on responses to anger by middle school students with chronic behavior problems. *Behavioral Disorders, 27*(3), 256–271.

Sanders, M. R. (1999). Triple p-positive parenting program: Towards an empirically validated multilevel parenting and family support strategy for the prevention of behavior and emotional problems in children. *Clinical Child and Family Psychology Review, 2*, 71–90.

Schur, S. B., Sikich, L., Findling, R. L., Malone, R. P., Crismon, M. L., Derivan, A., et al. (2003). Treatment recommendations for the use of antipsychotics for aggressive youth (TRAAY). Part I: A review. *Journal of the American Academy of Child and Adolescent Psychiatry, 42*(2), 132–144.

Snyder, K., & Kymissis, P. (1999). Anger management for adolescents: Efficacy of brief group therapy. *Journal of the American Academy of Child & Adolescent Psychiatry, 38*(11), 1409.

Steinberg, L. (2001). We know some things: Parent-adolescent relationships in retrospect and prospect. *Journal of Research on Adolescence, 11*, 1–19.

Szapocznik, J., Hervis, O. E., & Schwartz, S. J. (2003). *Brief strategic family therapy for adolescent drug abuse* (NIDA Therapy Manuals Series, NIH Publication 03-4751). Rockville, MD: National Institute on Drug Abuse.

Van Brunt, J., et al. (2005). Predictors of selecting atomoxetine therapy for children with attention-deficit-hyperactivity disorder. *Pharmacotherapy, 25*(11), 1541–1549.

Wachs, T. (2000). *Necessary but not sufficient.* Washington, DC: American Psychological Association.

Webster-Stratton, C., & Reid, M. (2003). Treating conduct problems and strengthening social and emotional competence in young children: The Dina dinosaur treatment program. *Journal of Emotional & Behavioral Disorders, 11*(3), 130.

Webster-Stratton, C., Reid, M.J., & Hammond, M. (2004). Treating children with early-onset conduct problems: intervention outcomes for parent, child, and teacher training. *Journal of Clinical Child and Adolescent Psychology, 33*(1), 105–24.

Weisz, J., Doss, A., & Hawley, K. (2005). Youth psychotherapy outcome research: A review and critique of the evidence base. *Annual Review of Psychology, 56*, 337–363.

Weisz, J. R., & Jensen, A. L. (2001). Child and adolescent psychotherapy in research and practice contexts: Review of the evidence and suggestions for improving the field. *European Child and Adolescent Psychiatry, 10*, 12–18.

Weisz, J., Jensen-Doss, A., & Hawley, K. (2006). Evidence-based youth psychotherapies versus usual clinical care. *American Psychologist, 61*(7), 671–689.

Werner, E. (2000). Protective factors and individual resilience. In J. Shonoff & S. Meisels (Eds.), *Handbook of early childhood intervention* (2nd ed., pp. 115–133). Cambridge: Cambridge University Press.

Wilson, S. J., & Lipsey, M. W. (2006a). The effectiveness of school-based social information processing programs: Part I: Universal programs. Center for Evaluation Research and Methodology, Vanderbilt University, Nashville, TN.

Wilson, S. J., & Lipsey, M. W. (2006b). The effectiveness of school-based social information processing programs: Part II: Selected/indicated pull out programs. Center for Evaluation Research and Methodology, Vanderbilt University, Nashville, TN.

Wilson, S. J., & Lipsey, M. W. (2007). School based interventions for aggressive and disruptive behavior: Update of a meta-analysis. *American Journal of Preventive Medicine, 33*(2S), S130–S143.

Wilson, S. J., Lipsey, M. W., & Soydan, H. (2003). Are mainstream programs for juvenile delinquency less effective with minority youth than majority youth? A meta-analysis of outcome research. *Research on Social Work Practice, 13*(1), 3–26.

Zisser, A., & Eyberg, S.M. (2010). Treating oppositional behavior in children using parent-child interaction therapy. In A.E. Kazdin & J.R. Weisz (Eds.) *Evidence-based psychotherapies for children and adolescents* (2nd ed., pp. 179–193). New York: Guilford.

CHAPTER 4

Alexander, J., & Parsons, B. V. (1982). *Functional family therapy.* Monterey, CA: Brooks-Cole.

American Psychiatric Association. (2000). *Diagnostic and statistical manual of mental disorders* (text revision). Washington, DC: Author.

American Psychological Association Task Force on Evidence-Based Practice for Children and Adolescents. (2008). *Disseminating evidence-based practice for children and adolescents: A systems approach to enhancing care.* Washington, DC: American Psychological Association.

Armelius, B. A., & Andreassen, T. H. (2007). Cognitive-behavioral treatment for antisocial behavior in youth in residential treatment. Retrieved January, 8, 2009 from The Campbell Collaboration website: http://www.campbellcollaboration.org/campbell_library/index.php.

Armstrong, T. D., & Costello, E. J. (2002). Community studies on adolescent substance use, abuse, or dependence and psychiatric comorbidity. *Journal of Consulting and Clinical Psychology, 70*(6), 1224–1239.

Azrin, N. H., Donohue, B., Besalel, V.A., Kogan, E. S., & Acierno, R. (1994). Youth drug abuse treatment: A controlled outcome study. *Journal of Child and Adolescent Substance Abuse, 3*, 1–16.

Azrin, N. H., Donohue, B., Teichner, G. A., Crum, T., Howell, J., & DeCato, L. A. (2001). A controlled evaluation and description of individual-cognitive problem solving and family behavior therapies in dually-diagnosed conduct disordered and substance-dependent youth. *Journal of Child & Adolescent Substance Abuse, 11*(1), 1–43.

Azrin, N. H., McMahon, P., Besalel, V. A., Donohue, B. C., Acierno, R., & Kogan, E. S. (1994). Behavior therapy for drug abuse: A controlled outcome study. *Behavior Research and Therapy, 32*, 857–866.

Battjes, R. J., Gordon, M. S., O'Grady, K. E., Kinlock, T. W., Katz, E. C., & Sears, E. A. (2004). Evaluation of a group-based substance abuse treatment program for adolescents. *Journal of Substance Abuse Treatment, 27*(2), 123–134.

Bender, K., Springer, D. W., & Kim, J. S. (2006). Treatment effectiveness with dually diagnosed adolescents: A systematic review. *Brief Treatment and Crisis Intervention, 6*(3), 177–205.

Block, J. (1978). Effects of a rational-emotive mental health program on poorly achieving, disruptive high school students. *Journal of Counseling Psychology, 25*, 61–65.

Borduin, C. M., Mann, B. J., Cone, L. T., Henggeler, S. W., Fucci, B. R., Blaske, D. M., et al. (1995). Multisystemic treatment of serious juvenile offenders: Long-term prevention of criminality and violence. *Journal of Consulting and Clinical Psychology*, 63, 569–578.

Bronfenbrenner, U. (1979). *The ecology of human development.* Cambridge, MA: Harvard University Press.

Bukstein, O., & Kaminer, Y. (1994). The nosology of adolescent substance abuse. *The American Journal on Addictions*, 3(1), 1–13.

Capaldi, D. M., & Patterson, G. R. (1994). Interrelated influences of contextual factors on antisocial behavior in childhood and adolescence for males. In D. C. Fowles, P. Sutker, & S. H. Goodman (Eds.), *Progress in experimental personality and psychopathology research* (pp. 165–198). New York: Springer.

Chamberlain, P., Leve, L. D., & DeGarmo, D. S. (2007). Multidimensional treatment foster care for girls in the juvenile justice system: 2-year follow-up of a randomized clinical trial. *Journal of Consulting and Clinical Psychology*, 75(1), 187–193.

Chamberlain, P., & Reid, J. B. (1998). Comparison of two community alternatives to incarceration for chronic juvenile offenders. *Journal of Consulting and Clinical Psychology*, 66(4), 624–633.

Chamberlain, P., & Smith, D. K. (2003). Antisocial behavior in children and adolescents: The Oregon Multidimensional Treatment Foster Care model. In A. E. Kazdin & J. R. Weisz (Eds.), *Evidence-based psychotherapies for children and adolescents* (pp. 282–300). New York: Guilford Press.

Chambless, D., & Hollon, S. (1998). Defining empirically supported therapies. *Journal of Consulting & Clinical Psychology*, 66(1), 7.

Chung, T., & Maisto, S. A. (2006). Relapse to alcohol and other drug use in treated adolescents: Review and reconsideration of relapse as a change point in clinical course. *Clinical Psychology Review*, 26(2), 149–161.

Cohen, J. (1988). *Statistical power analysis for the behavioral sciences* (2nd ed.). Hillsdale, NJ: Lawrence Erlbaum.

Creamer, M., Bell, R., & Failla, S. (2003). Psychometric properties of the Impact of Event Scale—Revised. *Behaviour Research and Therapy*, 41, 1489–1496.

Dennis, M., Godley, S. H., Diamond, G., Tims, F. M., Babor, T., & Donaldson, J., et al. (2004). The Cannabis Youth Treatment (CYT) Study: Main findings from two randomized trials. *Journal of Substance Abuse Treatment*, 27, 197–213.

Donohue, B., & Azrin, N. (2001). Family behavior therapy. In E. F. Wagner & H. B. Waldron (Eds.), *Innovations in adolescent substance abuse interventions* (pp. 205–227). Amsterdam, Netherlands: Pergamon/Elsevier Science.

Donohue, B., Azrin, N., Allen, D., Romero, V., Hill, H., Tracy, K., Lapota, H., Gorney, S., Abdel-Al, R., Caldas, D., Herdzik, K., Bradshaw, K., Valdez, R., & Van Hasselt, V. (2009). Family behavior therapy for substance abuse and other associated problems: A review of its intervention components and applicability. *Behavior Modification*, 33, 495–519.

Eddy, M. J., Whaley, R. B., & Chamberlain, P. (2004). The prevention of violent behavior by chronic and serious male juvenile offenders: A two year follow-up of a randomized clinical trial. *Journal of Emotional and Behavioral Disorders*, 12(1), 2–8.

Ehrensaft, M. K. (2005). Interpersonal relationships and sex differences in the development of conduct problems. *Clinical Child and Family Psychology Review*, 8(1), 39–63.

Eyberg, S. M., Nelson, M. M., & Boggs, S. R. (2008). Evidence-based psychosocial treatments for children and adolescents with disruptive behavior. *Journal of Clinical Child and Adolescent Psychology*, 37(1), 215–237.

Farrell, A. D., & White, K. S. (1998). Peer influences and drug use among urban adolescents: Family structure and parent-adolescent relationship as protective factors. *Journal of Consulting and Clinical Psychology*, 66(2), 248–258.

French, K., Finkbiner, R., & Duhamel, L. (2002). *Patterns of substance use among minority youth and adults in the United States: An overview and synthesis of national survey findings*. SAMHSA, Center for Substance Abuse Treatment, Washington, DC.

Frick, P. J. (2006). Developmental pathways to conduct disorder. *Child and Adolescent Psychiatric Clinics of North America*, 15(2), 311–331.

Friedman, A. S. (1989). Family therapy vs. parent groups: Effects on adolescent drug abusers. *American Journal of Family Therapy*, 17, 335–347.

Goldstein, A. P., Glick, B., & Gibbs, J. C. (1998). *Aggression replacement training: A comprehensive intervention for aggressive youth* (rev. ed.). Champaign, IL: Research Press.

Gordon, D. A., Arbuthnot, J., Gustafson, K. E., & McGreen, P. (1988). Home-based behavioral-systems family therapy with disadvantaged juvenile delinquents. *American Journal of Family Therapy*, 16(3), 243–255.

Hawkins, J. D., Catalano, R. F., & Miller, J. Y. (1992). Risk and protective factors for alcohol and other drug problems in adolescence and early adulthood: Implications for substance abuse prevention. *Psychological Bulletin*, 112(1), 64–105.

Henggeler, S. W. (1991). Multidimensional causal models of delinquent behavior and their implications for treatment. In R. Cohen & A. W. Siegel (Eds.), *Context and development* (pp. 211–231). Hillsdale, NJ: Erlbaum.

Henggeler, S., Borduin, C., Melton, G., & Mann, B. (1991). Effects of multisystemic therapy on drug use and abuse in serious juvenile offenders: A progress report from two outcome studies. *Family Dynamics of Addiction Quarterly*, 1(3), 40–51.

Henggeler, S. W., Clingempeel, W. G., Brondino, M. J., & Pickrel, S. G. (2002). Four-year follow-up of multisystemic therapy with substance-abusing and substance-dependent juvenile offenders. *Journal of the American Academy of Child & Adolescent Psychiatry*, 41(7), 868–874.

Henggeler, S. W., Cunningham, P. B., Pickrel, S. G., Schoenwald, S. K., & Brondino, M. J. (1996). Multisystemic therapy: An effective violence prevention approach for serious juvenile offenders. *Journal of Adolescence*, 19, 47–61.

Henggeler, S., Halliday-Boykins, C., Cunningham, P., Randall, J., Shapiro, S., & Chapman, J. (2006). Juvenile drug court: Enhancing outcomes by integrating evidence-based treatments. *Journal of Consulting and Clinical Psychology*, 74(1), 42–54. Retrieved March 11, 2008, doi:10.1037/0022-006X.74.1.42.

Henggeler, S. W., & Lee, T. (2003). Multisystemic treatment of serious clinical problems. In A. E. Kazdin & J. R. Weisz (Eds.), *Evidence-based psychotherapies for children and adolescents* (pp. 301–322). New York: Guilford Press.

Henggeler, S. W., Melton, G. B., Brondino, M. J., Scherer, D. G., & Hanley, J. H. (1997). Multisystemic therapy with violent and chronic juvenile offenders and their families: The role of treatment fidelity in successful dissemination. *Journal of Consulting and Clinical Psychology*, 65, 821–833.

Henggeler, S. W., Melton, G. B., & Smith, L. A. (1992). Family preservation using multisystemic therapy: An effective alternative to incarcerating serious juvenile offenders. *Journal of Consulting and Clinical Psychology*, 60(6), 953–961.

Henggeler, S., Pickrel, S., & Brondino, M. (1999). Multisystemic treatment of substance-abusing and -dependent delinquents: Outcomes, treatment fidelity, and transportability. *Mental Health Research*, 3(1), 171–184.

Higgins, S., & Silverman, K. (2008). Contingency management. In M. Galanter & H. Kleber (Eds.), *The American Psychiatric Publishing textbook of substance abuse treatment* (pp. 387–399). Arlington, VA: American Psychiatric Publishing.

Hingson, R.W., Heeren, T., & Winter, M. R. (2006). Age at drinking onset and alcohol dependence: Age at onset, duration, and severity. *Archives of Pediatrics and Adolescent Medicine*, 160(7), 739–746.

Hopfer, C. J., Stallings, M. C., Hewitt, J. K., & Crowley, T. J. (2003). Family transmission of marijuana use, abuse, and dependence. *Journal of the American Academy of Child & Adolescent Psychiatry*, 42(7), 834–841.

Hops, H., Waldron, H. B., Davis, B., Barrera, Jr., M., Turner, C. W., Brody, J., & Ozechowski, T. J. (2007). Ethnic influences on family processes and family therapy outcomes for substance-abusing adolescents. Unpublished manuscript, Oregon Research Institute.

Huey, S. J., Jr., & Polo, A. J. (2008). Evidence-based psychosocial treatments for ethnic minority youth. *Journal of Clinical Child and Adolescent Psychology*, 37(1), 262–301.

Huey, W. C., & Rank, R. C. (1984). Effects of counselor and peer-led group assertive training on black-adolescent aggression. *Journal of Counseling Psychology*, 31, 95–98.

Jessor, R., Van Den Bos, J., Vanderryn, J., Costa, F. M., & Turbin, M. S. (1995). Protective factors in adolescent problem behavior: Moderator effects and developmental change. *Developmental Psychology*, 31, 923–933.

Kaminer, Y., & Burleson, J. (1999). Psychotherapies for adolescent substance abusers: 15-month follow-up. *American Journal on Addictions*, 8, 114–119.

Kaminer, Y., Burleson, J. A., Blitz, C., Sussman, J., & Rounsaville, B. J. (1998). Psychotherapies for adolescent substance abuse: A pilot study. *The Journal of Nervous and Mental Disease*, 186, 684–690.

Kaminer, Y., Burleson, J. A., & Goldberger, R. (2002). Cognitive behavioral coping skills and psychoeducation therapies for adolescent substance abuse. *The Journal of Nervous and Mental Disease*, 190, 737–745.

Kaminer, Y.,& Waldron, H B. (2006). Evidence-based cognitive-behavioral therapies for adolescent substance use disorders: applications and challenges. In H. Liddle & C. Rowe (Eds.), *Adolescent substance abuse: Research and clinical advances* (pp. 396–420). New York: Cambridge University Press.

Kaplow, J. B., Curran, P. J., & Dodge, K. A. (2002). Child, parent, and peer predictors of early-onset substance use: A multisite longitudinal study. *Journal of Abnormal Child Psychology*, 30(3), 199–216.

Kessler, R. C., Berglund, P., Demler, O., Jin, R., Merikangas, K. R., & Walters, E. E. (2005). Lifetime prevalence and age-of-onset distributions of DSM-IV disorders in the National Comorbidity Survey Replication. *Archives of General Psychiatry*, 62(6), 593–602.

Kilpatrick, D. G., Acierno, R., Saunders, B., Resnick, H. S., Best, C. L., & Schnurr, P. P. (2000). Risk factors for adolescent substance abuse and dependence: Data from a national sample. *Journal of Consulting and Clinical Psychology, 68*(1), 19–30.

Latimer, W. W., Newcomb, M., Winters, K. C., & Stinchfield, R. D. (2000). Adolescent substance abuse treatment outcome: The role of substance abuse problem severity, psychosocial, and treatment factors. *Journal of Consulting and Clinical Psychology, 68*, 684–696.

Ledingham, J. E. (1999). Children and adolescents with oppositional defiant disorder and conduct disorder in the community: Experiences at school and with peers. In H. C. Quay & A. E. Hogan (Eds.), *Handbook of disruptive behavior disorders* (pp. 353–370). Dordrecht, Netherlands: Kluwer Academic Publishers.

Legrand, L. N., Keyes, M., McGue, M., Iacono, W. G., & Krueger, R. F. (2008). Rural environments reduce the genetic influence on adolescent substance use and rule-breaking behavior. *Psychological Medicine, 38*, 1341–1350.

Leve, L. D., Chamberlain, P., & Reid, J. B. (2005). Intervention outcomes for girls referred from juvenile justice: Effects on delinquency. *Journal of Consulting and Clinical Psychology, 73*(6), 1181–1185.

Liddle, H. A., Dakof, G. A., Diamond, G. S., Parker, G. S., Barrett, K., & Tejeda, M. (2001). Multidimensional family therapy for adolescent substance abuse: Results of a randomized clinical trial. *American Journal of Drug and Alcohol Abuse, 27*, 651–687.

Liddle, H. A., Dakof, G. A., Turner, M., & Tejeda, M. (2003). *Treating adolescent substance abuse: A comparison of individual and family therapy interventions.* Manuscript submitted for publication.

Liddle, H., Rowe, C., Dakof, G., Henderson, C., & Greenbaum, P. (2009). Multidimensional family therapy for young adolescent substance abuse: Twelve-month outcomes of a randomized controlled trial. *Journal of Consulting and Clinical Psychology, 77*, 12–25.

Liddle, H. A., Rowe, C. L., Dakof, G. A., Ungaro, R. A., & Henderson, C. E. (2004). Early intervention for adolescent substance abuse: Pretreatment to posttreatment outcomes of a randomized clinical trial comparing multidimensional family therapy and peer group treatment. *Journal of Psychoactive Drugs, 36*, 49–63.

Lipsey, M. W., Landenberger, N. A., & Wilson, S. J. (2007). Effects of cognitive-behavioral programs for criminal offenders. Retrieved January, 8, 2009 from The Campbell Collaboration website: http://www.campbellcollaboration.org/campbell_library/index.php.

Littell, J. H. (2005). Lessons from a systematic review of effects of multisystemic therapy. *Children and Youth Services Review, 27*(4), 445–463.

Littell, J. H., Bjørndal, A., Winsvold, A. & Hammerstrøm, K. (2008). Functional family therapy for families of youth (ages 11–18) with behaviour problems. Retrieved January, 8, 2009 from The Campbell Collaboration website: http://www.campbellcollaboration.org/campbell_library/index.php.

Littell, J. H., Popa, M., & Forsythe, B. (2005). Multisystemic therapy for social, emotional, and behavioral problems in youth aged 10–17. Retrieved January, 8, 2009 from The Campbell Collaboration website: http://www.campbellcollaboration.org/campbell_library/index.php.

Lochman, J. E., Coie, J. D., Underwood, M. K., & Terry, R. (1993). Effectiveness of a social relations intervention program for aggressive and nonaggressive, rejected children. *Journal of Consulting and Clinical Psychology, 61*, 1053–1058.

Lochman, J. E., & Wells, K. C. (2003). Effectiveness of the coping power program and of classroom intervention with aggressive children: Outcomes at a 1-year follow-up. *Behavior Therapy, 34*, 493–515.

Lochman, J. E., & Wells, K. C. (2004). The Coping Power Program for preadolescent aggressive boys and their parents: Outcome effects at the 1-year follow-up. *Journal of Consulting and Clinical Psychology, 72*, 571–578.

Loeber, R., Pardini, D. A., Stouthamer-Loeber, M., & Raine, A. (2007). Do cognitive, physiological, and psychosocial risk and promotive factors predict desistance from delinquency in males? *Development and Psychopathology, 19*(3), 867–887.

Macdonald, G., Higgins, J. P. T., & Ramchandani, P. (2006). Cognitive-behavioural interventions for children who have been sexually abused. *Cochrane Database of Systematic Reviews*, Issue 4, CD001930.

Macdonald, G., & Turner, W. (2008). Treatment foster care for improving outcomes in children and young people. *Cochrane Database of Systematic Reviews*, Issue 1, CD005649.

Marshal, M. P., Friedman, M. S., Stall, R., King, K. M., Miles, J., Gold, M. A., et al. (2008). Sexual orientation and adolescent substance use: A meta-analysis and methodological review. *Addiction, 103*(4), 546–556.

Martin, C., Kelly, T., Rayens, M. K., Brogli, B. R., Brenzel, A., Smith, W. J., et al. (2002). Sensation seeking, puberty and nicotine, alcohol and marijuana use in adolescence. *Journal of the American Academy of Child & Adolescent Psychiatry, 41*, 1495–1502.

Maughan, B., & Rutter, M. (2001). Antisocial children grown up. In J. Hill & B. Maughan (Eds.), *Conduct disorders in childhood and adolescence* (pp. 507–552). New York: Cambridge University Press.

McCart, M. R., Priester, P. E., Davies, W. H., & Azen, R. (2006). Differential effectiveness of behavioral parent-training and cognitive-behavioral therapy for antisocial youth: A meta-analysis. *Journal of Abnormal Child Psychology, 34*(4), 527–543.

McMahon, L. (1994). Responding to defenses against anxiety in daycare for young children. *Early Child Development and Care, 97*, 175–184.

Moffitt, T., Caspi, A., Harrington, H., & Milne, B. (2002). Males on the life-course persistent and adolescence-limited antisocial pathways among males and females. *Development and Psychopathology, 13*, 355–375.

Nathan, P. E., & Gorman, J.M. (2002). Efficacy, effectiveness, and the clinical utility of psychotherapy research. In P. E. Nathan & J. M. Gorman (Eds.), *A guide to treatments that work* (2nd ed., pp. 642–654). New York: Oxford University Press.

National Institute on Drug Abuse. (1997). Preventing drug use among children and adolescents: A research based guide for parents, educators, and community leaders. NIH Publication No. 04-4212(B).

Reddy, P., Resnicow, K., Omardien, R., & Kambaran, N. (2007). Prevalence and correlates of substance use among high school students in South Africa and the United States. *American Journal of Public Health, 97*(10), 1859–1864.

Rohde, P., Lewinsohn, P., Kahler, C., Seeley, J., & Brown, R. (2001). Natural course of alcohol use disorders from adolescence to young adulthood. *Journal of the American Academy of Child and Adolescent Psychiatry, 40*, 83–90.

Sattah, M. V., Supawitkul, S., Dondero, T. J., Kilmarx, P. H., Young, N. L., Mastro, T., et al. (2002). Prevalence of and risk factors for methamphetamine use in northern Thai youth: Results of an audio-computer-assisted self-interviewing survey with urine testing. *Addiction, 97*(7), 801–808.

Siebenbruner, J., Englund, M. M., Egeland, B., & Hudson, K. (2006). Developmental antecedents of late adolescence substance use patterns. *Development and Psychopathology, 18*(2), 551–571.

Smith, D. C., Hall, J. A., Williams, J. K., An, H., & Gotman, N. (2006). Comparative efficacy of family and group treatment for adolescent substance abuse. *The American Journal on Addictions, 15*, 131–136.

Snodgrass, R. (1989). Treatment foster care: A proposed definition. *Community Alternatives: International Journal of Family Care, 1*(2), 79–82.

Stanton, M. D., Rempala, H. A., & Conway, C. A. (2007). *Clinical techniques and outcomes for Transitional Family Therapy with adolescent alcohol and drug abusers.* Paper presented at the Joint Meeting on Adolescent Treatment Effectiveness, Washington, DC.

Substance Abuse and Mental Health Services Administration. (2006). *Results from the 2005 National Survey on Drug Use and Health: National Findings* (Office of Applied Studies, NSDUH Series H-30, DHHS Publication No. SMA 06-4194). Rockville, MD.

Waldron, H. B., Brody, J., & Turner, C. W. (2009). Group therapy for adolescent substance use disorders. In N. Jainchill (Ed.), *Understanding and treating adolescent substance use disorders.* Kingston, NJ: Civic Research Institute, Inc.

Waldron, H. B., Hops, H., Brody, J., Turner, C. W., Davis, B., Barrera, M., Jr., et al. (2007). Treatments for Hispanic and Anglo drug-abusing youth. Unpublished manuscript, Oregon Research Institute.

Waldron, H. B., & Kaminer, Y. (2004). On the learning curve: The emerging evidence supporting cognitive-behavioral therapies for adolescent substance abuse. *Addiction, 99*(Suppl. 2), 93–105.

Waldron, H. B., Ozechowski, T. J., Turner, C. W., & Brody, J. (2005). Treatment outcomes for youth with problem alcohol use. Paper presented at the 2005 Joint Meeting on Adolescent Treatment Effectiveness, Washington, DC.

Waldron, H. B., Slesnick, N., Brody, J. L., Turner, C. W., & Peterson, T. R. (2001). Treatment outcomes for adolescent substance abuse at 4- and 7-month assessments. *Journal of Consulting and Clinical Psychology, 69*, 802–813.

Waldron, H. B., & Turner, C. W. (2008). Evidence based psychosocial treatments for adolescent substance abuse. *Journal of Clinical Child & Adolescent Psychology, 37*(1), 238–261.

Wilson, S. J., Lipsey, M. W., & Soydan, H. (2003). Are mainstream programs for juvenile delinquency less effective with minority youth than majority youth? A meta-analysis of outcomes research. *Research on Social Work Practice, 13*(1), 3–26.

Woolfenden, S. R., Williams, K., & Peat, J. K. (2001). Family and parenting interventions in children and adolescents with conduct disorder and delinquency aged 10–17. *Cochrane Database of Systematic Reviews,* Issue 2.

Young, S. E., Rhee, S. H., Stallings, M. C., Corley, R. P., & Hewitt, J. K. (2006). Genetic and environmental vulnerabilities underlying adolescent substance use and problem use: General or specific? *Behavior Genetics, 36*(4), 603–615.

CHAPTER 5

American Academy of Child and Adolescent Psychiatry. (2007). Practice parameter for the assessment and treatment of children and adolescents with attention-deficit/hyperactivity disorder. *Journal of the American Academy of Child and Adolescent Psychiatry, 46,* 894–921.

Asbahr, F. R., Castillo, A. R., Ito, L. M., Latorre, M. D. O., Moreira, M. N., & Lotufo-Neto, F. (2005). Group cognitive-behavioral therapy versus sertraline for the treatment of children and adolescents with obsessive-compulsive disorder. *Journal of the American Academy of Child & Adolescent Psychiatry, 44*(11), 1128–1136.

Bandelow, B., Spaeth, C., Tichauer, A., Broocks, A., Hajak, G., & Ruther, E. (2002). Early traumatic life events, parental attitudes, family history, and birth risk factors in patients with panic disorder. *Comprehensive Psychiatry, 43,* 269–278.

Barrett, P. (1998). Evaluation of cognitive-behavioral group treatments for childhood anxiety disorders. *Journal of Clinical Child Psychology, 27*(4), 459–468.

Barrett, P., Dadds, M., & Rapee, R. (1996). Family treatment of childhood anxiety: A controlled trial. *Journal of Consulting and Clinical Psychology, 64*(2), 333–342.

Barrett, P., Farrell, L., Pina, A., Peris, T., & Piacentini, J. (2008). Evidence-based psychosocial treatments for child and adolescent obsessive-compulsive disorder. *Journal of Clinical Child & Adolescent Psychology, 37*(1), 131–155.

Beidel, D., & Turner, S. (2000). The social phobia and anxiety inventory for children (SPAI-C): External and discriminative validity. *Behavior Therapy, 31*(1), 75.

Boomsma, D., Van Beijsterveldt, C., & Hudziak, J. (2005). Genetic and environmental influences on anxious/depression during childhood: A study from the Netherlands Twin Register. *Genes, Brain & Behavior, 4*(8), 466–481.

Bridge, J. A., Iyengar, S., Salary, C. B., Barbe, R. P., Birmaher, B., Pincus, H. A., Ren, L., & Brent D. A. (2007). Clinical response and risk for reported suicidal ideation and suicide attempts in pediatric antidepressant treatment: A meta-analysis of randomized controlled trials. *JAMA, 297*(15), 1683–1696.

Brown R. T., Antonuccio, D. O., DuPaul G. J., Fristad M. A., King C. A., Leslie, L. K., McCormick G. S., Pelham W. E., Jr., Piacentini J. C., & Vitiello B. (2007). *Childhood mental health disorders: Evidence base and contextual factors for psychosocial, psychopharmacological and combined interventions.* Washington, DC: American Psychological Association.

Chu, B., & Harrison, T. (2007). Disorder-specific effects of CBT for anxious and depressed youth: A meta-analysis of candidate mediators of change. *Clinical Child & Family Psychology Review, 10*(4), 352–372.

Connolly, S., & Bernstein, G. (2007). Practice parameter for the assessment and treatment of children and adolescents with anxiety disorders. *Journal of the American Academy of Child & Adolescent Psychiatry, 46*(2), 267–283.

Costello, E., Egger, H., & Angold, A. (2005). the developmental epidemiology of anxiety disorders: phenomenology, prevalence, and comorbidity. *Child and Adolescent Psychiatric Clinics of North America, 14*(4), 631–648.

Donovan, C., & Spence, S. (2000). Prevention of childhood anxiety disorders. *Clinical Psychology Review, 20,* 509–531.

Flannery-Schroeder, E., & Kendall, P. (2000). Group and individual cognitive-behavioral treatments for youth with anxiety disorders: A randomized clinical trial. *Cognitive Therapy & Research*, 24(3), 251.

Gallagher, H., Rabian, B., & McCloskey, M. (2003). A brief group cognitive-behavioral intervention for social phobia in childhood. *Journal of Anxiety Disorders*, 18(4), 459–479.

Geller, D. A. Biederman, J., Stewart, S. E., Mullin, B., Martin, A., Spencer, T., & Faraone, S. V. (2003). Which SSRI? A meta-analysis of pharmacotherapy trials in pediatric obsessive-compulsive disorder. *American Journal of Psychiatry*, 160(11), 1919–1928.

Ginsburg, G. S., & Drake, K. L. (2002). School-based treatment for anxious African-American adolescents: A controlled pilot study. *Journal of the American Academy of Child and Adolescent Psychiatry*, 41(7), 768–775.

Gorman, J., Shear, K., Cowley, D., Cross, C. D., March, J., Roth, W., et al. (2002). Practice guideline for the treatment of patients with panic disorder. In *American Psychiatric Association practice guidelines for the treatment of psychiatric disorders. Compendium 2002* (pp. 635–696). Washington, DC: American Psychiatric Association.

Hagopian, L., & Ollendick, T. (1997). Anxiety disorders. In *Handbook of prevention and treatment with children and adolescents: Intervention in the real world context* (pp. 431–454). Hoboken, NJ: John Wiley & Sons Inc.

Hayward, P., Ahmad, T., & Wardle, J. (2000). Attention to bodily sensations: A test of the cognitive-attentional model of panic. *Depression & Anxiety* (1091-4269), 12(4), 203–208.

Huey, S. J., & Polo, A. J. (2008). Evidence-based psychosocial treatments for ethnic minority youth. *Clinical and Child Adolescent Psychology*, 37(1), 262–301.

In-Albon, T., & Schneider, S. (2006). Psychotherapy of childhood anxiety disorders: A meta-analysis. *Psychotherapy and Psychosomatics*, 76(1), 15–24.

James, A. A. C. J., Soler, A., & Weatherall, R. R. W. (2005). Cognitive behavioural therapy for anxiety disorders in children and adolescents. *Cochrane Database of Systematic Reviews*, 4, CD004690.

Kagan, J., Reznick, J., Snidman, N., Gibbons, J., & Johnson, M. (1988). Childhood derivatives of inhibition and lack of inhibition to the unfamiliar. *Child Development*, 59(6), 1580.

Kazdin, A. (2000). Perceived barriers to treatment participation and treatment acceptability among antisocial children and their families. *Journal of Child & Family Studies*, 9(2), 157–174.

Kendall, E. C. (1990). *Coping Cat workbook*. Ardmore, PA: Workbook.

Kendall, P. (1994). Treating anxiety disorders in children: Results of a randomized clinical trial. *Journal of Consulting and Clinical Psychology*, 62(1), 100–110.

Kendall, P., Flannery-Schroeder, E., Panichelli-Mindel, S., Southam-Gerow, M., Henin, A., & Warman, M. (1997). Therapy for youths with anxiety disorders: A second randomized clinical trial. *Journal of Consulting and Clinical Psychology*, 65(3), 366–380.

Kendall, P., Hudson, J., Gosch, E., Flannery-Schroeder, E., & Suveg, C. (2008). Cognitive-behavioral therapy for anxiety disordered youth: A randomized clinical trial evaluating child and family modalities. *Journal of Consulting and Clinical Psychology*, 76(2), 282–297.

Kendall, P., Kane, M., Howard, B., & Siqueland, L. (1990). *Cognitive-behavioral treatment of anxious children: Treatment manual*. (Available from P. C. Kendall, Department of Psychology, Temple University, Philadelphia, PA 19122.)

Lemstra, M., Neudorf, C., D'Arcy, C., Kunst, A., Warren, L. M, & Bennett N. R. (2008). A systematic review of depressed mood and anxiety by SES in youth aged 10–15 years. *Canadian Journal of Public Health*, 99(2), 125–129.

March, J. S., & Mulle, K. (1998). *OCD in children and adolescents: A cognitive–behavioral treatment manual.* New York: Guilford.

McLeod, B. D., Wood, J. J., & Weisz, J. R. (2007). Examining the association between parenting and childhood anxiety: A meta-analysis. *Clinical Psychology Review, 27*(2), 155–172.

Mendlowitz, S., Manassis, K., Bradley, S., Scapillato, D., Miezitis, S., & Shaw, B. (1999). Cognitive-behavioral group treatments in childhood anxiety disorders: The role of parental involvement. *Journal of the American Academy of Child & Adolescent Psychiatry, 38*(10), 1223–1229.

O'Kearney, R. (2007). Benefits of cognitive-behavioural therapy for children and youth with obsessive-compulsive disorder: Re-examination of the evidence. *Australian & New Zealand Journal of Psychiatry, 41*(3), 199–212.

O'Kearney, R. T., Anstey, K., & von Sanden, C. (2006). Behavioural and cognitive behavioural therapy for obsessive compulsive disorder in children and adolescents. *Cochrane Database of Systematic Reviews, 4,* CD004856.

Ozer, E., Best, S., Lipsey, T., & Weiss, D. (2003). Predictors of posttraumatic stress disorder and symptoms in adults: A meta-analysis. *Psychological Bulletin, 129,* 52–73.

Pediatric OCD Treatment Study (POTS) Team: (2004). Cognitive-behavior therapy, sertraline, and their combination for children and adolescents with obsessive-compulsive disorder: The Pediatric OCD Treatment Study (POTS) randomized controlled trial. *JAMA: Journal of the American Medical Association, 292*(16), 1969–1976.

Rapee, R., Abbott, M., & Lyneham, H. (2006). Bibliotherapy for children with anxiety disorders using written materials for parents: A randomized controlled trial. *Journal of Consulting and Clinical Psychology, 74*(3), 436–444.

Silverman, W. K., Kurtines, W. M., Ginsburg, G. S., Weems, C. F., Lumpkin, P. W., & Carmichael, D. H. (1999). Treating anxiety disorders in children with group cognitive-behavioral therapy: A randomized clinical trial. *Journal of Consulting and Clinical Psychology, 67*(6), 995–1003.

Silverman, W. K., Oritz, C. D., Viswesvaran, C., Burns, B., Kolko, D. J., Putnam, F. W., & Amaya-Jackson, L. (2008). Evidence-based psychosocial treatments for children and adolescents exposed to traumatic events. *Journal of Clinical Child & Adolescent Psychology, 37*(1), 156–183.

Silverman, W., Pina, A., & Viswesvaran, C. (2008). Evidence-based psychosocial treatments for phobic and anxiety disorders in children and adolescents. *Journal of Clinical Child & Adolescent Psychology, 37*(1), 105–130.

Spence, S., Donovan, C., & Brechman-Toussaint, M. (2000). The treatment of childhood social phobia: The effectiveness of a social skills training-based, cognitive-behavioural intervention, with and without parental involvement. *Journal of Child Psychology and Psychiatry, 41*(6), 713–726.

Spence, S. H., Holmes, J. M., March, S., & Lipp, O. V. (2006). The feasibility and outcome of clinic plus internet delivery of cognitive behavior therapy for childhood anxiety. *Journal of Consulting and Clinical Psychology, 74,* 614–621.

Spielmans, G., Pasek, L., & McFall, J. (2007). What are the active ingredients in cognitive and behavioral psychotherapy for anxious and depressed children? A meta-analytic review. *Clinical Psychology Review, 27*(5), 642–654.

Storch, E., Merlo, L., Larson, M., Geffken, G., Lehmkuhl, H., Jacob, M., et al. (2008). Impact of comorbidity on cognitive-behavioral therapy response in pediatric obsessive-compulsive disorder. *Journal of the American Academy of Child & Adolescent Psychiatry, 47*(5), 583–592.

Twenge, J. M. (2000). The age of anxiety? The birth cohort change in anxiety and neuroticism, 1952–1993. *Journal of Personality and Social Psychology, 79*(6), 1007–1021.

Velting, O., Setzer, N., & Albano, A. (2004). Update on and advances in assessment and cognitive-behavioral treatment of anxiety disorders in children and adolescents. *Professional Psychology: Research & Practice, 35*(1), 42–54.

Verdeli, H., Mufson, L., Lee, L., & Keith, J. A. (2006). Review of evidence-based psychotherapies for pediatric mood and anxiety disorders. *Current Psychiatry Reviews, 2*(3), 395–421.

Walkup, J. T., Albano, A. M., Piacentini, J., Birmaher, B., Compton, S. N., Sherrill, J. T., Ginsburg, G. S., Rynn, M. A., McCracken, J., Waslick, B., Iyengar, S., March, J. S., & Kendall, P. C. (2008). Cognitive behavioral therapy, sertraline, or a combination in childhood anxiety. *New England Journal of Medicine, 359*(26), 2753–2766.

Warren, S., Huston, L., Egeland, B., & Sroufe, L. (1997). Child and adolescent anxiety disorders and early attachment. *Journal of the American Academy of Child & Adolescent Psychiatry, 36*(5), 637–644.

Wilson, N. H., & Rotter, J. C. (1986). Anxiety management training and study skills counseling for students on self-esteem and test anxiety and performance. *School Counselor, 34*(1), 18–31.

CHAPTER 6

American Psychiatric Association. (2000). *Diagnostic and statistical manual of mental disorders,* 4th ed., Text Rev. Washington, DC: Author.

Brewin, C., Andrews, B., & Valentine, J. (2000). Meta-analysis of risk factors for posttraumatic stress disorder in trauma-exposed adults. *Journal of Consulting and Clinical Psychology, 68*, 748–766.

Bridge, J. A., Iyengar, S., Salary, C. B., Barbe, R. P., Birmaher, B., Pincus, H. A., Ren, L., & Brent, D. A. (2007). Clinical response and risk for reported suicidal ideation and suicide attempts in pediatric antidepressant treatment: A meta-analysis of randomized controlled trials. *JAMA, 297*(15), 1683–1696.

Broman-Fulks, J. J., Ruggiero, K. J., Green, B. A., Kilpatrick, D. G., Danielson, C. K., Resnick, H. S., & Saunders, B. (2006). Taxometric investigation of PTSD: Data from two nationally representative samples. *Behavior Therapy, 37*(4), 364–380.

Cohen, J. (1998). Practice parameters for the assessment and treatment of children and adolescents with posttraumatic stress disorder. *Journal of the American Academy of Child & Adolescent Psychiatry, 37*(10), 4S–26S.

Cohen, J. (2005). Treating Traumatized Children: Current Status and Future Directions. *Journal of Trauma & Dissociation, 6*(2), 109–121.

Cohen, J. A., Deblinger, E., Mannarino, A. P., & Steer, R. A. (2004). A multisite randomized controlled study of sexually abused, multiply traumatized children with PTSD: Initial treatment outcome. *Journal of the American Academy of Child & Adolescent Psychiatry, 43*, 393–402.

Cohen, J. A., & Mannarino, A. P. (1996). A treatment outcome study for sexually abused preschool children: Initial findings. *Journal of the American Academy of Child & Adolescent Psychiatry, 35*, 42–50.

Cohen, J. A., & Mannarino, A. P. (1998). Factors that mediate treatment outcome of sexually abused preschool children: Six- and 12-month follow up. *Journal of the American Academy of Child & Adolescent Psychiatry, 37*(1), 44–51.

Cohen, J. A., Mannarino, A. P., & Perel, J. M. (2007). A pilot randomized controlled trial of combined trauma-focused CBT and sertraline for childhood PSTD symptoms. *Journal of the American Academy of Child & Adolescent Psychiatry, 46*(7), 811–819.

Cohen, J. A., Mannarino, A. P., Perel, J. M., & Staron, V. (2007). A pilot randomized controlled trial of combined trauma-focused BCT and sertraline from childhood PTSD symptoms. *Journal of the American Academy of Child & Adolescent Psychiatry, 46*(7), 811–819.

Cohen, J., Mannarino, A., & Rogal, S. (2001). Treatment practices for childhood posttraumatic stress disorder. *Child Abuse and Neglect, 25*, 123–135.

Copeland, W. E., Keeler, G., Angold, A., & Costello, E. J. (2007). Traumatic events and posttraumatic stress in childhood. *Archives of General Psychiatry, 64*(5), 557–584.

Corcoran, J. (1998). In defense of mothers of sexual abuse victims. *Families in Society, 49*, 358–369.

Corcoran, J., & Pillai, V. (2007). Effectiveness of Secondary Pregnancy Prevention Programs: A Meta-Analysis. *Research on Social Work Practice, 17*(1), 5–18.

Corcoran, J., & Pillai, V. (2008). A meta-analysis of parent-involved treatment for child sexual abuse. *Research in Social Work Practice, 18*, 453–464.

Costello, E., Egger, H., & Angold, A. (2005). The developmental epidemiology of anxiety disorders: Phenomenology, prevalence, and comorbidity child adolescent. *Psychiatric Clinics of North America, 14*, 631–648.

Deblinger, E., & Heflin, A. H. (1996). *Treating sexually abused children and their nonoffending parents: A cognitive-behavioral approach*. Thousand Oaks, CA: Sage.

Deblinger, E., Lippman, J., & Steer, R. (1996). Sexually abused children suffering posttraumatic stress symptoms: Initial treatment outcome findings. *Child Maltreatment, 1*, 310–321.

Foa, E. B., Keane, T. M., & Friedman, M. J. (Eds.). (2000). *Effective treatments for PTSD: Practice guidelines from the International Society for Traumatic Stress Studies*. New York: Guilford Press.

Hetrick, S. E., Merry, S. N., McKenzie, J., Sindahl, P., & Proctor, M. (2007). Selective serotonin reuptake inhibitors (SSRIs) for depressive disorders in children and adolescents. *Cochrane Database of Systematic Reviews*, Issue 3, CD004851.

Huey, S. J., & Polo, A. J. (2008). Evidence-based psychosocial treatments for ethnic minority youth. *Journal of Clinical Child and Adolescent Psychology, 37*, 262–301.

Kataoka, S. A., Stein, B. D., Jaycox, L. H., Wong, M., Escudero, P., & Tu, W. (2003). A school-based mental health program for traumatized Latino immigrant children. *Journal of the American Academy of Child & Adolescent Psychiatry, 42*, 311–318.

Kazdin, A. (2001). *Behavior modification in applied settings* (6th ed.). Belmont, CA: Wadsworth/Thomson Learning.

Kolko, D. J. (1996). Individual cognitive behavioral treatment and family treatment and family therapy for physically abused brood and their offending parents: A comparison of clinical outcomes. *Child Maltreatment, 1*, 322–342.

Kowalik, S. (2004). Neurobiology of PTSD in children and adolescents. In R. Silva (Ed.), *Posttraumatic stress disorders in children and adolescents: Handbook* (pp. 83–122). New York: W.W. Norton & Co.

Linares, L. O., & Cloitre, M. (2004). Intergenerational links between mothers and children with PTSD spectrum illness. In R. Silva (Ed.), *Posttraumatic stress disorders in children and adolescents: Handbook*. New York: W.W. Norton & Co.

Macdonald, G., Higgins, J. P. T., & Ramchandani, P. (2006).Cognitive-behavioural interventions for children who have been sexually abused. *Cochrane Database of Systematic Reviews*, Issue 4, CD001930.

Ozer, E., Best, S., Lipsey, T., & Weiss, D. (2003). Predictors of posttraumatic stress disorder and symptoms in adults: A meta-analysis. *Psychological Bulletin, 129*, 52–73.

Rojas, V., & Pappagallo, M. (2004). Risk factors for PTSD in children and adolescents. In R. Silva (Ed.), *Posttraumatic stress disorders in children and adolescents: Handbook* (pp. 38–59). New York: W.W. Norton & Co.

Rothbaum, B., Meadows, E., Resick, P., & Foy, D. (2000). Cognitive-behavioral therapy. *Effective treatments for PTSD: Practice guidelines from the International Society for Traumatic Stress Studies* (pp. 320–325). New York: Guilford Press.

Saigh, P., Yasik, A., Oberfield, R., & Halamandaris, P. (2007). Self-reported anger among traumatized children and adolescents. *Journal of Psychopathology and Behavioral Assessment, 29*(1), 29–37.

Saigh, P., Yasik, A., Oberfield, R., Halamandaris, P., & Bremner, J. (2006). The intellectual performance of traumatized children and adolescents with or without posttraumatic stress disorder. *Journal of Abnormal Psychology, 115*(2), 332–340.

Saigh, P., Yasik, A., Sack, W., & Koplewicz, H. (1999). Child-adolescent posttraumatic stress disorder: Prevalence, risk factors, and comorbidity. In P. Saigh & J. Bremner (Eds.), *Posttraumatic stress disorder: A comprehensive text* (pp. 18–43). Needham Heights, MA: Allyn & Bacon.

Scheeringa, M. S., Wright, M. J., Hunt, J. P., & Zeanah, C. H. (2006). Factors affecting the diagnosis and prediction of PTSD symptomatology in children and adolescents. *American Journal of Psychiatry, 163*, 644–651.

Scheeringa, M. S., Zeanah, C. H., Drell, M. J., & Larrieu, J. A. (1995). Two approaches to the diagnosis of posttraumatic stress disorder in infancy and early childhood. *Journal of the American Academy of Child & Adolescent Psychiatry, 34*(2), 191–200.

Silva, R., & Kessler, L. (2004). Resiliency and vulnerability Factors in childhood PTSD. In R. Silva (Ed.), *Posttraumatic stress disorders in children and adolescents: Handbook* (pp. 18–37). New York: W.W. Norton & Co.

Silverman, W. K., Ortiz, C. D., Viswesvaran, C., Burns, B. J., Kolko, D. J., Putnam, F. W., et al. (2008). Evidence-based psychosocial treatments for children and adolescents exposed to traumatic events. *Journal of Clinical Child and Adolescent Psychology, 37*, 156–183.

Skowron, E., & Reinemann, D. H. (2005). Effectiveness of psychological interventions for child maltreatment: A meta-analysis. *Psychotherapy: Theory, Research, Practice, Training, 42*(1), 52–71.

Stein, D. J., Jaycox, L. H., Kataoka, S. H., Wong, M., Tu, W., & Elliott, M. N. (2003). A mental health intervention for school children exposed to violence. *Journal of the American Medical Association, 290*, 603–611.

Stein, D. J., Zungu-Dirwayi, N., Van der Linden, G. J. H., & Seedat, S. (2003). Pharmacotherapy for posttraumatic stress disorder (Cochrane Review). In *The Cochrane Library*, Issue 1. Oxford: Update Software.

Storr, C. L., Ialongo, N. S., Anthony, J. C., et al. (2007). Childhood antecedents of exposure to traumatic events and posttraumatic stress disorder. *The American Journal of Psychiatry, 164*(1), 119–125.

U.S. Department of Health and Human Services. (2001). Mental health: Culture, race and ethnicity—A supplement to mental health: A report of the surgeon general. Rockville, MD: U.S. Department of Health and Human Services, Substance Abuse and Mental Health Services Administration, Center for Mental Health Services, National Institutes of Health, National Institute of Mental Health.

Wethington, H., Hahn, R., Fuqua-Whitley, D., Sipe, T., Crosby, A., Johnson, R., Liberman, A., Mościcki, E., Price, L., Tuma, F., Kalra G., & Chattopadhyay, S. (2008). The effectiveness of interventions to reduce psychological harm from traumatic events among children and adolescents: A systematic review. *American Journal of Preventative Medicine, 35,* 287–313.

CHAPTER 7

Abela, J. R., Brozina, K., & Haigh, E. P. (2002). An examination of the response styles theory of depression in third-and seventh-grade children: A short-term longitudinal study. *Journal of Abnormal Child Psychology, 30*(5), 515–527.

Abramson, L., Metalsky, G., & Alloy, L. (1989). Hopelessness depression: A theory-based subtype of depression. *Psychological Review, 96*(2), 358–372.

Ackerson, J., Scogin, F., McKendree-Smith, N., & Lyman, R. D. (1998). Cognitive bibliotherapy for mild and moderate adolescent depressive symptomatology. *Journal of Consulting and Clinical Psychology, 66,* 685–690.

Alexandre, P K, Martins, S, & Richard, P. (2009). Disparities in adequate mental health care for past-year major depressive episodes among caucasian and hispanic youths. *Psychiatric Services, 60*(10), 1365–1371.

Beck, A. T. (1967). *Depression.* New York: Harper & Row.

Beck, A. T. (1970). *Depression: Causes and treatment.* Philadelphia: University of Pennsylvania Press.

Bolen, R., & Scannepeico, M. (1999). Prevalence of child sexual abuse: A corrective meta-analysis. *Social Service Review, 73,* 281–301.

Boomsma, D. I., Van Beijsterveldt, C. E., & Hudziak, J. J. (2005). Genetic and environmental influences on anxious/depression during childhood: A study from the Netherlands Twin Register. *Genes, Brain and Behavior, 4*(8), 466–481.

Brent, D. A. (2007). Clinical response and risk for reported suicidal ideation and suicide attempts in pediatric antidepressant treatment: A meta-analysis of randomized controlled trials. *The Journal of the American Medical Association, 297,* 1683–1696.

Brent, D., Emslie, G., Clarke, G., Wagner, K. D., Asarnow, J. R., Keller, M. Vitiello, B., Ritz, L., Lyengar, S., Abebe, K., Birmaher, B., Ryan, N., Kennard B., Hughes, C., DeBar, L., McCracken, J., Strober, M., Suddath, R., Spirito, A., Leonard, H., Melhem, N., Porta, G., Onorato, M., & Zelazny, J. (2008). Switching to another SSRI or to venlafaxine with or without cognitive behavioral therapy for adolescents with SSRI-resistant depression: The TORDIA randomized controlled trial. *Journal of the American Medical Association, 299*(8), 901–913.

Brent, D. A., & Poling, K. (1997). *Cognitive therapy treatment manual for depressed and suicidal youth.* Pittsburgh, PA: Star Center.

Brent, D., Roth, C., Holder, D., & Kolko, D. (1996). Psychosocial interventions for treating adolescent suicidal depression: A comparison of three psychosocial interventions. In *Psychosocial treatments for child and adolescent disorders: Empirically based strategies for clinical practice* (pp. 187–206). Washington, DC: American Psychological Association.

Bridge, J. A., Iyengar, S., Salary, C. B., Barbe, R. P., Birmaher, B., Pincus, H. A., Ren, L., & Brent, D. A. (2007). Clinical response and risk for reported suicidal ideation and suicide attempts in pediatric antidepressant treatment: A meta-analysis of randomized controlled trials. *The Journal of the American Medical Association, 297*, 1683–1696.

Brown, R. T., Antonuccio, D. O., Dupaul, G. J., Fristad, M. A., King, C. A., Leslie, L. K., McCormick, G. S., Pelham, W. E., Piacentini, J. C., & Vitiello, B. (2007). *Childhood mental health disorders: Evidence-base and contextual factors for psychosocial, psychopharmacological, and combined interventions.* Washington, DC: American Psychological Association.

Brunwasser, S., Gilham, J., & Kim, E. (2009). A meta-analytic review of the Penn Resiliency program's effect on depressive symptoms. *Journal of Consulting and Clinical Psychology, 77*, 1042–1054.

Burns, D. (1980). *Feeling good.* New York: Signet.

Centers for Disease Control and Prevention. (2004). *Youth risk behavior surveillance. Surveillance summaries,* May 21, 2004. MMWR 2004:53(No. SS-2).

Centers for Disease Control and Prevention. (2008). Youth risk behavior surveillance system (YRBS) survey. Health behaviors by race/ethnicity. National YRBS 2007. Downloaded on January 2, 2009 at http://www.cdc.gov/HealthyYouth/yrbs/pdf/yrbs07_us_disparity_race.pdf.

Cespedes, Y. M., & Huey, S. J. (2008). Depression in Latino adolescents. *Cultural Diversity and Ethnic Minority Psychology, 14*(2), 168–172.

Chu, B., & Harrison, T. (2007). Disorder-specific effects of CBT for anxious and depressed youth: A meta-analysis of candidate mediators of change. *Clinical Child & Family Psychology Review, 10*(4), 352–372.

Clarke, G. N., Debar, L., Lynch, F., Powell, J., Gale, J., & O'Connor, E. (2005). A randomized effectiveness trial of brief cognitive-behavioral therapy for depressed adolescents receiving antidepressant medication. *Journal of the American Academy of Child and Adolescent Psychiatry, 44*, 888–898.

Clarke, G. N., Hawkins, W., Murphy, M., Sheeber, L., Lewinsohn, P. M., & Seeley, J. (1995). Targeted prevention of unipolar depressive disorder in an at risk sample of high school adolescents: A randomized trial of a group cognitive intervention. *American Academy of Child and Adolescent Psychiatry, 34*, 312–321.

Clarke, G. N., Lewinsohn, P. M., & Hops, H. (1990). *Adolescent coping with depression course.* Kaiser Permanent, Portland, OR—retrieved from http://www.kpchr.org/acwd/acwd.html.

Corcoran, J., Dattalo, P., Grindle, L., & Brown, E. (2010, in preparation). Interventions for adolescent suicidality: A systematic review.

Costello, J. E., Erkanli, A., & Angold, A. (2006). Is there an epidemic of child or adolescent depression? *Journal of Child Psychology and Psychiatry, 47*(12), 1263–1271.

Curry, J., Rohde, P., Simons, A., Silva, S., Vitiello, B., & Kratochvil, C. J. (2006). Predictors and moderators of acute outcome in the Treatment for Adolescents with Depression Study (TADS). *Journal of the American Academy of Child and Adolescent Psychiatry, 45*, 1427–1439.

David-Ferdon, C., & Kaslow, N. J. (2008). Evidence-based psychosocial treatments for child and adolescent depression. *Journal of Clinical Child and Adolescent Psychology, 37*(1), 62–104.

Desai, H., & Jann, M. (2000). Major depression in women: A review of the literature. *Journal of the American Pharmaceutical Association, 40*, 525–537.

Diamond, G. S., Reis, B. F., Diamond, G. M., Siqueland, L., & Isaacs, L. (2002). Attachment-based family therapy for depressed adolescents: A treatment development study. *Journal of the American Academy of Child and Adolescent Psychiatry, 41*(10), 1190–1197.

Fergusson, D., Beautrais, A., & Horwood, L. (2003). Vulnerability and resiliency to suicidal behaviours in young people. *Psychological Medicine, 33*, 61–73.

Food and Drug Administration. (2004). FDA public health advisory. *Suicidality in children and adolescents being treated with antidepressant medications.* Rockville, MD: U.S. Food and Drug Administration.

Gillham, J. E., & Reivich, K. J. (1999). Prevention of depressive symptoms in school children: A research update. *Psychological Science, 10*, 461–462.

Gillham, J. E., Reivich, K., Freres, D. R., Lascher, M., Litzinger, S., & Shatte, A. J. (2006). School-based prevention of depression and anxiety symptoms in early adolescence: A pilot of a parent intervention component. *School Psychology Quarterly, 21*, 323–348.

Gillham, J. E., Reivich, K., Jaycox, L., & Seligman, M. E. P. (1995). Prevention of depressive symptoms in school children: Two year follow-up. *Psychological Science, 6*, 343–351.

Girgus, J., & Nolen-Hoeksema, S. (2006). Cognition and depression. In C.L. Keyes & S.H. Goodman (Eds.), *Women and depression: A handbook for the social, behavioral, and biomedical sciences* (pp. 147–175). New York: Cambridge University Press.

Gladstone, T. R., & Kaslow, N. J. (1995). Depression and attributions in children and adolescents: A meta-analytic review. *Journal of Abnormal Child Psychology, 23*(5), 597–606.

Gonzalez-Tejara, G., Canino, G., Ramirez, R., Chavez, L., Shrout, P., Bird, H., Bravo, M., Martinez-Taboas, A., Ribery, J., & Bauermeister, J. (2005). Examining minor and major depression in adolescents. *Journal of Child Psychology and Psychiatry, 46*, 888–899.

Goodman, S., & Gotlib, I. (1999). Risk for psychopathology in the children of depressed mothers: A developmental approach to the understanding of mechanisms. *Psychological Review, 106*(3), 458.

Goodyer, I. M., Dubicka, B., Wilkinson, P., Kelvin, R., Roberts, C., Byford, S., Breen, S., Ford, C., Barrett, B., Leech, A., Rothwell, J., White, L., & Harrington, R. (2008). A randomised controlled trial of cognitive behaviour therapy in adolescents with major depression treated by selective serotonin reuptake inhibitors. The ADAPT trial. *Health Technology Assessment, 12*(14), iii–iv, ix–60.

Gutman, L. M., & Sameroff, A. J. (2004). Continuities in depression from adolescence to young adulthood: Contrasting ecological influences. *Development and Psychopathology, 16*, 967–984.

Hazell, P., O'Connell, D., Heathcote, D., & Henry, D. (2002). Tricyclic drugs for depression in children and adolescents. *Cochrane Database of Systematic Reviews*, Issue 2, CD002317. DOI: 10.1002/14651858.CD002317.

Hetrick, S. E., Merry, S., McKenzie, J., Sindahl, P., & Proctor, M. (2007). Selective serotonin reuptake inhibitors (SSRIs) for depressive disorders in children and adolescents. *Cochrane Database of Systematic Reviews*, (3).

Huey, S., & Polo, A. (2008). Evidence-based psychosocial treatments for ethnic minority youth. *Journal of Clinical Child and Adolescent Psychology, 37*(1), 262–301.

Jaycox, L., Reivich, K., Gillham, J. E., & Seligman, M. E. P. (1994). Prevention of depressive symptoms in school children. *Behavioral Research and Therapy, 32*, 801–816.

Joiner, T. E., & Wagner, K. D. (1995). Attribution style and depression in children and adolescents: A meta-analytic review. *Clinical Psychology Review, 15*(8), 777–798.

Jose, P., & Brown, I. (2008). When does the gender difference in rumination begin? Gender and age differences in the use of rumination by adolescents. *Journal of Youth & Adolescence, 37*(2), 180–192.

Kagan, J., Reznick, J. S., & Snidman, N. (1987). The physiology and psychology of behavioral inhibition in children. *Child Development, 58*(6), 1459–1473.

Kaminski, K.M., & Garber, J. (2002). Depressive spectrum disorders in high-risk adolescents; Episode duration and predictors of time to recovery. *Journal of the American Academy of Child and Adolescent Psychiatry, 41*(4), 410–418.

Kane, P., & Garber, J. (2004). The relations among depression in fathers, children's psychopathology, and father-child conflict: A meta-analysis. *Clinical Psychology Review, 24*(3), 339–360.

Kaslow, N. J., & Thompson, M. (1998). Applying the criteria for empirically supported treatments to studies of psychosocial interventions for child and adolescent depression. *Journal of Clinical Child Psychology, 27*, 146–155.

Keenan, K., Hipwell, A., Feng, X., Babinski, D., Hinze, A., Rischall, M., & Henneberger, A. (2008). Subthreshold symptoms of depression in preadolescent girls are stable and predictive of depressive disorders. *Journal of the American Academy of Child and Adolescent Psychiatry, 47*, 1433–1442.

Kendler, K. S., Gatz, M., Gardner, C. O., & Pedersen, N. L. (2005). Age at onset and familial risk for major depression in a Swedish national twin sample. *Psychological Medicine, 35*(11), 1573–1579.

Kendler, K., Kuhn, J., Vittum, J., Prescott, C., & Riley, B. (2005). The interaction of stressful life events and a serotonin transporter polymorphism in the prediction of episodes of major depression. *Archives of General Psychiatry, 62*(5), 529–535.

Keenan, K., Hipwell, A., Xin, F., Babinski, D., Hinze, A., Rischall, M., et al. (2008). Subthreshold symptoms of depression in preadolescent girls are stable and predictive of depressive disorders. *Journal of the American Academy of Child & Adolescent Psychiatry, 47*(12), 1433–1442.

Kennard, B., Clarke, G., Weersing, V., Asarnow, J., Shamseddeen, W., Porta, G., Berk, M., Hughes, J. L., Spirito, A., Emslie, G. J., Keller, M. B., Wagner, K. D., Brent, D.A. (2009). Effective Components of TORDIA Cognitive-Behavioral Therapy for Adolescent Depression: Preliminary Findings. *Journal of Consulting & Clinical Psychology, 77*(6), 1033–1041.

Kessler, R. C. (2003). Epidemiology of women and depression. *Journal of Affective Disorders, 74*(1), 5–13.

Kolko, D. J., Brent, D. A., Baugher, M., Bridge, J., & Birmaher, B. (2000). Cognitive and family therapies for adolescent depression: Treatment specificity, medication, and moderation. *Journal of Consulting and Clinical Psychology, 68*, 303–314.

Kovacs, M. (2001). Gender and the course of major depressive disorder through adolescence in clinically referred youngsters. *Journal of the American Academy of Child and Adolescent Psychiatry, 40*, 1079–1085.

Le, H. N., Munoz, R., Ippen, C. G., & Stoddard, J. (2003). Treatment is not enough: We must prevent major depression in women. *Prevention and Treatment.* Retrieved on December 31, 2003 from http://80gateway1.ovid.com.proxy.library.vcu.edu/ovidweb.cgi.

Leech, S., Larkby, C., Day, R., & Day, N. (2006). Predictors and correlates of high levels of depression and anxiety symptoms among children at age 10. *Journal of the American Academy of Child and Adolescent Psychiatry, 45*(2), 223–230.

Lemstra, M., Neudorf, C., D'Arcy, C., Kunst, A., Warren, L., & Bennett, N. (2008). A systematic review of depressed mood and anxiety by SES in youth aged 10–15 years. *Canadian Journal of Public Health, 99*(2), 125–129.

Lewinsohn, P., & Clarke, G. (1999). Psychosocial treatments for adolescent depression. *Clinical Psychology Review, 19*(3), 329–342.

Lewinsohn, P. M., Clarke, G., Hops, H., & Andrews, J. (1990). Cognitive-behavioral treatment for depressed adolescents. *Behavior Therapy, 21,* 385–401.

Lewinsohn, P., Clarke, G., Rohde, P., & Hops, H. (1996). A course in coping: A cognitive-behavioral approach to the treatment of adolescent depression. In *Psychosocial treatments for child and adolescent disorders: Empirically based strategies for clinical practice* (pp. 109–135). Washington, DC: American Psychological Association.

Lewis, C., Simons, A., Nguyen, L., Murakami, J., Reid, M., Silva, S., & March, J. Impact of childhood trauma on treatment outcome in the treatment for adolescents with depression study (TADS). *Journal of the American Academy of Child and Adolescent Psychiatry, 49,* 132–140.

Luyten, P., Blatt, S. J., & Van Houdenhove, B. (2006). Depression research and treatment: Are we skating to where the puck is going to be? *Clinical Psychology Review, 26*(8), 985–999.

March, J., & Vitiello, B. (2009). Clinical messages from the treatment for adolescents with depression study (TADS). *American Journal of Psychiatry, 166*(10), 1118–1123.

McLeod, B. D., Weisz, J. R., & Wood, J. J. (2007). Examining the association between parenting and childhood depression: A meta-analysis. *Clinical Psychology Review, 27*(8), 986–1003.

Melvin, G. A., Tonge, B. J., King, N. J., Heyne, D., Gordon, M. S., & Klimkeit, E. (2006). A comparison of cognitive-behavioral therapy, sertraline, and their combination for adolescent depression. *Journal of the American Academy of Child and Adolescent Psychiatry, 45,* 1151–1161.

Michael, K. D., & Crowley, S. L. (2002). How effective are treatments for child and adolescent depression? A meta-analytic review. *Clinical Psychology Review, 22,* 247–269.

Mufson, L., Dorta, K. P., Moreau, D., & Weissman, M. M. (2005). Efficacy to effectiveness: Adaptations of interpersonal psychotherapy for adolescent depression. In E. Hibbs & P. Jensen (Eds.), *Psychosocial treatments for child and adolescent disorders: Empirically based strategies for clinical practice,* 2nd ed. (pp. 165–186). Washington, DC: American Psychological Association.

Nolen-Hoeksma, S. (2002). Gender differences in depression. In I. H. Gotlib (Ed.), *Handbook of depression* (pp. 492–509). New York: Guilford Press.

Olfson, M., Blanco, C., Liu, L., Moreno, C., & Laje, G. (2006). National trends in the outpatient treatment of children and adolescents with antipsychotic drugs. *Archives of General Psychiatry, 63*(6), 679–685.

Paolucci, E., Genuis, M., & Violato, C. (2001). A Meta-Analysis of the Published Research on the Effects of Child Sexual Abuse. *Journal of Psychology, 135*(1), 17.

Patton, G., Olsson, C., Bond, L., Toumbourou, J., Carlin, J., Hemphill, S., et al. (2008). Predicting female depression across puberty: A two-nation longitudinal study. *Journal of the American Academy of Child & Adolescent Psychiatry, 47*(12), 1424–1432.

Penza, K., Heim, C., & Nemeroff, C. (2006). Trauma and depression. In C. L. M. Keyes & S. H. Goodman (Eds.), *Women and depression, handbook for the social, behavioral, and biomedical sciences* (pp. 360–381). New York: Cambridge University Press.

Pilowsky, D., Wickramaratne, P., Rush, A., Hughes, C., Garber, J., Malloy, E., et al. (2006). Children of currently depressed mothers: A STAR*D ancillary study. *Journal of Clinical Psychiatry, 67*(1), 126–136.

Rao, U., Hammen, C., & Poland, R. (2010). Longitudinal course of adolescent depression: Neuroendocrine and psychosocial predictors. *Journal of the American Academy of Child and Adolescent Psychiatry, 49,* 141–151.

Reinecke, M. A., Ryan, N. E., & DuBois, D. L. (1998). Cognitive-behavioral therapy of depression and depressive symptoms during adolescence: A review and meta-analysis. *Journal of the American Academy of Child and Adolescent Psychiatry, 37,* 26–34.

Riggs, P. D., Mikulich-Gilbertson, S. K., Davies, R. D., Lohman, M., Klein, C., & Stover, S. K. (2007). A randomized controlled trial of fluoxetine and cognitive behavioral therapy in adolescents with major depression, behavior problems, and substance use disorders. *Archives of Pediatrics and Adolescent Medicine, 16*(11), 1026–1034.

Roberts, C., Kane, R., Thomson, H., Bishop, B. and Hart, B. (2003). The prevention of depressive symptoms in rural school children: A randomized controlled trial. *Journal of Consulting and Clinical Psychology, 71,* 622–628.

Rossello, J., & Bernal, G. (1999). The efficacy of cognitive-behavioral and interpersonal treatments for depression in Puerto Rican adolescents. *Journal of Consulting and Clinical Psychology, 67,* 734–745.

Rossello, J., Bernal, G., & Rivera-Medina, C. (2008). Individual and group CBT and IPT for Puerto Rican adolescents with depressive symptoms. *Cultural Diversity and Ethnic Minority Psychology, 14*(3), 234–245.

Rudolph, K. (2002). Gender differences in emotional responses to interpersonal stress during adolescence. *Journal of Adolescent Health, 30,* 3–13.

Rushton, J., Forcier, M., & Schectman, R. (2002). Epidemiology of depressive symptoms in the national longitudinal study of adolescent health. *Journal of American Academy of Child and Adolescent Psychiatry, 41,* 199–205.

Rutter, M., Kim-Cohen, J., & Maughan, B. (2006). Continuities and discontinuities in psycho-pathology between childhood and adult life. *Journal of Child Psychology and Psychiatry, 47*(3–4), 276–295.

Sander, J. B., & McCarty, C. A. (2005). Youth depression in the family context: Familial risk factors and models of treatment. *Clinical Child and Family Psychology Review, 8*(3), 203–219.

Sanford, M., Boyle, M., McCleary, L., Miller, J. G., Steele, M. & Duku, E. (2006). A pilot study of adjunctive family psychoeducation in adolescent major depression: Feasibility and treatment effect. *Journal of the American Academy of Child and Adolescent Psychiatry, 45,* 386–395.

Silk, J. S., Vanderbilt-Adriance, E., Shaw, D. S., Forbes, E. E., Whalen, D. J., Ryan, N. D., & Dahl, R. E. (2007). Resilience among children and adolescents at risk for depression: Mediation and moderation across social and neurobiological contexts. *Development and Psychopathology, 19*(3), 841–865.

Simons, R., Murry, V., McLoyd, V., Kueihsiu, L., Cutrona, C., & Conger, R. (2002). Discrimination, crime, ethnic identity, and parenting as correlates of depressive symptoms among African American children: A multilevel analysis. *Development and Psychopathology, 14,* 371–393.

Spielmans, G. I., Pasek, L. F., & McFall, J. P. (2007). What are the active ingredients in cognitive and behavioral psychotherapy for anxious and depressed children? A meta-analytic review. *Clinical Psychology Review, 27*(5), 642–654.

Stark, K. D., Hargrave, J., Sander, J., Custer, G., Schnoebelen, S., Simpson, J., & Molnar, J. (2006). Treatment of childhood depression: The ACTION treatment program. In P. C. Kendall (Ed.), *Child and adolescent therapy: Cognitive-behavioral procedures* (3rd ed., pp. 169–216). New York: Guilford Press.

Stark, K. D., Reynolds, W. M., & Kaslow, N. J. (1987). A comparison of the relative efficacy of self-control therapy and behavior problem-solving therapy for depression in children. *Journal of Abnormal Child Psychology, 15*, 91–113.

Stark, K. D., Rouse, L., & Livingston, R. (1991). In P. Kendall (Ed.), *Child and adolescent therapy* (pp. 165–206). New York: Guilford Press.

Taylor, T. L., & Montgomery, P. (2007). Can cognitive-behavioral therapy increase self-esteem among depressed adolescents? A systematic review. *Children and Youth Services Review, 29*(7), 823–839.

The TADS Team. (2007). The treatment for adolescents with depression study (TADS): Long-term effectiveness and safety outcomes. The TADS Team. *Archives of General Psychiatry, 64*(10), 1132–1144.

Twenge, J. M., & Nolen-Hoeksema, S. (2002). Age, gender, race, socioeconomic status, and birth cohort difference on the children's depression inventory: A meta-analysis. *Journal of Abnormal Psychology, 111*(4), 578–588.

Umaña-Taylor, A., & Updegraff, K. (2007). Latino adolescents' mental health: Exploring the interrelations among discrimination, ethnic identity, cultural orientation, self-esteem, and depressive symptoms. *Journal of Adolescence, 30*(4), 549–567.

Usala, T., Clavenna, A., Zuddas, A., & Bonati, M. (2008). Randomised controlled trials of selective serotonin reuptake inhibitors in treating depression in children and adolescents: A systematic review and meta-analysis. *European Neuropsychopharmacology, 18*(1), 62–73.

Verdeli, H., Mufson, L., Lee, L., & Keith, J. A. (2006). Review of evidence-based psychotherapies for pediatric mood and anxiety disorders. *Current Psychiatry Reviews, 2*(3), 395–421.

Vitiello, B. (2009). Treatment of adolescent depression: what we have come to know. *Depression & Anxiety (1091-4269), 26*(5), 393–395.

Wade, T. J., Cairney, J., & Pevalin, D. J. (2002). Emergence of gender differences in depression during adolescence: National panel results from three countries. *Journal of the American Academy of Child and Adolescent Psychiatry, 41*, 190–199.

Watanabe, N., Hunot, V., Omori, I. M., Churchill, R., & Furukawa, T. A. (2007). Psychotherapy for depression among children and adolescents: A systematic review. *Acta Psychiatrica Scandinavica, 116*(2), 84–95.

Weisz, J. R., McCarty, C. A., & Valeri, S. M. (2006). Effects of psychotherapy for depression in children and adolescents: A meta-analysis. *Psychological Bulletin, 132*, 132–149.

Whittington, C. J., Kendall, T., Fonagy, P., Cottrell, D., Cotgrove, A., & Boddington, E. (2004). Selective serotonin reuptake inhibitors in childhood depression: Systematic review of published versus unpublished data. *Lancet, 363*(9418), 1341–1345.

Yu, D. L. and Seligman, M. E. P. (2002). Preventing depressive symptoms in Chinese children. *Prevention and Treatment, 5*(9), 1–39.

CHAPTER 8

Agras, W. S., Brandt, H. A., Bulik, C. M., Dolan-Sewell, R., Fairburn, C. G., Halmi, K. A., Herzog, D. B., Jimerson, D. C., Kaplan, A. S., Kaye, W. H., Le Grange, D., Lock, J., Mitchell, J., Rudorfer, M. V., Street, L. L., Striegel-Moore, R., Vitousek, K. M., Walsh, B. T., & Wilfley, D. E. (2004). Report of National Institutes of Health workshop on overcoming barriers to treatment research in anorexia nervosa. *International Journal of Eating Disorders, 35*(4), 509–521.

Agras, W. S., Bryson, S., Hammer, L. D., & Kraemer, H. C. (2007). Childhood risk factors for thin body preoccupation and social pressure to be thin. *Journal of the American Academy of Child & Adolescent Psychiatry, 46*(2), 171–178.

American Psychiatric Association. (2000). *Diagnostic and Statistical Manual of Mental Disorders* (4th ed., Text Revision). Washington, DC: Author.

Anderson, A. E., Bowers, W. A., & Watson, T. (2001). A slimming program for eating disorders not otherwise specified: Reconceptualizing a confusing, residual diagnostic category. *Psychiatric Clinics of North America, 24*(2), 271–280.

Bacaltchuk, J., & Hay, P. (2003). *Antidepressants versus placebo for people with bulimianervosa* (Cochrane Review). In: *The Cochrane Library*, Issue 4. Chichester, UK: John Wiley & Sons, Ltd.

Bacaltchuk, J., Hay, P., & Trefiglio, R. (2001). Antidepressants verses psychological treatments and their combination for bulimia nervosa. *Cochrane Database System Review, 24*, CD003385.

Ball, J., & Mitchell, P. (2004). A randomized controlled study of cognitive behavior therapy and behavioral family therapy for anorexia nervosa patients. *Eating disorders, 12*(4), 303–314.

Bell, L. (2003). What can we learn from consumer studies and qualitative research in the treatment of eating disorders?. *Eating Weight Disorders, 8*, 181–187.

Berkman, N. D., Lohr, K. N., & Bulik, C. M. (2007). Outcomes of eating disorders: A systematic review of the literature. *International Journal of Eating Disorders, 40*(4), 293–309.

Bulik, C. M., Sullivan, P. F., Tozzi, F., Furberg, H., Lichtenstein, P., & Pedersen, N. L. (2006). Prevalence, heritability, and prospective risk factors for anorexia nervosa. *Archives of General Psychiatry, 63*, 305–312.

Cassin, S. E., & von Ranson, K. M (2005). Personality and eating disorders: A decade in review. *Clinical Psychology Review, 25*(7), 895–916.

Chen, E., Touyz, S. W., Beumont, J. V., Fairburn, C. G., Griffiths, R., Butow, P., Russell, J., Schotte, D. E., Gertler, R., & Basten, C. (2003). Comparison of group and individual cognitive-behavioral therapy for patients with bulimia nervosa. *International Journal of Eating Disorders, 33*(3), 241–254.

Christoph-Steinhausen, H., Grigoroiu-Serbanescu, M., Boyadjieva, S., Neumärker, K. J., & Metzke, C. W. (2008). Course and predictors of rehospitalization in adolescent anorexia nervosa in a multisite study. *International Journal of Eating Disorders, 41*(1), 29–36.

Claudino, A. M., Hay, P., Lima, M. S., Bacaltchuk, J., Schmidt, U., & Treasure, J. (2006). Antidepressants for anorexia nervosa. *Cochrane Database of Systematic Reviews*, Issue 1, CD004365. DOI: 10.1002/14651858.CD004365.pub2.

Commission on Adolescent Eating Disorders. (2005). In D. L. Evans, E. B. Foa, R. E. Gur, H. Hendin, C. P. O'Brien, M. E. P. Seligman, & B. T. Walsh (Eds.), *Treating and preventing adolescent mental health disorders: What we know and what we don't know* (pp. 283–302). New York: Oxford University Press.

Cooper, Z. (1995). The development and maintenance of eating disorders. In K. D. Brownell & C. G. Fairburn (Eds.), *Eating disorders and obesity: A comprehensive handbook* (pp. 199–206). New York: Guilford Press.

Crow, S., Eisenberg, M. E., Story, M., & Neumark-Sztainer, D. (2008). Are body dissatisfaction, eating disturbance, and body mass index predictors of suicidal behavior in adolescents? A longitudinal study. *Journal of Consulting and Clinical Psychology, 76*(5), 887–892.

Eddy, K. T., Doyle, A. C., Hoste, R. R., Herzog, D. B., & Le Grange, D. (2008). Eating disorder not otherwise specified in adolescents. *Journal of the American Academy of Child & Adolescent Psychiatry, 47*(2), 156–164.

Eisler, I., Dare, C., Hodes, M., Russell, G., Dodge, E., & Le Grange, D. (2000). Family therapy for adolescent anorexia nervosa: The results of a controlled comparison of two family interventions. *Journal of Child Psychology and Psychiatry and Allied Disciplines, 41*, 727–736.

Fairburn, C.G. (2008). *Cognitive behavior therapy and eating disorders.* New York: Guilford Publications.

Fairburn, C. G., Agras, W. S., Walsh, B. T., Wilson, G. T., & Stice, E. (2004). Prediction of outcome in bulimia nervosa by early change in treatment. *The American Journal of Psychiatry, 161*, 2322–2324.

Fairburn, C. G., Cooper, Z., Doll, H. A., & Davies, B. A. (2005). Identifying dieters who will develop an eating disorder: A prospective, population-based study. *The American Journal of Psychiatry, 162*, 2249–2255.

Fairburn, C. G., Cooper, Z., Doll, H. A., O'Connor, M. E., Bohn, K., Hawker, D. M., Wales, J.A., & Palmer, R.L. (2009). Transdiagnostic cognitive-behavioral therapy for patients with eating disorders: A two-site trial with 60-week follow-up. *American Journal of Psychiatry, 166*, 311–319.

Fairburn, C. G., Jones, R., Peveler, R. C., Carr, S. J., et al. (1991). Three psychological treatments for bulimia nervosa: A comparative trial. *Archives of General Psychiatry, 48*(5), 463–469.

Fairburn, C. G., Marcus, M. D., & Wilson, G. T. (1993). Cognitive-behavioral therapy for binge eating and bulimia nervosa: A comprehensive treatment manual. In C. G. Fairburn & G. T. Wilson (Eds.), *Binge eating: Nature, assessment, and treatment* (pp. 361–404). New York: Guilford Press.

Fairburn, C. G., Norman, P. A., Welch, S. A., O'Connor, M. E., et al. (1995). A prospective study of outcome in bulimia nervosa and the long-term effects of three psychological treatments. *Archives of General Psychiatry, 52*(4), 304–312.

Favaro, A., Tenconi, E., & Santonastaso, P. (2006). Prenatal factors and the risk of developing anorexia nervosa and bulimia nervosa. *Archives of General Psychiatry, 63*, 82–88.

Feld, R., Woodside, D., Kaplan, A., Olmsted, M., & Carter, J. (2001). Pretreatment motivational enhancement therapy for eating disorders: A pilot study. *International Journal of Eating Disorders, 29*(4), 393–400.

Fonagy, P., Target, M., Cottrell, D., Phillips, J., & Kurtz, Z. (2002). *What works for whom? A critical review of treatments for children and adolescents.* New York: Guilford Press.

Foreyt, J., Poston, W., Winebarger, A., & McGavin, J. (1998). Anorexia nervosa and bulimia nervosa. In E. Mash & R. Barkley (Eds.), *Treatment of childhood disorders* (2nd ed., pp. 647–691). New York: Guilford Press.

Franko, D. L., Dorer, D. J., Keel, P. K., Jackson, S., Manzo, M. P., & Herzog, D. B. (2005). How do eating disorders and alcohol use disorder influence each other? *International Journal of Eating Disorders, 38*, 200–207.

Franko, D., Wonderlich, S., Little, D., & Herzog, D. (2004). Diagnosis and classification of eating disorders. In J. K. Thompson (Ed.), *Handbook of eating disorders and obesity* (pp. 58–80). Hoboken, NJ: John Wiley & Sons.

Golden, N. H., Katzman, D. K., Kreipe, R. E., Stevens, S. L., Sawyer, S. M., Rees, J., Nicholls, D., Rome, E. S., & the Society for Adolescent Medicine. (2003). Eating disorders in adolescents: Position paper of the Society of Adolescent Medicine. *Journal of Adolescent Health, 33*(6), 496–503.

Gowers, S., & Bryant-Waugh, R. (2004). Management of child and adolescent eating disorders: The current evidence base and future directions. *Journal of Child Psychology and Psychiatry, 45*, 63–83.

Grabe, S., Ward, L. M., & Hyde, J. S. (2008). The role of the media in body image concerns among women: A meta-analysis of experimental and correlational studies. *Psychological Buletinl, 134*(3), 460–476.

Hay, P. J., Bacaltchuk, J., Byrnes, R. T., Claudino, A. M., Ekmejian, A. A., & Yong, P. Y. (2003). Individual psychotherapy in the outpatient treatment of adults with anorexia nervosa. *Cochrane Database of Systematic Reviews*, Issue 4, CD003909. DOI: 10.1002/14651858.CD003909.

Hay, P. J., Bacaltchuk, J., & Stefano, S. (2004). Psychotherapy for bulimia nervosa and binging. *Cochrane Database of Systematic Reviews, 3*, CD000562.

Hoek, H. W., & van Hoeken, D. (2003). Review of the prevalence and incidence of eating disorders. *International Journal of Eating Disorders, 34*(4), 383–396.

Hudson, J., Hiripi, E., Pope, H., & Kessler, R. (2006). The prevalence and correlates of eating disorders in the National Comorbidity Survey Replication. *Biological Psychiatry, 61*, 348–358.

Johnson, M., Woolf, K., Milliron, B., & Smith, K. (2007). Markers of eating behaviors in a diverse group of obese and normal weight women. *FASEB Journal, 21*(6).

Johnston, O., Fornai, G., Cabrini, S., & Kendrik, T. (2007). Feasibility and acceptability of screening for eating disorders in primary care. *Family Practice, 24*(5), 511–517.

Keel, P. K., Dorer, D. J., Franko, D. L., Jackson, S. C., & Herzog, D. B. (2005). Postremission predictors of relapse in women with eating disorders. *Amercan Journal of Psychiatry, 162*(12), 2263–2268.

Keel, P., & Mitchell, J. (1997). Outcome in bulimia nervosa. *American Journal of Psychiatry, 154*, 313–321.

Kelly, A., Wall, M., Eisenberg, M., Story, M., & Neumark-Sztainer, D. (2004). Adolescent girls with high body satisfaction: Who are they and what can they teach us? *Journal of Adolescent Health, 37*, 391–396.

Kotler, L. A., Boudreau, G. S., & Devlin, M. J. (2003). Emerging psychotherapies for eating disorders. *Journal of Psychiatric Practice, 9*(6), 431–441.

Kotler, L. A., Cohen, P., Davies, M., Pine, D. S., & Walsh, B. D. (2001). Longitudinal relationships between childhood, adolescent, and adult eating disorders. *Journal of the American Academy of Child and Adolescent Psychiatry, 40*, 1434–1441.

Le Grange, D., Crosby, R. D., Rathouz, P. J., & Leventhal, B. L. (2007). A randomized controlled comparison of family-based treatment and supportive psychotherapy for adolescent bulimia nervosa. *Archives of General Psychiatry, 64*(9), 1049–1056.

Le Grange, D., Eisler, I., Dare, C., & Russell, G. F. M. (1992). Evaluation of family treatments in adolescent anorexia nervosa: A pilot study. *International Journal of Eating Disorders, 12,* 347–357.

Leon, G. R., Fulkerson, J. A., Perry, C. L., Keel, P. K., & Klump, K. L. (1999). Three to four year prospective evaluation of personality and behavioral risk factors for later disordered eating in adolescent girls and boys. *Journal of Youth and Adolescence, 28,* 181.

Lewandowski, L., Gebing, T., Anthony, J., & O'Brien, W. (1997). Meta-analysis of cognitive-behavioral treatment studies for bulimia. *Clinical Psychology Review, 17,* 703–718.

Lewinsohn, P. M., Streigel-Moore, R. H., & Seeley, J. R. (2000). Epidemiology and natural course of eating disorders in young women from adolescence to young adulthood. *Journal of the American Academy of Child and Adolescent Psychiatry, 39,* 1284–1292.

Lock, J. (2005). Adjusting cognitive behavior therapy for adolescents with bulimia nervosa: Results of case series. *American Journal of Psychotherapy, 59*(3), 267–281.

Lock, J., Agras, W. S., Bryson, S., & Kraemer, H. C. (2005). A comparison of short- and long-term family therapy for adolescent anorexia nervosa. *Journal of the American Academy of Child and Adolescent Psychiatry, 44*(7), 632–639.

Lock, J., Le Grange, D., Agras, W. S., & Dare, C. (2001). *Treatment manual for anorexia nervosa: A family-based approach.* New York: Guilford Press.

Lowe, M. R. (2002). Dietary restraint and overeating. In K. D. Brownell (Ed.), *Eating disorders and obesity* (pp. 88–92). New York: Guildford Press.

Lowe, M. R., & Timko, C. A. (2004). What a difference a diet makes: Towards an understanding of differences between restrained dieters and restrained nondieters. *Eating Behaviors, 5*(3), 199–208.

Miller, W., & Rollnick, S. (2002). *Motivational interviewing* (2nd ed.). New York: Guilford Press.

Minuchin, S., Rosman, B. L., & Baker, L. (1978). *Psychosomatic families: Anorexia in context.* Cambridge, MA: Harvard University Press.

Mizes, J. S., & Palermo, T. M. (1997). Eating disorders. In R. T Ammerman & M. Hersen (Eds.), *Handbook of prevention and treatment with children and adolescents: Intervention in the real world context* (pp. 238–258). New York: John Wiley & Sons, Inc.

Nevonen, L., & Broberg, A. G. (2006). A comparison of sequenced individual and group psycho-therapy for patients with bulimia nervosa. *International Journal of Eating Disorders, 39*(2), 117–127.

NICE. (2004). Eating disorders: Core interventions in the treatment and management of anorexia nervosa, bulimia nervosa, and related eating disorders. Downloaded on July 17, 2009 from http://www.nice.org.uk/nicemedia/pdf/cg009niceguidance.pdf.

O'Neill, S. (2003). African American women and eating disturbances: A meta-analysis. *Journal of Black Psychology, 29,* 3–16.

Patton, G. C., Selzer, R., Coffey, C., Carlin, J. B., & Wolfe, R. (1999). Onset of adolescent eating disorders: Population based cohort study over 3 years. *British Medical Journal, 318,* 765–768.

Perkins, S. J., Murphy, R., Schmidt, U., & Williams, C. (2006). Self-help and guided self-help for eating disorders. *Cochrane Database of SystematicReviews,* Issue 3, CD004191. DOI: 10.1002/14651858.CD004191.pub2.

Pompili, M., Mancinelli, I., Girardi, P., Ruberto, A., & Tatarelli, R. (2004). Suicide in anorexia nervosa: A meta-analysis. *International Journal of Eating Disorders, 36*(1), 99–103.

Robin, A. L., Siegel, P. T., & Moye, A. (1995). Family versus individual therapy for anorexia: Impact on family conflict. *International Journal of Eating Disorders, 17*(4), 313–322.

Robin, A. L., Siegel, P. T., Koepke, T., Moye, A. W., & Tice, S. (1994). Family therapy versus individual therapy for adolescent females with anorexia nervosa. *Developmental and Behavioral Pediatrics, 15*(2), 111–116.

Robin, A. L., Seigel, P. T., Moye, A. W., Gilroy, M., Barker, D. A., & Sikand, A. (1999). A controlled comparison of family versus individual therapy for adolescents with anorexia nervosa. *Journal of the American Academy of Child and Adolescent Psychiatry, 38*, 1482–1489.

Rome, E., & Ammerman, S. (2003). Medical complications of eating disorders: An update. *Journal of Adolescent Health, 33*, 418–426.

Russell, G. F., Szmukler, G. I., Dare, C., & Eisler, I. (1987). An evaluation of family therapy in anorexia nervosa and bulimia nervosa. *Archives of General Psychiatry, 44*(12), 1047–1056.

Safer, D. L., Telch, C. F., & Agras, W. S. (2001). Dialectical behavior therapy for bulimia nervosa. *American Journal of Psychiatry, 158*, 632–634.

Salbach, H., Klinkowski, N., Pfeiffer, E., Lehmkuhl, U., & Korte, A. (2007). Dialectical behavior therapy for adolescents with anorexia and bulimia nervosa (DBT-AN/ BN)—A pilot study. *Praxis der Kinderpsychologie und Kinderpsychiatrie, 56*(2), 91–108.

Schmidt, U. (2009). Cognitive behavioral approaches in adolescent anorexia and bulimia nervosa. *Child and Adolescent Psychiatric Clinics of North America, 18*, 147–158.

Schmidt, U., Lee, S., Beecham, J., Perkins, S., Treasure, J., Yi, I., Winn, S., Robinson, P., Murphy, R., Keville, S., Johnson-Sabine, E., Jenkins, M., Frost, S., Dodge, L., Berelowitz, M., & Eisler, I. (2007). A randomized controlled trial of family therapy and cognitive behavior therapy guided self-care for adolescents with bulimia nervosa and related disorders. *American Journal of Psychiatry, 164*(4), 591–598.

Shapiro, J., Berkman, N., Brownley, K., Sedway, J., Lohr, K., & Bulik, C. (2007). Bulimia nervosa treatment: A systematic review of randomized controlled trials. *International Journal of Eating Disorders, 40*(4), 321–336.

Stice, E., (2002). Risk and maintenance factors for eating pathology: A meta-analytic review. *Psychological Bulletin, 128*(5), 825–848.

Striegel-Moore, R. H. (1993). Etiology of binge eating: A developmental perspective. *International Journal of Social Psychiatry, 32*, 383–387.

Striegel-Moore, R. H., & Cachelin, F. M. (1999). Body image concerns and disordered eating in adolescent girls: Risk and protective factors. In N. G. Johnson, M. C. Roberts, & J. Worell (Eds.), *Beyond appearance: A new look at adolescent girls* (pp. 85–108). Washington, DC: American Psychological Association.

Thompson-Brenner, H., Glass, S., & Westen, D. (2003). A Multidimensional meta-analysis of psychotherapy for bulimia nervosa. *Clinical Psychological Science Practice, 10*, 269–287.

Treasure, J., Katzman, M., Schmidt, U., Troop, N., Todd, G., & de Silva, P. (1999). Engagement and outcome in treatment of bulimia nervosa: First phase of a sequential design comparing motivation enhancement therapy and cognitive behavioural therapy. *Behaviour Research and Therapy, 37*, 405–418.

Von Ranson, K. M., & Robinson, K. E. (2006). Who is providing what type of psychotherapy to eating disorder client? A survey. *International Journal of Eating Disorders, 39*(1), 27–34.

Wertheim, E. H., Koerner, J., & Paxton, S. J. (2001). Longitudinal predictors of restrictive eating and bulimic tendencies in three different age groups of adolescent girls. *Journal of Youth & Adolescence, 30*(1), 69–81.

White, J. (2000). The prevention of eating disorders: A review of the research on risk factors with implications for practice. *Journal of Child and Adolescent Psychiatric Nursing, 13*, 76–88.

Whittal, M., Agras, W. S., & Gould, R. (1999). Bulimia nervosa: A meta-analysis of psychosocial and pharmacological treatments. *Behavior Therapy, 30*, 117–135.

Wildes, A. J., Emery, R. E., & Simons, A.D. (2001). The roles of ethnicity and culture in the development of eating disturbance and body dissatisfaction: A meta-analytic review. *Clinical Psychology Review, 21*(4), 521–551.

Wilfley, D. E., Bishop, M. E., Wilson, G. T., & Agras W.S. (2007). Classification of eating disorders: Toward DSM-V. *The International Journal of Eating Disorders, 40*, S123–S129.

Wilson, G. T., Grilo, C. M., & Vitousek, K. M. (2007). Psychological treatment of eating disorders. *American Psychology, 62*(3), 199–216.

Wilson, G., Heffernan, K., & Black, C. (1996). Eating disorders. In E. Mash & R. Barkley (Eds.), *Child psychopathology* (pp. 541–571). New York: Guilford Press.

Wilson, G. T., & Latner, J. (2001). Eating disorders and addiction. In M. M. Hetherington (Ed.), *Food cravings and addiction* (pp. 585–605). Leatherhead, Surrey, England: Leatherhead Food Research Association.

Wilson, G. T., & Sysko, R. (2006). Cognitive-behavioural therapy for adolescents with bulimia nervosa. *European Eating Disorders Review, 14*(1), 8–16.

Wilson, G., Terence L., Loeb, K. L., Walsh, B. T., Labouvie, E., Petkova, E., et al. (1999). Psychological versus pharmacological treatments of bulimia nervosa: Predictors and processes of change. *Journal of Consulting and Clinical Psychology, 67*(4), 451–459.

Wildes, J. E., Emery, R. E., & Simons, A. D. (2001). The roles of ethnicity and culture in the development of eating disturbance and body dissatisfaction: A meta-analytic review. *Clinical Psychology Review, 21*(4), 521–551.

Yager, J., Anderson, A., Devlin, M., Egger, H., Herzog, D., Mitchell, J., Powers, P., Yates, A., & Zerbe, K. (2002). Practice guideline for the treatment of patients with eating disorders. In *American Psychiatric Association practice guidelines for the treatment of psychiatric disorders: Compendium 2002* (2nd ed., pp. 697–766). Washington, DC: American Psychiatric Association.

CHAPTER 9

American Psychological Association Task Force on Evidence-Based Practice for Children and Adolescents. (2008). *Disseminating evidence-based practice for children and adolescents: A systems approach to enhancing care.* Washington, DC: American Psychological Association.

Armelius, B. A., & Andreassen, T. H. (2007). Cognitive-behavioral treatment for antisocial behavior in youth in residential treatment. Retrieved January, 8, 2009 from The Campbell Collaboration website: http://www.campbellcollaboration.org/campbell_library/index.php.

Brown, R. T., Antonuccio, D. O., Dupaul, G. J., Fristad, M. A., King, C. A., Leslie, L. K., McCormick, G. S., Pelham, W. E., Piacentini, J. C., & Vitiello, B. (2007). *Childhood mental health disorders: Evidence-base and contextual factors for psychosocial, psychopharmacological, and combined interventions.* Washington, DC: American Psychological Association.

Caetano, P. (2004). Standards for reporting non-randomized evaluations of behavioral and public health interventions: The TREND statement. *Society for the Study of Addiction, 99,* 1075–1080.

Chorpita, B. F., Becker, K. D., & Daleiden, E. L. (2007). Understanding the common elements of evidence-based practice: Misconceptions and clinical examples. *Journal of the American Academy of Child & Adolescent Psychiatry, 46*(5), 647–652.

Cooper, J. L., Aratani, Y., Knitzer, J., Douglas-Hall, A., Masi, R., Banghart, P., & Dababnahet, S. (2008). Unclaimed children revisited: The status of children's mentalhealth policy in the United States. Downloaded 2009 from http://www.nccp.org/publications/pub_853.html.

Crystal, S., Olfson, M., Huang, C., Pincus, H., & Gerhard, T. (2009). Broadened use of atypical antipsychotics: Safety, effectiveness, and policy challenges. *Health Affairs, 28*, w770–w781.

Gambrill, E. (2007). Transparency as the route to evidence-informed professional education. *Research on Social Work Practice, 17*(5), 553–560.

Gilgun, J. (2005). The four cornerstones of evidence-based practice. *Research on Social Work Practice, 15,* 52–61.

Huang, L., Stroul, B., Friedman, R., Mrazek, P., Friesen, B., Pires, S., & Mayberg, S. (2005). Transforming mental health care for children and their families. *American Psychologist, 60,* 615–627.

Karver, M. S., Handelsman, J. B., & Fields, S. (2006). Meta-analysis of therapeutic relationship variables in youth and family therapy: The evidence for different relationship variables in the child and adolescent treatment outcome literature. *Clinical Psychology Review, 26*(1), 50–65.

Kazdin, A. E. (2008). Evidence-based treatment and practice: New opportunities to bridge clinical research and practice, enhance the knowledge base, and improve patient care. *American psychologist, 63*(3), 146–159.

Lipsey, M. W., Landenberger, N. A., & Wilson, S. J. (2007). Effects of cognitive-behavioral programs for criminal offenders. Retrieved January, 8, 2009 from The Campbell Collaboration website: http://www.campbellcollaboration.org/campbell_library/index.php.

Littell, J. H. (2005). Lessons from a systematic review of effects of multisystemic therapy. *Children and Youth Services Review, 27*(4), 445–463.

Littel, J., Corcoran, J., & Pillai, V. (2008). *Systematic reviews and meta-analysis.* New York: Oxford University Press.

Littell, J. H., Popa, M., & Forsythe. B. (2005). Multisystemic therapy for social, emotional, and behavioral problems in youth aged 10–17. *The Cochrane Library, 4,* CD004797.

Miller, S., Wampold, B., & Varhely, K. (2008). Direct comparisons of treatment modalities for youth disorders: a meta-analysis. *Psychotherapy Research, 18*(1), 5–14.

Mills, C., Stephan, S., Moore, E., Weist, M., Daly, B., & Edwards, M. (2006). The President's New Freedom Commission: Capitalizing on opportunities to advance school-based mental health services. *Clinical Child and Family Psychology Review, 9,* 149–161.

Moher, D., Cook, D. J., Eastwood, S., Olkin, I., Rennie, D., Stroup, D. F., et al. (1999). Improving the quality of reports of meta-analyses of randomised controlled trials: The QUOROM statement. *The Lancet, 354,* 1896–1900.

Moher, D., Schulz, K., & Altman, D. (2001). The CONSORT statement: Revised recommendations for improving the quality of parallel-group randomized trials. *Annals of Internal Medicine, 134*, 657–662.

Mullen, E., Bellamy, J., Bledsoe, S., & Francois, J. (2007). Teaching evidence-based practice. *Research on Social Work Practice, 17*, 574–582.

Nathan, P. E., & Gorman, J. M. (Eds.), (2007). *A guide to treatments that work* (2nd ed.). New York: Oxford University Press.

National Association of Social Work (1999). Code of Ethics. Downloaded 2010 from http://www.naswdc.org/pubs/code/Default.asp

Nock, M. K., Goldman, J. L., & Wang, Y. (2004). From science to practice: The flexible use of evidence-based treatments in clinical settings. *Journal of the American Academy of Child & Adolescent Psychiatry, 43*, 777–780.

Norcross, J., Beutler, L., & Levant, R. (2005). *Evidence-based practices in mental health: Debate and dialogue on the fundamental questions.* Washington, DC: American Psychological Association.

Roth, A., & Fonagy, P. (2005). *What Works for Whom? A Critical Review of Psychotherapy Research*, 2nd ed. New York: Guilford Press.

Sackett, D. L., Richardson, W. S., Rosenberg, W., & Haynes, R. B. (1997). *Evidence-Based Medicine—How to Practice and Teach EBM.* New York: Churchill Livingstone.

Silverman, W. K., & Kurtines, W. M. (2005). Progress in developing an exposure-based transfer-of-control approach to treating internalizing disorders in youth. In E. D. Hibbs & P. S. Jensen (Eds.), *Psychosocial treatments for child and adolescent disorders: Empirically based strategies for clinical practice* (2nd ed., pp. 97–119). Washington, DC: American Psychological Association.

Wampold, B. (2001). *The great psychotherapy debate.* Mahwah, NJ: Lawrence Erlbaum Associates.

Weissman, M., Verdeli, H., Gameroff, M., Bledsoe, S., Betts, K., Mufson, L., Fitterling, H., & Wickramaratne, P. (2006). National survey of psychotherapy training in psychiatry, psychology, and social work. *Archives of General Psychiatry, 63*, 925–934.

Weisz, J. R., & Addis, M. (2006). The research-practice tango and other choreographic challenges: Using and testing evidence-based psychotherapies in clinical care setting. In C. Goodheart, A. Kazdin, & R. Sternberg (Eds.), *Evidence-based psychotherapy: Where practice and research meet* (pp. 179–206). Washington, DC: American Psychological Association.

Weisz, J. R., Doss, A. J., & Hawley, K. M. (2006). Evidence-based youth psychotherapies versus usual clinical care: A meta-analysis of direct comparisons. *American Psychologist, 61*(7), 671–689.

Weisz, J., Jensen, A., & McLeod, B. (2005). Development and dissemination of child and adolescent psychotherapies: Milestones, methods, and a new deployment-focused model. In E. D. Hibbs & P. S. Jensen (Eds.), *Psychosocial treatments for child and adolescent disorders: Empirically based strategies for clinical practice* (2nd. ed., pp. 9–39). Washington, DC: American Psychological Association.

Weisz, J., Sandler, I., Durlak, J., & Anton, B. (2005). Promoting and protecting youth mental health through evidence-based prevention and treatment. *American Psychologist, 60*, 628–648.

Wilson, S., Lipsey, M. W., & Soydan, H. (2003). Are mainstream programs for juvenile delinquency less effective with minority youth than majority youth? A meta-analysis of outcomes research. *Research on Social Work Practice, 13*(1), 3–26.

INDEX

Note: Page numbers followed by "*t*" denote tables.

Cognitive–behavioral therapy (CBT) (*cont.*)
  for anorexia nervosa, 172–73, 175–80
  for anxiety disorder, 93, 95, 101, 104*t*, 105
  for bulimia nervosa, 164–65, 172–73, 175–80
  for depressive disorders, 129–37, 140–41,
    145–46, 150–55
    research recommendations, 147–48
  plus fluoxetine, 140
  for oppositional defiant disorder/conduct
    disorder, 37–38
  for posttraumatic stress disorder, 114, 124
  plus sertraline, 140
  for substance use disorders, 66, 82
Cohen's d. See Standardized mean differences
    (SMD)
Combination therapy
  for anxiety disorder, 101
  for attention deficit hyperactivity disorder,
    18–20
  for depressive disorders, 140–41
  for posttraumatic stress disorder, 120
Comorbidity, 185
  and adolescent antisocial behavior/substance
    use disorders, 83–84
  and attention deficit hyperactivity
    disorder, 23
Conditioning, 102, 121–23
  classical, 67, 122
  operant, 45
Conduct disorder (CD), 36–65, 86, 141
  case study, 61–65
  cognitive–behavioral therapy for, 37–38
  gender and, 83
  onset of
    biological influences, 53
    psychological influences, 53–54
    social influences, 54–55
  prevalence of, 36
  psychosocial interventions, 39–43*t*
    child-focused interventions, 37–45
    family-focused interventions, 45–48
  research recommendations for, 58, 60–61
  treatment and recovery
    biological influences, 55–57
    psychological influences, 57
    social influences, 57–58, 59*t*
Coping Cat program, 98, 110–12
Coping Power program, 82
Coping with Depression for Adolescents, 130, 135
Correlation coefficient, 9

DBT. *See* Dialectical behavior therapy (DBT)
Depressive disorders, 129–55
  biopsychosocial risk and protective
      factors
    for onset of, 141–47, 146*t*
    for treatment and recovery, 147*t*
  case study, 150–55
  cognitive–behavioral therapies for, 129–37,
    140–41, 145–48
  combination therapy for, 140–41
  family therapy for, 136
  interpersonal therapy for, 130, 135–36, 145–46,
    148, 163
  medication treatment for, 137–40, 138–39*t*
  prevalence of, 129
  psychosocial treatment for, 129–37
    APA Task Force 12 Criteria for, 134–35,
      145, 150
    systematic reviews/meta-analyses of,
      130–34, 132–33*t*
  research recommendations, 147–50
  selective serotonin reuptake
      inhibitors for, 137
  Self-Control Therapy for, 129–30, 134–35
*Diagnostic and Statistical Manual of Mental
    Disorders* (DSM), 5–6
Dialectical behavior therapy (DBT)
  for anorexia/bulimia nervosa, 167–68
Dysthymic disorder, 129, 152–53

Eating Disorder Not Otherwise Specified
    (EDNOS), 160, 167, 173–74, 189
Eating disorders
  anorexia nervosa, 159–63, 167–80, 171*t*
  binge-eating disorder, 164
  bulimia nervosa, 159–60, 163–80, 172*t*
EBP. *See* Evidence-based practice (EBP)
EDNOS. *See* Eating Disorder Not Otherwise
    Specified (EDNOS)
Effexor, for depressive disorders, 141
Empirically supported treatment
  APA Task Force 12 Criteria for. *See* APA Task
    Force 12 Criteria
  systematic reviews/meta-analyses of. *See*
    Systematic reviews/meta-analyses
Ethnicity
  and adolescent antisocial behavior/substance
    use disorders
    APA Task Force 12 Criteria for, 82
    systematic reviews/meta-analyses, 81–82